D0893411

Networking

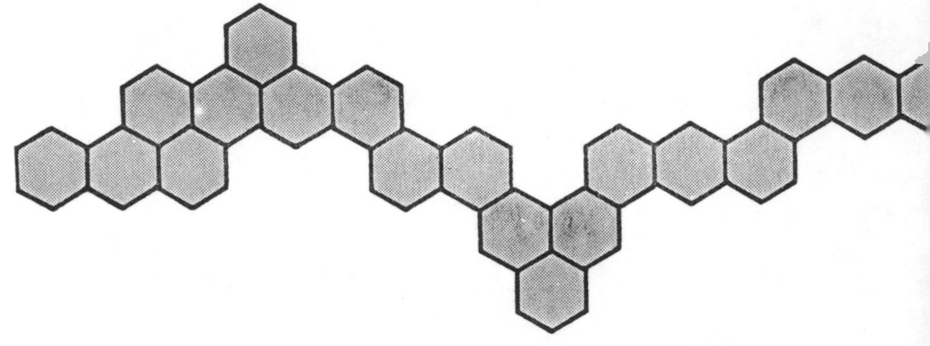

NETW

The Great New Way for

Harcourt Brace Jovanovic

Mary Scott Welch

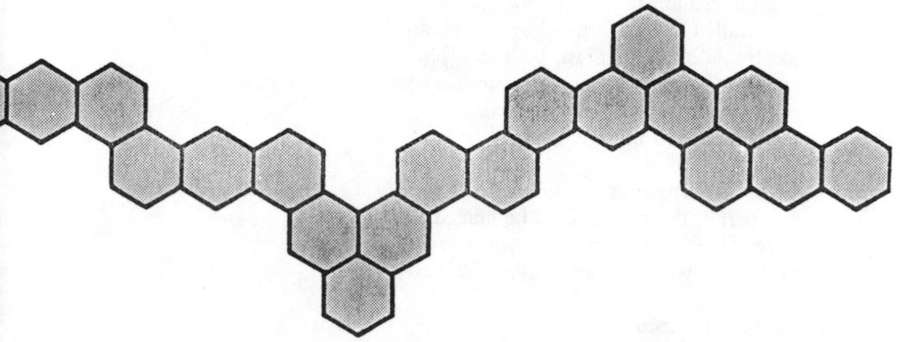

RKING

Women to Get Ahead

ew York and London

Requests for permission to make copies of
any part of the work should be mailed to:
Permissions, Harcourt Brace Jovanovich, Inc.
757 Third Avenue, New York, N.Y. 10017

Set in VIP Electra

Printed in the United States of America

Library of Congress Cataloging in Publication Data

Welch, Mary Scott.
Networking.

Bibliography: p.
Includes index.
1. Women—Employment. 2. Women in business.
3. Success. I. Title.
HD6053.W44 650'.14'024042 79-2767
ISBN 0-15-165199-X

First edition

B C D E

**Dedicated to Barrett,
Farley, Laurie, Maggie, and Molly**

Acknowledgments

A far-flung network of informants and encouragers has helped this book come to life. In addition to those whose names appear in the text, my deep sigh of thanks goes to: Beth Adams, Mary Albro, Holly Alderman, Donna Allen, Madeline Appel, Charles Blake, Kathy Bonk, Mary Boyette, Agnes Braganza, Peggy Brooks, Ellen Cassidy, Sylvia Chambers, Dorothy Chappel, Sey Chassler, Jean Col, Belita Cowan, Jeannine Dowling, Catherine East, Michal Feder, Chris Filner, Joan Foden, Nancy Ford, Diane Freaney, Sylvia Freeman, Carol Gaffney, Eileen Galley, Beverly Gandy, Madeline Gardner, Patricia Goldman, Nikki Green, Gloria Griffin, Sue Gutterson, Susan Hager, M. L. Hanson, Mary Hardy, Alexandria Hatcher, Eileen Hendry, Cheryl Lou Hepburn, Alice Herb, Mary Hilton, Julie Hoover, Kate Hunter, Norma Jackman, Thelma Jackson, Joy Jensen, Judith Johnson, Pauline Johnson, Winifred Kessler, Joanne Koltnow, Silvia Koner, Anne Lang, Deane Laycock, Marge Lucas, Hermine Lueders, Susan McIlhenny, Lucille Maddalena, Patsy Martin, Barbara Micale, Ann Miner, Jean Munk, Karen Nussbaum, Terry Odendahl, Dorothy Orr, Linda Phillips, Michael Riddell, William Robbins, Aura Rossi, Frieda Rozen, Pat Russell, Claire Safran, Ruth Shaeffer, Marcia Sharp, Florence Spillinger, Lael Stegall, Bill Stewart, Maxine Stewart, Susan Strecker, Judy Tisdale, Judith Turner, Pat Wagner, Evelyne Walborsky, Ronnie Welch, Sarah Welch, Karen Wellish, Barbara Wertheimer, Kay Wight, Diane Willett, Woodrow Wirsig, Charlotte Wood, and Linzy Zuker.

M.S.W.

Contents

Networking

"Where you are tomorrow may well depend on whom you meet tonight."

—SARAH WEDDINGTON

Assistant to the President of the United States
addressing a meeting of the Washington Women's Network,
Washington, D.C.

Introduction —to a Concept, a Technique, a Process

. . . that can help you get ahead in your chosen career, even if you think you don't need any help (yet). It can help you feel more comfortable and be more effective where you are, especially if you're "playing hardball," as the men say—if, that is, you're personally ambitious and professionally serious about your work.

Magic? No, *networking*.* As a concept, it can change your whole way of thinking about what it takes to succeed in business. As a technique, it will introduce you to stimulating, knowledgeable allies you didn't know you had. As a process, it knows no limits—and neither will you if you use it to its fullest potential.

This book will show you how to network. It will show you how to do deliberately what men have always done without having to think about it—that is, develop and use your contacts. For inside information. For advice and ideas. For leads and referrals. For moral support when the going gets rough. Or just for someone to talk to

* Note from a formerly fussy grammarian: *network* is a noun, and the practice of making nouns into verbs is rightly condemned by those of us who respect the language, but for once this word coinage is warranted. For networking is very definitely an *action*, a *doing*, so vital, so lively, that it could never be described by an inert noun.

in confidence, someone who understands what you're talking about without the need for a lot of background explanation of what it's like to be a woman working in a man's world.

You've probably heard the system referred to as the "old boys' network." When a job opens, a contract goes out for bids, a stock splits, a story breaks, a rumor spreads, a war threatens—whatever—this "old boy" calls that "old boy" on the phone, or they meet for a drink or a game of golf, and before long some business gets done, to the satisfaction of both. Hundreds of other people may have been involved in the transaction, in one way or another—personnel departments, stockholders, trade associations, public relations assistants, secretaries, even bartenders—but it's the "old boys" who will have maneuvered it. They'll have cut through all the resistance and red tape with ease, simply because they knew each other (or knew *of* each other) well enough to get in touch informally. The old boys' network may not be the *fairest* method of operation you ever heard of—it tends to leave out anyone who is not an "old boy"—but it is certainly effective. It's worth study and, to a certain degree, emulation.

And now women are creating their own version, at once an answer to being left out by the "old boys" and a wonderful new way of relating to each other. The "new girls' network," as it is sometimes called, even by women who bristle at being called "girls" in any other context, is springing up all over, growing almost faster than a reporter like me can keep up with it. From coast to coast, wherever the 43 million women now in the labor force are working, women are getting together to help each other get better jobs and/or to be more effective on the jobs they already have. That's what this book is all about. It's about what's happening, and why, and how you can get into the exciting new action.

A Martian would wonder what's new about women

getting together in groups: haven't they always, from quilting bees to garden or civic clubs to professional associations? Yes, and a good networker will use the old-line organizations as well as the new groups for her personal networking activity. But a network of the kind described in this book has a more specific focus and, at least in my observation, a much, much livelier animus—as you'll see and *feel* once you are caught up in it.

How *I* got into it is a networking example in itself.

Until about five years ago, I had never heard the term *network* applied to interpersonal relations. In my mind, *network* meant ABC, CBS, or NBC.

But then my friend Sue Ambler Roberts introduced me to her friend Marilyn Moats Kennedy. Sue, whom I now realize I'd met through another network (corporate wives), was plugging me into her Chicago women's resources network, although neither of us was thinking in those terms at the time. I had been writing a series of articles on women's jobs for a national magazine, and Sue said I "ought to know" Marilyn, a career counselor, because she had a lot of good ideas. I was in Chicago for quite another purpose, and I was not working on any specific job-related assignment at the moment, so I have to admit I wasn't too keen about spending my limited time in the city just getting acquainted with someone new, however interesting she might prove to be. (Ah, yes, I am a living example of what "they" say about working women: I'm extremely task-oriented, and I hate to "waste" time; both traits are drawbacks when it comes to networking.) But Sue was firm, and I was her houseguest, so we went to Marilyn's office.

In the course of our conversation, Marilyn said, "You are the center of your own universe. You have lines strung out to all parts of it. Where your universe intersects or overlaps someone else's, your lines cross that person's. Hundreds, maybe thousands of other people's universes feed into yours. If you could draw a map of them all, you'd have a mesh or a web, a huge fishnet—a *network*. Everyone is set smack-dab in the middle of a vast network, if only she realized it."

I wish I could say that Sue and I turned to each other, instantly recognizing the importance of what we were hearing, but it's only now, looking back, that I mark that day as the beginning of my network consciousness. I typed up a suggestion to the editor of my magazine series, proposing a piece on how to expand one's network, but nothing came of it. I called Marilyn with other questions in subsequent years, and once or twice I quoted her by name in the magazine articles I wrote, but she and I never discussed networking again.

It wasn't until 1977 that the great dawn broke in my consciousness. I woke up to the fact that women all over this country had an informal, unofficial network of their own—and I was in it. They were talking to each other, and to me, outside and behind official channels of communication. My "discovery" came about this way:

Redbook's editors had asked me to write an article they titled, in advance, "The Ten Best Corporations for Women to Work For." Most would have affirmative action plans, we knew—*affirmative action* meaning the taking of positive steps to recruit, hire, train, and promote women, in accordance with government guidelines growing out of Title VII, the amendment to the Civil Rights Act of 1964 that prohibits discrimination in employment based on sex. I had to find out which companies were doing the best job of moving women up out of the lowest-paid, least-appreciated jobs in what has been called the "female ghetto," those clerical and unskilled labor jobs traditionally performed by mostly women, and which companies had more than token women in management roles.

In my research for the article, I was running into puzzling resistance from the corporations. Contrary to expectations, they were in no hurry to make anybody's "ten best" list. Their representatives were putting me off; they couldn't (or wouldn't) give me the personnel numbers I needed, so that I could see how many women had been hired or promoted. They spoke in terms of percentages, but clearly a 100-percent increase in women in supervisory positions, say, could mean only that two women now worked where one had before. I pressed for *numbers*. They changed the subject, inviting me to interview their stars, women who were "firsts" in high positions. But by that time we had all had enough of that kind of "information." One woman manager does not equal opportunity make.

I was stymied. I was afraid I'd have to give up the whole assignment, when I heard about a women's caucus at ABC-TV, a small group of women who met regularly to discuss the job situation. It turned out that they also met from time to time with similar groups at the two other broadcasting networks, so through them I met women at CBS and NBC. They in turn told me about groups in other companies—*Reader's Digest*, Chase Manhattan Bank, *Newsweek*, *The New York Times*. Soon I was talking directly to women all over the country—not to the public relations or personnel departments of the corporations where they worked, but to the women themselves. Each woman I talked to said, in effect, "My company doesn't belong to any 'ten best' list, but I hear X company is doing well by women. Call my friend A over there. She'll give you a sense of what's going on." And friend A would indeed do that, again saying, "Not *my* company," and passing me on to her friend B in still another company. I was being plugged into a women's network I hadn't known existed. The women were being amazingly candid and revealing, giving me the information I needed even though they didn't know *me*—they only knew A or B, who had referred me.

(In the end I wrote about those women and their groups, not the "ten best" I'd set out to find, for it turned out that *no* corporation was living up to its affirmative action plan. Changes were in the works, but moving slowly.)

So began what has become for me the very exciting experience of seeing networks spring into being everywhere. They are not, so far, affiliated with each other. Most don't know about the others' existence—or didn't, until I became an inadvertent link while doing research for this book. Every group I talked to wanted to know what other groups I'd uncovered, where, and how the others were different from or the same as theirs. But a network of networks is bound to happen eventually, a clearinghouse of information, perhaps, a pooling of services. It makes sense. Maybe this book can contribute to that end.

But its major purpose is to get you started on networking in your own career, to tell you how to go about it and why. You'll read about how other women are doing it, both individually and in groups they form for the purpose. You'll read about real careers that have been advanced by networking. You'll see how the networking technique applies to every kind of work, at every level: a secretary can profit by talking to another secretary, one who works down the hall or across town, just as a corporate executive benefits by discussing her management problems with another executive who works for another company. You'll see how to go about it if you want to join a network group that's already under way, or to organize a group of your own.

What you *won't* see in this book is:

• *A philosophical discussion of whether or not "getting ahead" is an admirable goal for a woman to have.* This book is for and about women who have already decided that point: they are frankly ambitious.

• *How to write your résumé to conceal your "dumb" jobs, poor salaries, or years out of the labor market altogether.* Network groups are imparting these skills to their members by way of their educational programs, but this book is about the people part of networking, not the paper part. It's the people part that gets the jobs. You can fill out all those job applications and personnel forms the way the men do—*after* you've got the job.

• *Ten tough questions of the job interview and how to handle them.* Your network will tell you, rather, what your potential interviewer is like as a person, what contacts will impress him or her, how many others with what credentials are being interviewed for the same job, or even (just as usefully, if this is one of those jobs that the old boys' network closed out before going through the motions of looking for a woman) why you shouldn't bother.

• *How to get a raise.* If you're networking in the style this book recommends, you won't be asking that question as such. You'll be finding out what your job is worth (what your peers are being paid to carry comparable responsibilities in other companies), what you're worth apart from your job (your market value), what besides money you ought to be thinking about (perks? status symbols? titles?).

• *How to be more assertive.* When you know more, feel more confident, put a higher value on your own experience, and simply spend more time with gutsier women—all of which will happen in the course of good networking—you'll wonder why you thought you needed any other kind of assertiveness training.

• *Job strategies that work.* A good network will provide a safe climate in which you can try out your ideas on your knowledgeable friends before you risk them on your job. Networking will also expose you to other job histories: you'll hear a lot about this ploy and that and pick up a lot of the atmosphere of politicking. But this book is not about office politics. It will give you the method to use, not the strategy itself.

In short, this is not a career-counseling book, except

that after traveling from coast to coast, talking to women who are getting together in just this way, I think the best counsel I can give any woman who is serious about getting ahead in her career is, simply, *network.*

Start now. Here's how.

NOTE: In this book I have referred to individual women initially by their full names, but thereafter I've used their first names only. Since this practice is counter-trend, I'd like you to know why I chose it.

During the sixties, as the women's movement revived, women became painfully aware that their last names were male names—their fathers', their husbands'. The only names they could call their own were their first names, which they hoped had been chosen for them by their nameless mothers. So they referred to each other, in person and in print, by their first names only.

It made good feminist sense, at the time.

But then the first-name practice came up against another rationale: women so addressed were being trivialized and made childlike in the minds of men, for *they* used first names only with servants, tradesmen, children, and other "inferiors." *They* were the model, because *they* were in charge. Therefore, women began referring to themselves, in print if not in person, by their last names. Mary Jones, in the first paragraph, became simply Jones farther down in the story, just as John Jones had always been treated in print. (Except for *The New York Times*, which persisted in calling him Mr. Jones down the page, whether he had just invented perpetual motion or had been convicted of rape. Other papers used the last name without honorarium. Women began to do the same.) This being the style for men, it should be the same for women.

There is a history for last-naming women. It wasn't unusual for "girls" in school to be so called. I remember Bass and Chandler and Bergen and Wade in my college house; I don't remember thinking about the last-name usage one way or another at the time. I still think of those women in those terms, although of course some have had several other last names since. It didn't matter.

Now, apparently, it does. That's why I now feel I have to explain why I have reverted to the use of Betty and Ann and Peggy instead of the currently conventional Harragan, Peterson, Brooks.

The reason is that one of the aims of women's networking is to establish first-name relationships with each other. Knowing whom to call about what, then being able to speak to her as informally as use of her first name implies—that's what this book is about. So, without further ado about Miss, Mrs., Ms., or Madam President, let's network.

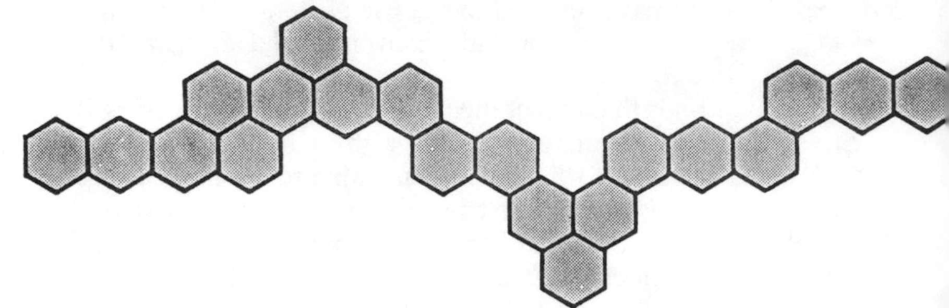

Personal

Part One

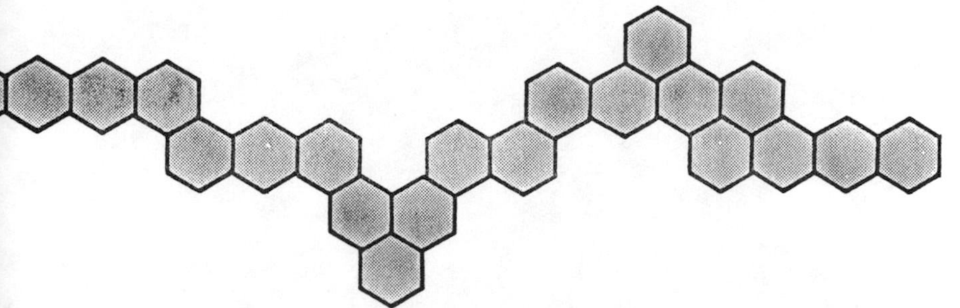

Networking

□1 What Is Networking?

It's the process of developing and using your contacts for information, advice, and moral support as you pursue your career. It's linking the women you know to the women they know in an ever-expanding communications network. It's building a community of working women, across professional and occupational lines, outside the old boys' network. It's helping each other to become more effective in the work world—with more clout, more money, more know-how, more self-confidence. It's beating the system that isolates women as they move up in male-dominated environments. It's asking for help when you need it—knowing *when* you need it, knowing whom and how to ask for it. It's *giving* help, too, serving as a resource for other women. In sum, it's getting together to get ahead.

Who needs it—and why?

We all need it—all women who work outside our homes, all 43 million of us—because we're still not getting our fair share of the employment pie. We need to get together to help each other to understand "the system," so that we can improve our lot.

We're 42 percent of the labor force, but we have nowhere near 42 percent of the good jobs. Eighty percent of us are still concentrated in lower-paying, lower-status jobs—in service industries, clerical fields, retail sales, manufacturing plants. Where 5,377,000 men were making $25,000 a year or more in 1977, the latest year for this particular breakdown of the figures, only 200,000 women were in that income bracket. That year, the average annual earnings of full-time women workers were $9,535, only 56 percent of men's average annual earnings of $16,929. That wage gap was greater still in sales, where women earn 45 cents of the men's dollar. Even in clerical work, "woman's work," women earn less than men: female clericals earn 61 cents for every dollar earned by male clericals. (In 1956, women in clerical occupations earned 72 percent of what their male counterparts were earning; in 1962, 69 percent; in 1976, 64 percent. They've come a long way—down.)

We're 1 percent of the U.S. Senate, 4 percent of the House of Representatives, zero percent of the Supreme Court. We're 99 percent of all secretaries, hold fewer than 2 percent of the seats on the top 1,300 corporations' boards of directors. Sixteen percent of us are classified as "professional and technical workers," but whereas women professionals tend to be schoolteachers or nurses, men are lawyers, doctors, or college professors. As for managers and administrators, the category where we're supposed to be making such huge strides, we're only 6.3 percent of those. Managers and administrators are 93.7 percent male.

Ten years ago, most of us weren't aware of numbers like those. Five years ago the facts may have seeped into our consciousness, but if we were advancing in our careers ourselves, we figured they didn't concern us: we were "different"; we were "making it." And if we were stuck, we thought it was our own fault: we hadn't tried hard enough; late in coming to the realization that work is central to our lives, regardless of marriage and motherhood, we hadn't been serious enough about our jobs.

Only now do we begin to get the picture. Only now do we see that where women are in the work world has little to do with themselves and everything to do with "the system." And vis-à-vis "the system," we're still on the outside looking in.

True, some of the numbers are improving. In 1950, women were 6 percent of doctors, 4 percent of lawyers. Today we're 12 and 10 percent of those professions, respectively. With a degree in chemistry, engineering, or business administration, a woman graduating from college today starts even in salary with the men in her class. It remains to be seen whether she stays even as the class of 1979 moves up. More often the men shoot ahead, claiming executive titles, while the women are shunted aside into professional slots or nonsupervisory staff jobs—doing their own thing, and doing it well, but not running the company.

For despite laws against sex discrimination in employment, and despite what are probably good intentions on the part of many corporations, "the system" is resistant to change. The resistance creates a great deal of frustration, especially among well-qualified women who are seriously dedicated to their careers. They need a means of dealing with that frustration in a constructive way, and sharing their feelings with other women is the best means available. They also need encouragement in continuing to bang away at the barriers against them, wherever and whenever they find them. Alone, they might be tempted to give up, or to settle for whatever they can easily get without making a fuss. Together, they can renew each other's will to find a way up the career ladder. And when they can be together with their "role models," women who are succeeding to formerly all-male heights, the encouragement and renewal take on extra strength.

"Women need the support of other women, not because they are extra-fragile but because they are outside the male apprentice and support network." So say Barbara Benedict Bunker and Edith Whitford Seashore, of the prestigious National Training Laboratories Institute, headquartered in Arlington, Virginia. "In most organizations, the more established officers of the company keep a sharp eye on and encourage younger men of promise. Frequently, they advise them, take them in as protégés, and use influence to make possible their advancement. This is infrequently true of women. Therefore, if they are to realize their potential, women need other women to make the climate one in which they, too, feel supported."

That's exactly the climate women are providing for each other through networking.

Are women networking only with other women?

No. A good networker uses every resource available to her, and that includes men. Besides, as Boston career counselor and Massachusetts municipal official Marcia Crowley points out, in some situations, men are the only ones out there. But it's the phenomenon of women networking with other women that is creating the most excitement today and the most promise for the future.

Women are seeking out other women—for information, for advice, for moral support—because only other working women can truly understand what working women are up against. Men don't understand that women in business have problems that their male colleagues simply don't have. Not least among those problems is the fact that men don't acknowledge that such problems exist.

Let's take a very elementary problem as an example. A woman executive, included for the first time in a weekly meeting that has been, until then, all male, enters the conference room and finds that the men expect her to take notes for the meeting—because most of the women they've dealt with in the past have been secretaries, and "secretaries take notes."

The men in the meeting didn't think about the fact that they were all men, before—that was just the way they were—but now a woman joins them, so they notice. Even now they may not notice in the sense of "Hey, we were all men before, weren't we?" It will be more like "Hey, what's this woman doing here?" What happens in the next hour or two may be of absolutely no consequence to the company, to the business at hand, or to the men present; it may not be important to the woman, either, in the long run; but it is a problem, let's agree, that no man would ever have—not even a black man.

For exactly that reason, it's a problem that the woman can't discuss with a man, at least not without a lot of prior explanation, leading no doubt to defensiveness on her part. That is, if she made the mistake of supposing the man would understand what she was talking about and said, "They assumed I'd take the notes for the meeting!" the man would say, "Well, why not? I always take notes, myself."

But another *woman* would probably raise her eyes to the sky, sighing, understanding instantly that the men in the conference room had tried to force the lone woman into the stereotype of secretary and that the woman reporting the event felt in her gut that it was important *not* to accept that role, *not* to take notes. Another woman would understand that it was not a matter of note taking at all, just as the famous controversy over who makes the coffee is not about coffee making: these are all status questions. Those who have status (men) can afford to pooh-pooh it. The president of the company could work in a windowless office without a carpet and he'd still be president. (Not that he would do so. The president usually pooh-poohs status symbols from the grandest office in the company.) Those who have no status, or are just coming into a little of it, can't afford not to insist on having the symbols.

Another woman would not have to have all this explained to her, so the conversation could proceed from there: What should I have said? Should I have just taken the notes—and then managed to lose them? How do *you* handle situations like that? Am I overreacting?

That's just one of the reasons why women need other women to talk to. Another reason goes back to the old boys' network. Men are leaving the women they work with out of their informal information channels. Men aren't telling women what they tell each other as a matter of course. Whether this is deliberate or not is a moot point.

It may be simply an outcome of the fact that men and women don't socialize off the job, at least not yet, not much. Women don't belong to the same golf and tennis and health clubs; they don't frequent the same bars, either. It may be merely thoughtless, as it may have been when four male colleagues failed to tell Donna Widman that their General Electric sales team was expected to set up the exhibition materials before the big conference. The men arrived in blue jeans, appropriately dressed for the physical labor ahead; Donna, unknowing, was wearing her best $350 suit. Men can be pretty dumb about things like that, but they can also be smart—street smart. So Donna's associates may have deliberately withheld that information from her to make her look foolish and/or helpless—"as I most certainly did," she told me, "standing around, handicapped by my clothes, feeling positively superfluous."

But whether it's malicious or careless, withholding information has the same effect: it puts women at a disadvantage, for information is power.

Without adequate information, anyone is bound to make mistakes, serious mistakes, so women are using each other to close the gap, wherever possible, between what they know and what else they *need* to know. Some of those gaps are not specific to the particular jobs the women hold—that is, they concern attitudes and types of behavior that have not figured into the average woman's upbringing, as they have in the average man's. Network groups are filling these gaps by sponsoring seminars, holding workshops, bringing in speakers on subjects such as management skills, financial planning, career goal setting, and so on.

Other gaps relate more directly to the individual woman's job situation. Rather than ask "dumb" questions of her male colleagues, she looks to her network for the answers.

A third reason why women need other women to talk to is an extension of the first two: they're lonely. The higher a woman moves up in the work world, the more likely she is to be entirely surrounded by men. She feels conspicuous, and she is. Whatever she does is apt to be judged in terms of her womanness. If she succeeds it's because she's different from most women; if she fails it's because she's just like a woman. Dr. Rosabeth Moss Kanter, Yale sociologist, has reported that in this situation the token person can develop "deviant behavior," literally, thus making matters worse. This woman needs one of her own kind to talk to.

The Executive Women's Council, a network group in Baltimore, describes the situation tellingly in a brochure about itself:

"Women of high rank in management are still very few, and the traditional prejudices against women in positions of authority are still widespread, though often subtle. Consequently, despite the appearance of career success, executive women experience isolation and encounter discrimination. . . . Without the support of a peer group, they can be psychologically alone. They face many invisible barriers, some only vaguely sensed by themselves, that belie or qualify their apparent success and restrict future opportunity."

A male vice-president with a business problem he wants to kick around informally can drop in the next office and find another man, another vice-president. The two can then "get their act together" before going to a meeting where their division may be under siege. A female vice-president will have to call around town before she can check out her own strategy for the meeting.

If she's a good networker, that's exactly what she'll do. She will already have built up a relationship with that other vice-president across town; she will already have checked out the other woman's business acumen and tested how far she can go in asking for advice. Now, as she picks up the phone, she'll be entering into a conversation just as easy and almost as informal as that between the male vice-presidents who are next-door neighbors. And maybe one even more helpful, because the person at the other end of the line will know, in the current phrase, "where she's coming from." She'll still have to go to that meeting alone; she'll still be surprised, probably, by whatever strategy the men have worked out together (leaving her out); but at least she'll have had a chance to discuss and rehearse her own act, without fear of put-down.

How does networking work?

- "Hello, Alice? Joan. Good meeting last night, wasn't it? Say, I have a letter here from a consultant who says he's dealt with your firm. . . ."
- "Diane? This is Reggie. I get back from the conference and find this new guy has put a totally different training program in place of the one you and I worked

out. Joe was all set to sign off on mine when I left. This new thing is a disaster, but before I go in and scream, tell me—what the hell happened?"

• "May I speak to Ms. Commissioner, please? I'm calling at the suggestion of Mary Jones, about a possible opening on the commissioner's staff."

• "I understand you worked for Blodgett's when they were handling P.R. for Widgets. I'm considering a job at Widgets. Do you have time to give me a little background on the management over there, or do you know anyone who still works there?"

• "We have to pay our own laundry charges for our smocks. Do you?"

• "He said I should grow up: it's childish to make such a fuss over where my desk is placed. What's the difference as long as I'm getting the same pay as the men in the inside room? What do you think? Am I getting upset over the wrong thing?"

• "I finally got to go out to lunch with them, just like one of the guys, but all they talked about was football. When they tried to include me in the conversation—I really think they *were* trying—they asked my opinion of the Dallas Cowgirls. Did I blow it? What would *you* have said?"

• "Did you get this wacky memo from quality control? What in the world does it mean?"

• "Can I get you to look at a draft of my memo, unofficially? Tell me if it sounds at all angry. I'm trying to keep my cool about this."

• "Some of us are getting together to talk about personal days. Would you like to join us? Do you know anyone you could bring from another company?"

• "What's this I hear about awards for productivity? Is it happening over your way? Is your shop going to go for that?"

• "Your guy is going to be getting a copy of my boss's report to personnel, about some new affirmative action guidelines. Make sure he understands paragraph c on page four, will you? It's a sleeper."

• "We're going to be looking for a librarian who also has a law degree. I thought I'd call before the order goes out, in case one of your former students . . ."

• "My manager acts as though I'm his property when we're traveling together. Or like we're out on a date. I'm sure the field men think I'm sleeping with him, but he'd be the first to deny it if anyone dared say so. Just as he would if it were true, of course. What a bind this is! Do I have to quit to get out of it? Is that maybe what he wants?"

• "I have this job interview—it's the third, so I think they're serious—and I have no idea what salary to ask for. I'm calling around to see what different houses are paying commodity analysts. Could you give me a guess as to the range in your place?"

• "Listen, am I going crazy, or what?"

That's a sample of how networking works, especially that last quote. Women are checking with each other about all kinds of job-related problems, particularly the kind that make them feel that the men they work with know something they don't know.

In so doing, they are establishing connections with each other both inside and outside the places where they work, both in groups formed for the purpose and in one-to-one relationships they develop informally. Although many of them have comparable jobs, at much the same levels in their professions or occupations (which helps and may even be necessary when they call upon each other's expertise to solve specific work problems), just as many are talking to other women over and around the abyss that employment hierarchies create between a secretary, say, and a vice-president. In such instances, their common bond is their gender and the societal conditioning that so often handicaps women in the work world.

They can talk easily and openly to each other, as they usually cannot to men, because they share the common experience of feeling odd.

They don't have to explain this feeling to each other, much less justify it. They don't even have to mention it: it goes without saying. But it's the thread that runs through the entire fabric of their communications with each other these days. As such, it holds together women who may in many other respects be altogether different from each other and makes them intelligible to each other.

But aren't women supposed to mistrust each other?

That's a common view, but good networkers are trusting and helping other women to a degree that defies the old stereotype.

"They" say that women mistrust other women because we've been raised to compete with each other for men. In that sense, "the other woman" is my natural enemy. But networking isn't about finding and keeping husbands; it's about work.

"They" also say that women try to separate themselves from other women, not to join them, so that they can be seen as themselves, as individuals, rather than as part of a generally looked-down-upon group. That's partly true, and it's understandable, particularly in older women. Twenty years ago, a career woman almost *had* to distance herself from her sisters; employers wouldn't take her seriously otherwise, for they believed that women worked only until they got married or became pregnant. In those days the assumption was based on fact: most women really were not serious about their jobs because they expected to marry and stay home forever after. So women who thought in terms of serious, lifelong careers, regardless of marriage and motherhood, set out to prove they were not like other women. To them, "you think like a man"* was the ultimate compliment; they shared the male opinion of female mentality. At parties, career women wanted to talk shop with men, not to talk babies and recipes with women, a wish usually frustrated. Wanting only to be accepted by men, they were shunted off with the women—who didn't accept them, either, because they really *were* "different." They ended up in limbo, not "one of the guys," but not "one of the girls" either.

Some of those women are still around, bearing the scars of those days, still bogged down in attitudes and forms of behavior no longer called for. Unless they went through consciousness-raising ten years ago, or have since come to realize that they're no longer alone out there (or needn't be), they still tend to separate themselves from other women, still buying into male belief in the stereotypes. They're not good networkers.

But some others of them have grown with the opportunity and the times, dropping their armor with grateful relief as they align themselves with the women of today. They make excellent mentors, expert networkers.

Women are human, and we carry our history within us, so we do not *all* give the lie to stereotypes. Nor is our sex without its fair share of scoundrels. But as you get into networking you'll find a level of trust and candor beyond the belief of anyone who thinks women are invariably suspicious of each other. You've heard of male bonding. You've read countless books, seen innumerable movies, about male buddies standing by each other. Wait until you become a part of the new *female* buddy system: as Assistant Professor Susan B. Ogden has ob-

* Current riposte, courtesy of Congresswoman Gladys Spellman: "I know, I'm having a bad day. I'll be all right tomorrow."

served, in her management classes at Seattle University's School of Business, this is, truly, female bonding. It's less dramatic than what happens among men on the battlefield, although you might say that the male-dominated work world is a kind of battlefield for women today. It's less grounded in our shared biology than the kind of help women used to give each other during childbirth, although biology does indeed color the experience of women among men. But women are now helping other women, just because they are women.

We don't always know quite how to do this. Some of the process has to be learned. Even Edith Seashore had to teach it to herself, she whose business it is to sensitize others to the special needs of women in male environments. (She was the consultant the Naval Academy called in when it decided to admit women.) As she tells the story, she was one of two women on a board of directors. She never saw or talked to the other woman outside the board room. It didn't occur to her to align herself with the other woman, for they were opposites in everything from points of view to personality traits. But during one meeting she began to notice how often the men interrupted the other woman or, after hearing her out, continued the discussion without regard for what she had said. They did this almost as often to Edith, she tardily realized, although her own remarks were usually on the other side of any subject. It began to seem that the governing factor was not what either of them said but that they were women. Outsiders, interlopers.

Edith began to say things like "Just a minute. I'm not sure Ms. X has finished what she was saying." Or, to the woman, "Could you say a little more about that? I don't agree, so far, but I'd like to know more about this." Or "Were you satisfied with the board's response to your point? It seems to me we went too fast."

In time, the other woman began to do the same for her. They never discussed this; they just did it. "And I like to think that gradually the tone of the meetings changed. It became more accepting of us as equal members, as persons."

Networking is much less subtle than that. It has a distinct quality of "You scratch my back, I'll scratch yours."

A good networker is not so much nurturing others, as is said to be woman's bent and fulfillment, as she is looking after "Number One." But underlying her businesslike trading of information and favors is the sense that what's good for women in general is good for her in particular. She has the not-always-conscious feeling that anything she can do to improve the image and the effectiveness of women, as a class, will improve her own position as an individual. Attorney Lee Kraft, a member of an influential network group in Washington State, put it this way: "It is the philosophy of the group that the more women we can get into the very highest echelons of power, the more successful our total network will be."

How are women getting to know each other?

Through networking groups. The groups come in all sizes, shapes, and styles. They may be merely spontaneous, informal lunch groups where just a few women get together, each woman gradually introducing a new person to the original group, until finally, in many cases, the size of the group outgrows the time and space it originally used, so that more formal arrangements have to be made to accommodate it. Such as:

In-house groups

Groups of women who work in the same company get together on a regular basis just to talk things over. Their meetings can range from gripe sessions to preplanned attempts to help each other become more knowledgeable about their company. They can be vertical groups, meaning they include women holding all levels of jobs, top to bottom; or horizontal, meaning they are composed of women who work at comparable levels: secretaries get together with other secretaries, v.p.'s with other v.p.'s.

Same-company groups that organize around an issue. The issue may be a broad one: is this company discriminating against women? Or a narrow one: can the docking of employees who are three minutes late be corrected? These issue-oriented groups may be committed to dealing amicably with their management, being very careful from the outset not to seem in any way militant. Or they may be frankly angry, eventually taking the company to court. (The possibility that the amiable group or any group will turn into a litigious group is what worries management from the first—which explains why some of the most innocent in-house groups come up against what would otherwise be mystifying resistance and disapproval from on high.)

In addition to these differences among same-company groups, a major distinction in each category is whether they are overground or underground:

Overground groups meet in company space, sometimes even on company time; use the interoffice mails, the copy machines, and the official bulletin boards; sometimes have a small expense budget allotted them by a cooperative management. They are usually autonomous; management exerts no obvious control. But it goes without saying that these groups are not troublemaking. Their focus is usually on self-education and internal communication, not reform.

Underground groups, out of preference or necessity, keep their activities carefully separate from the workplace. They meet in the members' homes or in restaurants and other public places. They pay their own expenses. Sometimes their membership is secret. They are not necessarily any more action-oriented or more demanding than the overground groups, but they feel free to be so if the need arises.

Across company lines

All those same variations on the theme may occur in groups formed across company lines. Thus we have:

Vertical networks. Every working woman in town is welcome. An interest in advancing on the job is just about the only membership requirement.

Vertical/occupational. The job level doesn't matter but the type of job or the field of work does. Thus, Women in Communications includes everyone from a production assistant on a trade paper to Barbara Walters, but all the members are in some form of communications work. Women in Construction can be contractors or carpenters.

Horizontal networks. The members may work in different fields but they hold jobs at somewhat the same level. The level may be determined by salary and/or title or certain professional credentials, but the idea is to bring peers together—women who have comparable responsibilities and experience, who can talk each other's language as equals. Thus we have many networks with the term *executive* or *professional* in their names, each with its own criteria by which it defines the terms. Some are frankly elitist. Others include any woman in the field who is committed to becoming an executive or a professional.

Horizontal/occupational or professional. The finest refinement of all. Members work at the same level in the same field. For example, they're vice-presidents in financial organizations, or agents in commercial real estate, or sales reps of industrial products, or general counsels in corporations.

Multi-nets

The woman who belongs to an in-house vertical group may also belong to an outside group, or two or three, horizontal or vertical, or both. She may not devote equal time and energy to them all, but she makes a point of touching base with as many networks as she can. Her object is to get to know as many women as possible, as well as possible, against the day when she'll want to call on them for concrete help.

Is networking difficult?

Not really. It's easy, and fun, once you understand what you're doing and why.

Still, a few stumbling blocks may lie in your path as you begin. It may not "feel" right. In a funny kind of way, it seems unfeminine. (For all the years that have elapsed since Betty Friedan wrote *The Feminine Mystique*, and for all the changes that have come about as a result, many women still worry about losing their "femininity"; and we still allow the male culture to define femininity for us.)

Why should it feel unfeminine to reach out to others, to initiate contact? Maybe *scary* is a better word. The average woman grows up waiting for the phone to ring, waiting to be asked (to dance, to marry), not choosing but waiting to be chosen. Even if she later rejects that lady-in-waiting concept intellectually, she still "feels funny" about pushing herself forward. She's never crashed a party in her life; the very thought of doing so is repugnant.

Networkers have to rise above all that negative conditioning, for it is all passive. Networking is *active*. Networkers take the initiative in introducing themselves, telephoning, making dates, writing notes, "keeping in touch." For women who find it difficult to shed "feminine" habits, network groups make it easier. They create a supportive atmosphere in which to try reaching out.

Two other aspects of networking go against our usual cast of mind. First, the prospect of *using* people. It does sound crass, doesn't it? Cultivating other women, creating relationships with them, not because we like and enjoy them but because they can be *useful* to us? Asking for help is hard enough for a lot of us, but asking someone we've consciously set up for the purpose? It goes against the feminine grain somehow.

As an antidote to that crass-sounding prospect, remind yourself that you are a good resource for others, just as good a resource as they are for you. Yes, you'll be using people, but in good networking, the people you use will also be using you. The exchange may not always be immediate, with instant mutual payoff, but it will all come out even in the end.

A second element of networking may bother you: it takes time. Women who work are pressed for time, at best. Juggling a career along with home and family or along with an active social and civic life keeps a woman's schedule more than full. To manage it all, she's had to be very time-conscious, and meeting with other women can seem like a waste of time. (Interestingly, a recent survey showed that men "waste" more time on the job than women. The men around the proverbial water cooler are networking, although they don't call it that.) She'll have to make a conscious effort to discard that attitude at first, but when she sees the value of networking she'll know that it's worth every "wasted" minute it takes.

See if you can't set aside all those objections, from questions of femininity to matters of time. And yes, include that one about "My best friends have always been men." And that other one, "I'm not a joiner." Mind cleared of such debris, suspend your disbelief in women working with women and decide to become a networker.

What's in it for me?

Probably the biggest benefits of effective networking are psychological—a sense of community, for example, as opposed to the feeling of separateness so many women experience in "man's world." To find role models, to see how successful women talk and act, can give your psyche a tremendous uplift. As for learning that other women have the same "crazy" feelings as you, sometimes—who can measure the salubrious effects?

But precise, pragmatic rewards are there to be claimed as well. They fall into these general categories:

1. *Information*. Information is power. What you don't know *can* hurt you. A network is your conduit to the kind of information you need in order to advance in your career. You don't even have to know what kind of information that is; in fact, you probably *don't* know at this juncture. (As former New York State legislator Constance Cook has said, "If I knew the right questions, I'd know how to find the answers.") The larger your network, the better your chance of finding out exactly what you need to know.

2. *Referrals*. Sometimes the best kind of information is a referral. "I don't know," your networker will say, "but you should talk to X and Y." Knowing whom to call is almost as good as knowing.

3. *Feedback*. A network helps you check out your behavior, your ideas, your strategies for success—before you risk them in "the real world." When the feedback is positive, the effect is one of moral support: you're encouraged to greater heights than you might otherwise

have attempted. But negative feedback can be just as valuable, and when given in the supportive climate of a network relationship, it helps without hurting.

As one woman said, "I get strokes from my network, and heaven knows I need all the strokes I can get, but I count on them to give me kicks, too. I don't want blanket approval."

How can I get into all this action?

The first step is to realize that you really need other people: you can't go it alone. You need other women to consult about your career, about small problems and large ones as they arise on your job. In fact, you need a network to let you know you're *having* problems. It's truly amazing how much can go on over your head if you're at all naïve about the way the workplace operates.

Most of the events that ultimately have a negative effect on a career—a lost contract or account, a change in management, a budget cut—seem to be impersonal, beyond our control one way or another, and often that's the case. But sometimes the events can be anticipated, their personal effects blunted, if you make the right move at the right time. This means acting, as opposed to reacting, and it requires an enormous switch in the way most of us think and behave on the job.

The first step in making that switch is to become more aware of what's going on around us. "Work 80 percent as hard," one career counselor advises. "Spend 20 percent more time and thought on the environment you're working in."

Spend part of that 20 percent time and effort on getting acquainted with the other women who work where you do, finding out what they do, how their jobs fit into the total picture. If there's an employee group or a women's caucus, join it; if not, think about starting one, using the methods outlined in this book.

Next, step two, start seeking out women outside your own workplace. You'll find them in any number of gathering places—in professional associations, at conferences and seminars, in activist organizations. Ask every woman you meet if there's a networking group, of the kind described in this book, in your city. If so, join and begin to take part in it. If not, again, consider starting your own.

As you meet new women, find out as much as you can about their career plans, and tell them about yours. Figure out how you can help each other. And do it. If you do, you will see how quickly your personal network expands and how useful it can become in ways far beyond your imagining now.

The process requires certain people skills and a few mechanics, as we'll discuss, but it's nothing you can't pick up in short order. And once you do, you'll be absolutely amazed at the change it can bring about in yourself.

That's really not too much to promise you. Networking can cause a real turnaround in your attitude toward work, an enormous boost in your self-confidence, and a sense of great things to come that is quite impossible to describe.

Deanna Spooner was feeling its effects when she wrote from Portland, Oregon, to two easterners she had met at an Organizational Development Network conference, "After sharing so intensely the conference experience, I feel a real need to maintain some communication with you. . . . I returned to my OD [Organizational Development] specialist job at Kaiser with new vigor and excitement. The conference was my first, and I can't wait for my second! It must have been one of the loudest *aha*'s of my life."

I've seen and felt this effect myself, yet when I get back to my typewriter after experiencing a "high" at a network meeting, I can't seem to find the words to explain what happens.

Neither can Frances Lear, a Los Angeles management consultant, whose network consists of sixteen to eighteen high-powered women she entertains at dinner once a month. "I don't know why it's so great," she says, "but it's a kind of magic time."

Theodora Wells, career counselor, whose network includes Women in Business (Los Angeles), gropes for words too. "The energy flow is so exciting!" she says. "I have never experienced this where men are involved. I think it's because women would rather collaborate than compete, if we could have our way, which is not true of men. Very few men, even in team situations, are without a hidden agenda of competition. Women share more freely, without putting a price tag on what we give to each other. It's—wonderful!"

Dr. Jean Baker Miller, a Boston psychiatrist, addressed this difference between men and women in her book *Toward a New Psychology of Women*. "Men very early in life acquire the sense that they are members of a superior group. Things are supposed to be done for them by those lesser people who work at trying to do so. From then on, cooperativeness may appear to men as if it were somehow detracting from themselves. To cooperate, to share, means somehow to lose something, or, at best, altruistically, to give something away. All this is greatly augmented by men's notions that they must be independent, go it alone, win.

"To women, who do not have the same experience, cooperativeness does not have the same quality of loss. In the first place, most women have not been imbued with a spurious sense of advantage over a group of other people. . . .

"Women are more practiced in cooperation and at present more able to seek out and enjoy situations that require that quality. I do not mean that women have any greater inherent saintliness. We all know that women have many competitive aspects, too. In the past, many women competed with each other for men, for obvious reasons. But today, as women try to move on, they are trying to turn away from this sort of competition with other women, shifting the balance even further toward cooperativeness."

Alice Armstrong, Ph.D., the executive director of the Institute for Managerial and Professional Women in Portland, Oregon, doesn't agree with these ideas about collaboration and cooperativeness, but she, too, marvels at the high energy level of networking groups. She views the phenomenon in terms of power. Her doctoral dissertation showed that there was no significant difference between women and men in their need for power, for the feeling of dominance. Dr. Abraham Maslow, the late, noted psychologist, found that women who tested low in dominance were repressing their natural feelings. Alice says, "Networking releases energies long held in check because women have been afraid of losing their 'femininity.' Once women experience their own power they have a flood of energy that is exciting to share. Networking permits this shared excitement that comes with competing and winning. We have never before had a cheering section to encourage us to reach for the top. With this supportive networking, the 'fear of success' that we have heard so much about is dead."

"They're smelling success!" said another observer, in yet another attempt to describe the excitement.

But maybe the best way to predict what can happen to your career, once you get into networking, is to tell you how certain other women have advanced by using this process.

□2 Networking Success Stories

Illustrating the network process is easier than explaining it, so here's a collection of case histories to show you how other women have used networking in their careers. These are all true stories about real people, although in some cases the women have asked me to disguise identifiable details and give them fictitious names so as not to jeopardize network connections they're still using.

As you read over these examples, notice particularly how each woman met the others who were to become so useful to her. These same means of connecting are available to you.

Loré Caulfield, NBC-TV producer-writer-director in Los Angeles, wanted to give herself a special reward to celebrate the airing of her documentary, "The Quiet Revolution of Mrs. Harris." She decided on that ultimate extravagance, pure silk lingerie, and went shopping for silk-satin bikinis. After looking everywhere, with no success, she bought silk yardage and found a dressmaker to make up a few according to her dream design. They were so great-looking (and feeling) that friends wanted copies; they encouraged her to show them to Robinson's, a store that promptly ordered twenty dozen.

"I'd always wanted a cottage industry," she says, "but for retirement, not for now. I wasn't ready to leave my TV job. I thought I could do both. Mistake."

In addition to a full-time job and a business that was exploding, she had on her hands "a monster organization"—Women in Business, a network group she started. "I was already going crazy when the crisis to end all crises loomed: I was expecting a $5,000 silk shipment, and I didn't have the cash to pay for it; my customers owed me, but I couldn't put my hands on that. Banks don't lend to women entrepreneurs, as I already knew, so I thought, 'This is it. I'll have to give up.'"

It was in that despairing mood that she talked to her network, just complaining, not for a moment expecting what would happen: they volunteered to lend her the $5,000 for ninety days, which was all she needed. She was in.

You can now find Loré Lingerie in all the best stores around the country: Saks Fifth Avenue, Neiman-Marcus, and Marshall Field, for example. Bergdorf Goodman, New York, has a Loré boutique. Loré Caulfield, former TV employee, now runs a million-dollar business.

As to what her network means to her: "It wasn't so much the money," she recalls, "although that was absolutely crucial at the time. More important was the trust, the confidence in me that the other women demonstrated with their generous offer."

Networking is *power*!

At age twenty-eight, *Kathleen Housley* is the first woman and the youngest person ever to become editor of *Grumman Plane News*, a biweekly employee publication with a circulation of thirty-six thousand. She credits her promotion from editorial assistant ("basically a secretary") to the network she has developed over six years of working at Grumman—three years of summer jobs, while she was in college, three years since her graduation with a bachelor of arts degree. Grumman's twenty thousand employees include three thousand women, but they're so widely distributed, among the aircraft manufacturer's fourteen work centers on Long Island (New York), that Kathy wouldn't have known more than a few of them except for—shades of the old boys' network itself—golf.

While playing in the golf league, she met about ninety women, mostly secretaries, and within a year her career had taken off. Those who managed their bosses' appointment schedules were helpful in "sneaking" her in to v.p.'s offices, for interviews she wrote up for *Plane News*. Although she didn't realize it at the time, the women were also talking her up—so when the editor's job opened, she was appointed.

"Some of the women who have helped me are now calling me to help them," says Kathy. "They've been asking me how to start their own newsletters. I'm glad I'm able to return the favor they did me. That's what networking is all about, isn't it?"

Just before she went to Paris to address a conference on "Women in a Changing Society," Maggie Tripp, lecturer on women's studies at the New School for Social Research, New York City, attended a meeting of the Thursday Caucus, where Sarah Weddington, newly appointed assistant to President Carter, spoke. After the talk, Maggie quickly introduced herself to Sarah and told her of a forthcoming trip to France. "Would you like me to take a message from you to the French minister for women's affairs?" Maggie asked. Sarah said she'd prepare a letter of introduction, but Maggie thought, "Sure, sure; she'll forget." Not so. The letter arrived in plenty of time for Maggie's departure, and it opened doors magically in Paris. If there had been no Thursday Caucus . . . if

Maggie hadn't gone to the meeting . . . if she'd hung back instead of going up to the podium afterward . . . But no: this was networking at its best.

In return, Maggie will be able to supply Sarah with Parisian introductions, if or when Sarah goes abroad.

Constance Cook, former assemblywoman in the New York State legislature, was being considered for a gubernatorial appointment. As her final interview approached, she was fretting over what salary to ask for when in the mail, unsigned, there arrived a printout on salary ranges for the job. She went into the interview with confidence and came out with the job: vice-president for land grant affairs, Cornell University, Ithaca, New York.

When she arrived at her office on her first day on the new job, she found a vase of roses, the card saying, "Congratulations, from the network!" As she later learned, her benefactors were the secretaries in the office, women who didn't know her personally but knew her record as a battler for women's rights. (She had led the fight against antiabortion laws in the state.) The "network" wanted the appointment to go to a woman, and especially to this woman.

Marie O'Connor was in a dead-end job, as she describes it, when she took an insurance class at Marymount Manhattan College, in New York, where she met Marie Coleman. The two Maries worked for the same company, the Equitable Life Assurance Society, but they had never met before. Thanks to this meeting, Marie O. heard about an opening in Marie C.'s area and, with Marie C.'s support in talking to her manager, got the job—a three-grade jump and an $86-a-week raise. "Plus a chance to use my brain a little," says Marie O. She's a payroll analyst now. "Such networking is especially useful for a senior woman like me." She's fifty-one and has been with the company twenty-five years. "We're the women who are most often overlooked by management."

Janice La Rouche called Jackie Ceballos, public relations counsel, whom she knew through work with the National Organization for Women (NOW), to find out how her idea of feminist career counseling could be written up in *The New York Times*. She wanted to protect it from copiers by getting her name attached to it in the public prints. Jackie knew Marylin Bender, then a writer for the women's page at *The Times*. "She made the phone call for me," Janice now recalls. "I wouldn't have dared, myself, but Jackie's very outgoing. She'll call anybody." As it happened, far from being annoyed, Marylin was delighted to be given a fresh story idea. Marylin wrote what was to be the first in a long list of news breaks, stories about Janice. That was back in 1970, but Janice still remembers it as an example of how women can help each other, and how networking works. "We didn't call it that, then," as she says. "We called it 'using your contacts.' But it came hard for me—I never have wanted to ask anyone for anything—so I remember it well." Marylin Bender went on to become editor of the Sunday financial section of *The Times* and is now writing a book. Janice is the most quoted and probably the most sought-after career counselor in New York City. But they're still a part of each other's network.

Ruth Moghadam, a free-lance training and development consultant, happened to sit next to Fran Laprad, director of client services, Automatic Data Processing Company, at a networking program. After Ruth described the kind of management development seminars she puts on, Fran said, "My company needs someone like you." The end result was a substantial contract for Ruth, who designed a program, produced the training materials (including videotapes), and ran workshops that eventually all the executives and potential executives attended, in small groups throughout the winter. One network contact. Six months of lucrative work.

"She told me I was being set up. I wouldn't have known!" says Jennifer Owens, a middle manager in the oil business. She had been going great guns on her job as energy conservation coordinator for a refinery. The only woman and the only nonengineer in her area, she had had earlier problems in being accepted, but her last evaluation had shown her to be, "if not walking on water, swimming very quickly." Now, suddenly, out of the blue it seemed, she got a bad performance evaluation.

She was distraught. She kept going over and over her recent job efforts, day and sleepless night, trying to figure out what she had done wrong, for, typically, she thought it was her own fault. She was a hard worker, a good worker, and a loyal company person. It didn't occur to her to do anything about the evaluation except work harder and better so that it wouldn't happen again. It didn't even occur to her to talk to anyone about it—that would have been like washing her laundry in public. But then, her friend in employee relations—"the only female I felt I could talk to, the only one who is as serious about her career as I am about mine"—dropped a hint. She had seen the part of Jenny's evaluation that the employee is not privy to. "Did you ever threaten a discrimination suit?" she asked. That was her way of suggesting a reason why Jenny's manager might want to start giving her bad reports, so that if she were fired or passed over for promotion she couldn't holler "Sexism!" Proof that she was not qualified for the next step up would lie in the personnel files.

Jennifer had never threatened suit, but now she recalled asking, at an orientation meeting about promotion procedures, "Is there some requirement about sex?" The man sitting next to her had nudged her in the ribs, warning her, but she had followed up her question with another one: why were all the women except her in one area (computers)? The orientation leader had said, weakly, "Maybe they have never voiced a desire to move." But within six months another female had been moved out of computing, and within a year, two.

Jenny had been rather proud of having prodded the company into action, but now she wondered: had she come through as a troublemaker?

She decided to consult the Network, an invitational group she belonged to. One member, whom she had never met before, was a lawyer skilled in discrimination suits; she advised Jenny against taking that kind of action, because of the cost, the risk, and the emotional strain litigation entails, but helped her work out a strategy for having her performance evaluation corrected. The first step was to have a showdown with her manager, asking for details: what did he mean, she "tended to adopt less than optimum solutions"? What solutions, to what problems, when? (Turned out he was thinking of a time when she had adopted *his* solution, operating on *his* orders. He had to back down on that one.) What did he mean by "needs help in technical areas"? Did he mean she should go back to school? She had a B.A. in math and an M.B.A.; did he want her to become an engineer? The answer was no, and he couldn't produce any evidence that she lacked technical know-how, so he agreed to scratch that one. But then he said, "Well, if I take that back, I'll also have to take back 'universal agreement that she has improved her interpersonal skills.' I'll have to say you're still too aggressive to be a good manager."

Jenny didn't understand this kind of horse trading. To her, "universal agreement" meant "universal agreement," and if her manager was going to take it back just because she was challenging him on the performance evaluation, maybe she'd better quit. She now thinks she'd have thrown in the towel but for her network.

One woman said, "Wait, let me check around and see what other jobs there might be for someone in your salary bracket. I can do it without letting anyone know who's looking." But she came back with bad news on that front. Jenny would have to move to another city to come anywhere near matching her present job. She wasn't willing to move—her husband and children were dug in right there—so she had to keep on trying to get her evaluation cleaned up.

The network finally persuaded her to do what she had at first said she couldn't do—go over her immediate boss's head. She told the whole story to a higher-up who proved to be friendly, who, in fact, said, "This company isn't always as fair as it might be." The upshot was: she got to write her own evaluation, complimentary adjectives and all. From "treading water," she was back to "swimming quickly."

"I'm not on the fast track anymore; I can see that," she says. "That's mostly because I'm not willing to relocate. But I think they'll be pretty careful with me from here on out.

"Thanks to my network, I think I hit just the right tone in speaking up for myself. I didn't shrivel up and die, but I didn't threaten them, either.

"I really like my job. I'm glad to put in fifty to sixty hours a week when I need to, because this is really exciting work. I got to do the whole process design on a $3 million crude distillation; who could ask for anything more?

"I shudder to think what might have happened if I hadn't had my network to talk to. The men I work with weren't helping me any. I didn't even ask them to. This was a woman's problem, and women helped me resolve it."

Kate Rand Lloyd's story proves that networking is valuable even at the top. She was articles editor of *Vogue* when she decided she was stuck; she'd never be editor-in-chief. She talked it over with Eleanor Thomas Elliott, who had been on *Vogue* with her in the past but had since concentrated on volunteer work. "We decided I had to come out of hiding. Condé Nast [which publishes *Vogue*] can be like a convent. I knew everybody there, but no one outside, in the real world."

Elly introduced Kate into two of her own networks—an arts and literature committee, and a small women's discussion group. In the discussion group, Kate met Eleanor Clark French, prominent in Democratic party politics. As Jimmy Carter's 1976 campaign for the presidential nomination began, Kate decided to volunteer to help. She wanted to be seen out in the world. She called Eleanor Clark French, who by then knew Kate's professional standing; appreciating that Kate wasn't volunteering to stuff envelopes, Eleanor said she'd help line up a suitable assignment.

The scene shifts to the national nominating convention where, in the lower reaches of the Americana Hotel, Kate and a small, hard-pressed crew are writing and editing "Carter Convention News," two issues of which are to hit the convention floor before the wild week ends with Carter's nomination. Among those who stop by Kate's news desk is Elizabeth Forsling Harris, then publisher of a new magazine called *Working Woman*. Kate and Betty say, "When this is over, let's have lunch."

And they do. So when, later, Betty Harris is asked to find a replacement for the founding editor of the magazine, Betty thinks of—guess who? Kate becomes editor of *Working Woman*. It is close to two years since she decided to leave *Vogue*.

Jeri Jackson Feagans was administering a program for training minorities at the public television station in New York, when the president who had supported this program was replaced by one who didn't seem to care about it. She didn't appreciate the trouble she was in until she found herself describing it to three men she met at the annual public broadcasting convention, in Washington. "You need some support," they told her. "You are too insulated." And they invited her to call them any time she needed feedback. She did just that, calling their various offices in Los Angeles, Washington, and Cambridge, Massachusetts, as her job situation became more and more precarious.

That particular network helped her through a difficult period, but other networks were called into play when she found herself out of a job.

First, Eleanor Brown, director of management development for Westinghouse Broadcasting, whom she had met at a communications conference, advised, "Don't close any doors. Follow all leads." Without that advice she might have turned away when Lucile Cliete, administrator of compensation for NBC personnel and like Jackie a member of the National Association of Media Women, told her of an opening at Avis. She thought, "Me, a broadcast executive? What do I want with the rent-a-car business?" But she remembered Eleanor's advice and called for the interview at Avis. There she was interviewed by "the best interviewer I've ever encountered. She encouraged me to list my volunteer activities on the application, which wouldn't have occurred to me, and my volunteer work included managing the campaign office for David Dinkins. That name apparently leaped off the paper when William Schechter, the vice-president in charge of public relations for Avis, was interviewing me. He had been active in Democratic politics, working for Bobby Kennedy, and he knew a lot of the same people I had met when working for Dinkins." She got the job.

Jeri Jackson Feagans is now community relations and publicity manager for Avis. As such, she has expanded her network to include people working in all kinds of community organizations. But she has also kept up with her broadcast-media network. She's in this book because of another network—Women Business Owners. She was on a panel; I was in the workshop!

The first woman principal of a high school on the east side of Seattle got there because of her network. After her first interview, she told other network members she had an uneasy feeling about her prospects. "I can tell by the questions that they don't think a woman can handle the job," she said. "Can you help?" They could and did: members who had influence with the school board telephoned in her behalf. Others wrote letters.

From that same network, in Bellevue, Washington, comes a story that illustrates the importance of getting inside information before going after a job. One member of the network was interviewed for a position as consultant to the school district but was turned down because she already held elective office. She then passed word of the opening along to another member of the network and proceeded to brief her thoroughly on the post, giving her all the information she'd collected through several weeks of discussion and negotiation for the job. So equipped, the second networker was able to convince the school authorities that she was just the person they needed as a consultant.

Network groups sometimes go to bat officially for their members. "We recently had two women call us about career problems," reports Joretta J. White, vice-president of the Network of Women in Business in Indianapolis, Indiana. "I personally worked with one woman and helped her put together a series of answers to questions raised by her employer. I also called her immediate supervisor about her problem; happily, the supervisor was glad to talk to me, and everything worked out to everyone's satisfaction." And the supervisor later joined the Network herself!

Joretta's own job is that of principal planner for the Department of Metropolitan Development in Indianapolis. Other networkers include ten presidents, directors, or owners of businesses; eight attorneys; nineteen communications professionals, including representatives of all media; nine salespeople; six real estate specialists; four advertising executives; four vice-presidents of corporations. "With so much expertise to call upon in time of need, we all feel more secure in our jobs," says Roberta Broderick, an insurance broker who is president of the Network.

Here's a four-step chain that is typical of the networking process:

STEP 1: At a 1977 seminar of the Bay Area Executive Women's Forum (BAEWF), Diane Winokur meets Karen Torrey. They maintain infrequent contact but mutual respect.

STEP 2: Two years later, a young woman new to San Francisco is introduced to Karen. Karen refers her to Diane.

STEP 3: Diane makes some suggestions for job hunting and invites young woman to BAEWF meeting.

STEP 4: At BAEWF meeting, the young woman is introduced to Betty Burr, who has a job available in her department, one that fits the young woman's needs and abilities.

Marilyn Schultz had been out of the film business, and out of New York, for four years; she knew she had to let people know she was back if she expected to make a go of it as a free-lance film producer, so she began telephoning around her old network ("although I hadn't called it that at the time"). These were contacts she'd made when on the news staff at NBC. "I didn't think anybody would remember me, and I hate making those 'Hello-how-are-you?' kinds of calls, but I knew I had to do it." She called Marjorie Guthrie, the widow of Woodie Guthrie, who started the Committee to End Huntington's Disease after his death. Marjorie came on the phone with a happy "How nice to hear from you! We show your film all the time!"

"I had completely forgotten the 'film,' which was a videotape I had put together for her as a favor, using news clips we had broadcast from time to time at the station. It turned out she'd been showing it at fund raisers ever since."

With that beginning, the two took up where they'd left off five years before. They're talking about doing a new film, with Marilyn this time serving as a free-lance producer-writer. To be called *A House United*, it will further Marjorie's dream of getting the different committees for all neurological diseases together in a single campaign to raise money for research and patient care.

Marilyn says, "When I think how I had to force myself to make that call! Now it looks as though I'll be helping Marjorie realize a dream, just as she'll be helping me get back into the film business."

When Beverly Rivers came to New York from Toronto, she knew no one. All she knew was that she wanted to go into business for herself, not work for someone else. She'd need a partner, she figured, one with the financial skills she felt shaky about, so she ran an ad of her own and also began to answer "Partner Wanted" ads in *The New York Times* and the *Wall Street Journal*. The leads thus produced were useless—"Nothing but pizza parlors and schlocky investment 'opportunities' "—so it dawned on Beverly that the city needed a clearinghouse where partners could find each other. But she couldn't believe in her own idea; she just kept looking for a partner.

That she did by attending every career-oriented lecture, seminar, panel, and class she heard about, "networking off each event." Three women she met turned out to be important to her: Mary Ellen Spiegel, marketing director for *Chain Store Age*, whom she met at one of Sharon Bermon's "Counseling Women" seminars; Alexandria Hatcher, a member (later president) of Women Business Owners, whom she met at one of the dinners that Executive Woman holds; and Mildred Tuffield, a prominent financial consultant who gives a course on starting your own business at Hunter College, whom Beverly met by taking the course, then asking for a private conference. "Mildred said, 'You're dynamic enough; you have the idea; *go*!' It was what I needed—an authority figure, to whom I had transferred power, giving me the go-ahead. Next day I went to Citibank, where I talked my way into a start-up loan."

The result is Business Partner Search, Inc., for which, ironically, Beverly has no partner. She runs forums at which businessmen (mostly men) take the mike to outline the ventures for which they seek partners and, during the evening, match their needs with others' expertise. Mary Ellen Spiegel has been a speaker and has turned up other speakers; Alexandria Hatcher has run a pre-forum workshop on how to present yourself and your business effectively in a short speech; and Mildred Tuffield has "provided me with the most powerful networking I've ever done. She must have led me to fifteen or twenty people by now, including the prestigious authorities on my advisory board, with three or four intervening contacts on the way to each."

When Letitia Baldrige was ill, she called on members of the Women's Forum to write her syndicated column, "Contemporary Living." "I use the Forum in many other ways," says Tish, "always when checking someone out, as in: 'Would X make a good director?' They're all just great. Nobody ever turns you down. When they don't know something, they find out."

Like most successful women, Tish belongs to more

than one network. Her others include Trends, a small monthly luncheon group of fashion executives; the National Home Fashions League; and the Fashion Group. Men as well as women belong to two others, the American Society of Interior Designers and the Public Relations Society of America.

Alice Ely, editor of a trade publication called *Non-Foods Merchandising*, needed pictures to accompany a feature about Seattle, and she needed them fast. A member of Women in Communications, a national network, she called the job "chair" of the Seattle chapter, who said she'd check her list of member free-lancers and get back in touch. "Within minutes," Alice says, "Peg Keene, part-time writer-photographer for the *Washington Food Dealer*, called me back and offered to do the job for me the next day. Peg was ideal; I needed a supermarket photo, and that was where her expertise lay. The entire hunt for a free-lance photographer had taken half an hour.

"When I told my publisher I'd found a photographer, he could not believe how fast I'd done it. And, because I gave the credit to WIC connections, he's shown a marked interest in my 'women's group' ever since."

Vivian Raskin was a hospital management consultant in Baltimore, working for a firm in Chicago, when her husband, a physician, asked her to fill in for his secretary for a week or two. While seeing how badly her own husband's office was run, she conceived the idea of going into business for herself, as a management consultant to physicians, dentists, lawyers, and other professionals who could use a computerized billing service she would set up. She needed technical advice on the computer part. As she tried to find it, she had an unsettling experience she still doesn't like to talk about.

"Let's just say the people I had been working with were

untrustworthy," says Vivian. "I suspected some infringement on ideas and concepts. It took me a while to retrust." But through Ruth Adams, chair of the board of her network, she met Patricia Meyer, national accounts manager for the Commercial Credit Services Corporation, who understood computers. Pat helped Vivian research her project, directing her to people who proved helpful—including two women bankers through whom she got financing she couldn't get anywhere else (because she had never established a credit rating in her own name).

"I couldn't believe how many women were so very willing to help me get my business started. The feeling of support and encouragement I've gotten from the network is absolutely incredible," says Vivian. "I've leased my computer and signed my first client, my husband. Medicharge is under way!"

Carol Angstman Maul, then in business for herself as Creative Images, in San Francisco, was asked to speak to other members of Women Entrepreneurs there, a network of women business owners. She talked about her work, which was coordinating logos and letterheads and brochures for new companies, telling how she was managing on a low budget. "My phone started ringing at nine the next morning, with clients. The women saw something they wanted, including the low overhead that kept my fees down, and I looked successful to them. Women are very much into using the services of other women—a phenomenal exchange—and it meant a lot to me."

Soon afterward, though, Carol moved to Portland, Oregon. She couldn't take her San Francisco clients with her, but she certainly took the idea of establishing a network of other women entrepreneurs. In the spring of 1979, with a core group of about twenty, to be augmented by a story that reporter Judy McDermott was then writing for the Portland paper, the *Oregonian*,

Carol was in the process of starting a new Women Entrepreneurs group. "We all need this," she said. "The message we all brought each other was 'Hey, we can do it!' And a woman struggling along on her own can't hear too much of that!"

Carin A. Clauss, solicitor, U.S. Department of Labor, says the network was primarily responsible for her appointment. She had been an assistant solicitor and didn't know anyone in the new Carter administration. Because of the Hatch Act, which forbids political activity by federal employees, she couldn't establish her own political base. But Mary King, who had worked hard in the Carter campaign, knew of her, and at the beginning of the administration, Mary was meeting with every cabinet officer, usually before his or her confirmation, to suggest women who could be appointed to the subcabinet level. Mary suggested Carin. Carin got the appointment.

Carin pooh-poohs the idea of a merit promotion at her level. "I was on all kinds of lists, but lists get stuck into desk drawers. I needed someone to make direct and personal contact on my behalf. That's what Mary did for me."

The new ambassador to Barbados, Sally Shelton, says the same. So does Richard F. Celeste, the new Peace Corps director: "You've heard of the old boys' network?" he said, in a speech. "I am here as a result of the old girls' network."

"The network continues to work," says Carin. "All the women who got in are able to throw out the net to bring in other women. Mary started this."

Mary King is deputy director of an agency that might have been named after her—Action. (It's the federal agency for volunteerism.)

The Women's Media Group, an invitational network of one hundred or so women working in New York City publishing, advertising, and broadcasting, conducted an anonymous wage and salary study of its membership a few years ago. "We all suspected we were underpaid," says Fredrica Friedman, a senior editor at *Reader's Digest* and (in 1979) treasurer for the group, "but we really didn't *know*, until we put our survey information together with what the men we knew told us about what they were making. It was devastating! The upshot was that many of us demanded more money. And got it!"

Like many other women, B.N. (before networking), the media women had been operating out of ignorance. Sitting across the desk from a man who said, "What salary do you want?" they didn't know what to ask for. Sharing the results of the membership survey changed all that.

Suzanne Jeffers was new in New York. She went to see her friend Lou Willett Stanke, who worked in personnel at Philip Morris. Lou made three phone calls, with the result that Suzanne found herself teamed up with Cathy Willis to write a proposal for a training program, which was sold to Chase Manhattan Bank. This created a job for Cathy, who then hired Suzanne to do the training. She in turn hired another member of the network to help her.

Suzanne has now incorporated herself and is making $70,000 a year, touring the country as spokeswoman for Du Pont, talking about women in business.

"My network has become national," she says, "now that women who see me on television are writing me, and I'm hearing, too, from universities and organizations that ask me to speak. It's very exciting. I love my work; I love being able to help other women. And, you know, the help always comes back, in some way or another. I think this is really the only way for women to move ahead—to reach back and pull forward the next woman in the line. The jobs and the entrepreneurial opportunities that are the most fun and the best-paying are, as we all know, filled from the inside. The more women we get on the inside, the more other women will hear about these opportunities.

"I find that women who operate from a position of strength are the most willing to share, to help. It's those who haven't a lot to offer, unfortunately, who misunderstand and misuse this fabulous networking system we have going for us.

"But as one who came to New York from California, cold, a year and a half ago, at the time thoroughly intimidated by the idea of moving to the big city, I can say absolutely that anyone who follows up on the leads offered, who takes the action step, as I call it, will get in on the excitement—and the profits. I see no end to this. The future is ours."

And lastly, a fitting climax.

The scene is the "ladies'" room.

The time is after a lunch for Sarah Weddington, sponsored by a combination of networks in San Francisco, at the instigation of the Professional Women's Alliance. Six hundred women have turned out for the $20-a-ticket affair, although only four hundred could be accommodated. In the ladies' room there is a crush.

A voice from a stall is apparently continuing a conversation with another woman in the line. The voice is that of Roxanne Mankin, president of her own investment real estate syndication company—meaning she buys, manages, and improves real estate worth $15 million for seventy investors. The voice says, "I'm looking for a comptroller for my company. Do you know a CPA with heavy financial experience?" An excited voice from the next stall: "I'll be right out!" So there, in the perfect locker room atmosphere of the old boys' network, Joan Mills, an executive searcher specializing in women in the financial area, finds a new client in Roxanne.

"The network has been a lot more help to me than that," says Roxanne. She has had "a hard time," with "a lot of pushing around," in being taken seriously, because she's an attractive, young (thirty-five) woman making big deals. "When I go in to talk about a $2 or $3 million loan, say, it helps to have had someone call ahead and say, 'Listen, she's competent, she knows her business, and she *does* close her deals.' Saves me a lot of time in proving and re-proving myself."

She can do the same for other women in her network, adding to their credibility.

"That's how it works. And it's terrific," she says.

The Alliance plans to affiliate with the Women's Forum in New York. Manhattan ladies' rooms, take notice.

Equally pertinent are unsuccess stories. Here are a few cases in which the women concerned had no network to help them.

Abby C. was hired to put out a newsletter for a nonprofit agency. The executive director, who hired her, told her he wanted a balance in newsletter coverage of the various volunteer committees and their work. She took that to mean she shouldn't feature six pictures in which the same woman appeared, but when she printed an issue without the pictures a certain volunteer expected to see, the woman complained—not to her, but to the director. The director then called Abby in and told her she had offended the volunteer. He put it to her that she had a personality problem!

That's just one incident, and it's oversimplified, but it's an example of what kept happening. Abby would do what her boss wanted; a volunteer would want something else; Abby would be in the middle. And whenever such a conflict came to a head, the director would back off, never acknowledging that she was carrying out his orders.

Looking back, Abby says she made two mistakes that could have been avoided if she'd had anyone to talk to about her job. One was taking the director's word for what the volunteers said about her, instead of hearing the complaints firsthand. She should have insisted on a three-way meeting, or at least she should have talked directly to the volunteers. (When she finally did the latter, she learned that the director had overstated the facts.) The other was not appreciating the importance of the volunteer committee members. "I thought the committees were a nuisance; I thought the executive director was my boss," she says. "Actually, the volunteers were *his* boss, and he was putting me out in front with them, trying out his ideas. When his ideas were acceptable, they were his; when they drew complaints, they were mine."

Abby had been "too busy trying to stay on top of the job" to seek out her predecessor or talk to other people in the office about why that woman had left and why the post had been unfilled for three months before Abby was hired. Otherwise she'd have known the director had pulled these tricks before, and she'd have figured out how to protect herself. She'd also have seen that her own interests lay with the volunteers, who were mostly prominent people from whom future leads and recommendations would be invaluable. As it was, when she finally was put in the position of being offered another job in the agency, because of her "personality problem," she not only didn't have a network she might have cultivated, she didn't even have good references.

Marilyn Moats Kennedy says, "If anything that happened in your office in the past six months surprised you, you aren't plugged in."

Mary L. was totally surprised. It wasn't until years later, in fact, that she realized what had happened, not just to her but to Jerry T., the man who had hired her to produce a monthly children's page for the women's magazine of which he was managing editor. Although Mary had known Jerry for many years, she had no reason to think he was hiring her out of friendship: she was a pro; she had written several children's books; she believed him when he said she was exactly right for the job.

She was excited about the possibilities and full of ideas, which she submitted to Jerry in outline form. He okayed a few and she produced them in rough layout form, at which point they went to the editorial board for approval. They were turned down. Mary was not included in the board meetings—only the top editors attended—so she didn't hear exactly what was said about her roughs, but Jerry told her it was a question of hitting the right tone. He said not to be discouraged—it always takes a new editor a few false starts before she or he finds the right "voice" for this magazine—but Mary couldn't help feeling inadequate. She also felt that she was letting Jerry down.

She tried again and again, with the same results. Meanwhile, the magazine she was supposed to be contributing to continued to be published without a children's page of any kind. She could see why they would want the first such page to be just right, but the concept of what would be right became more and more elusive. She began to wonder how they could afford to pay her salary if she was not producing.

Her ideas began to dry up. She could criticize everything she thought of almost before she thought of it. Her enthusiasm gone, she couldn't muster the energy necessary to produce roughs. In the beginning, when the art department said they were too busy to work on her material, she pressed and nagged until she got what she needed. Now she didn't blame them for being too busy:

why should they spend their valuable time on pages that were not going to get into the magazine anyway?

After months of this stalemate, at a time when the managing editor was away on an extended trip (which he hadn't bothered to tell Mary he was taking), the executive editor called her into his office. He and Jerry were of equal rank, with an editor-in-chief above them both. Mary had not met with him before because the children's page was meant for what's called the front of the book, which was Jerry's domain. The executive editor inquired into her background in a conversation that seemed very much like a job interview; she realized he didn't know anything about her. Then he told her there was to be no children's page. He had been persuaded against his better judgment to experiment with the idea, but he had known from the start, and the board had agreed, that it wasn't going to work. He offered to try Mary out on other assignments, but at that exact moment she realized she'd rather be home writing children's books. If she still could. She "quit."

It was weeks later, but she was still licking her wounds when Jerry called. He said he was surprised on his return to find her gone. "I wish you'd talked to me before you decided to quit," he said, and he sounded rather put-upon. He implied that she shouldn't have accepted the job if she hadn't been willing to give it more time than she had. Astounded by his tone, Mary went on the defensive: why hadn't he told her at the outset that the executive editor was against the whole idea, which was in any case experimental? Jerry said new ideas were always experimental; nobody had to be told that. He said if she'd stuck it out they could have pulled it off, but now, of course, the idea was dead. He couldn't blame the board if they weren't willing to hire someone else to work it out. It was easier to drop the whole thing. He was disappointed.

Now Mary felt herself to be a double failure: she had failed the magazine by not coming up with the "right" children's page; she had failed Jerry by not staying on, at least until his return.

Within three months, Jerry had been fired. Mary read the news in the paper. The news account said he had resigned "for reasons of health," and the executive editor was quoted as regretting the magazine's loss, but even a person of Mary's naïveté could read the truth between the lines. Two editors of equal rank had been struggling for dominance. Jerry had lost. Mary hadn't even known there was a war going on; nevertheless, she had been on the losing side.

By the time Mary realized that even a genius couldn't have devised a suitable children's page, or anything else that could be seen as Jerry's project, the damage had been done to her ego. Even today, although she knows that the quality of her work had nothing to do with anything, she says things like "My style doesn't lend itself to magazine work" and "I'm not a staff person." She says Jerry should have leveled with her from the beginning—he could have trusted her—but she thinks the reason he didn't was that she was not important enough to be taken into his confidence. (Notice the self-deprecation.) "Or," she speculates, "maybe he didn't know what was happening either." Innocence dies hard.

Mary was accustomed to working alone—most writers are—so it hadn't occurred to her to involve anyone else on the magazine in what she was trying to do. She chatted with the rest of the staff, at least that part of it officed near her, but she didn't ask them questions about anything more serious than how to requisition supplies. She usually had errands to run on her lunch hour, and she dashed home to her family every night after work, so she didn't hear any of the rumors that the others might be discussing over lunch or drinks. Maybe the others wouldn't have told them to her anyway—they probably identified her with Jerry—but she didn't give them the chance.

A network could not have changed the situation for her, but it could have saved her the grief and self-doubt she suffered. At least she'd have known what was going on around her.

"I've just left Al Clark," her ex-boss, Hugh, said, naming the creative director of one of the best advertising agencies in town. "He's licking his wounds on the squash court. I told him all about you and he's interested. He's going to be in his office all afternoon. Give him about twenty more minutes to get there, then give him a call. He'll be expecting to hear from you."

Cynthia should have been jubilant. Al Clark was exactly the man she'd been hoping to see in exactly the agency she'd like to join, and having Hugh put in a good word for her, in person, was invaluable. But as she hung up the phone she had mixed feelings. She had already had an interview at Clark's agency, a good interview with a man in personnel. He had been enthusiastic about her book (the collection of samples of her work that every advertising copywriter uses as her résumé); he had told her he'd arrange further interviews for her. It wouldn't be right to go over his head, would it? No. And besides, she had an ad to get out that afternoon on her present job. And besides . . . she needed a haircut.

Cynthia didn't make that call.

Four months later (by which time she needed another haircut!) she still hadn't reached Al Clark on the phone. He was always either out of town, out of the office, or in a meeting. The personnel man said he had put in a good word for her, but "Mr. Clark is a very difficult man to get hold of."

Six years later, when she was working at another, much less prestigious agency, she met Al Clark and told him the story in a kind of here's-a-joke-on-me manner. He looked blank, then incredulous. "There must be a place in heaven for people like you," he said. "Personnel heaven." Cynthia understood that she had done something utterly stupid by putting personnel's interests before her own.

"I had the uncomfortable feeling that he was glad he hadn't made the mistake of hiring me," she says. "And he certainly didn't say anything remotely like 'Well, now that we've met, call me next Tuesday at two.' He just moved on, shaking his head."

Could a network have helped? She could have asked someone how important it was to go the personnel route just because she'd started there. (Anyone could have told her this was misplaced loyalty. Even the personnel man would have understood the importance of direct access to the person with hiring power.) She could even have asked if her hair looked all right, that strictly female type of reassurance being helpful before a job interview.

But, of course, she had made her decision all alone, without talking to anyone. It wasn't until years later that she realized how naïve she had been, what a mistake she had made in her priorities.

□3 Square One

The networking phenomenon finds you where you are. How you use it, and for what purposes, will depend on your current situation and your career goal.

Talk of goals makes a lot of women nervous. They're not used to planning their careers. When asked to, as in career development seminars, they sometimes balk. It's as though one should, rather, sneak up on success, or have it "just happen." Also, not having announced that one is in the running makes possible a whole set of excuses for not winning: from "I didn't want it anyway," to "I could have had it if I'd really tried."

Even fully committed, up-front career women sometimes have a problem with goal setting: they set their sights lower than their capabilities, aspiring only to what they think might conceivably be attainable. They don't know that's what they're doing, of course, any more than I knew I was unnecessarily stereotyping myself when I set out to write for women's magazines, never even trying for the *New Yorker*, say, or *Scientific American*. Often it takes an outsider to point out the self-limitations of women. As a *Fortune* magazine writer did when Theresa Wyszkowski, Harvard 1973 M.B.A., said her "ultimate" goal was to be a plant manager for Digital

Equipment Company, where she then had a job in inventory accounting. "Would an ambitious *male* M.B.A. give plant manager as an ultimate goal?" the *Fortune* reporter wondered. "It seems unlikely. For Wyszkowski, it would be a breakthrough—no woman has ever held such a job; for a man equally motivated, just another job on the way to something bigger. Differences like these may help explain why women's aspirations—which after all have something to do with how far they go—are usually lower than men's."

Women who have already "made it" reflect the prevalent, rather superstitious attitude toward goal setting when they say, as so many do, "I was lucky. I was in the right place at the right time." Usually a more careful examination of such a career will reveal that the "right place" was a logical way station en route to the top, and the "right time" came after twenty-odd years of hard, qualifying labor. But on being so reminded, will the subject of this scrutiny then confess that she *wanted* to achieve her present pinnacle? Never, or almost never. It's as if she believes, even now, that her "luck" will run out if she admits to giving it a carefully orchestrated assist. She's Cinderella, nervously watching the clock.

It's the special beauty of networking that it can help women on every rung of the career ladder. It can help women who haven't yet faced up to the fact that they're probably going to be working for twenty years or more, with or without time out for child rearing. It can help them make up their minds to commit themselves to a serious career, or at least get them out where they can see where commitment might lead if and when they're ready.

At the same time, networking can help the woman who is frankly out to become chairman of the board, the one who is clear about her goals and is shooting high. She'll be networking in different places from both the one who is "just looking, thanks" and the "lucky" woman who has already achieved her goal, but the process will be the same for them all.

To begin, let's see where *you* are.

First, what kind of networking are you already doing?

One way to check up on yourself, in this regard, is to look at the appointment book on your desk and/or the pocket calendar you carry around with you. Note how many lunch dates you've had with how many persons of value to your career in the last month. Make the same check of your drink-after-work activities and, if you're free to make evening plans apart from your family, your dinner engagements.

Let's suppose you now discover that you have been lunching with friends only, and the same friends over and over at that; that you never go out for drinks (you don't drink); and that the evening hours in your date books are clean, white blanks.

Worse, let's suppose you don't even *have* an appointment book or a pocket calendar.

Never mind. You're in no worse shape than many of the members of a professional women's association who drew similar blanks when a workshop on networking opened with this exercise of the date books. "I use my lunch hour for shopping," said one. "I don't have to write my lunch dates down," said another. "I make them on the spot, usually falling in with whatever group is going out when I am." Others actually raised objections to this whole idea of what they referred to as "working" on their own time: they considered it work to talk business and career over lunch!

Most of the women in that group have good jobs, and they're enough committed to work to belong to the professional association in their field, so their reaction to the date book exercise cannot be attributed to lack of interest in their careers. They just didn't know about networking, or, if they did, they didn't know how to go about it.

If your calendar shows many appointments, with

many different people, the next step in assessing your present networking activity is to remember what you talked about during those meetings. Did you let those other persons know what you do in your job and how well you do it? Did you convey the impression that you're going places, not being too specific (it's not a good idea to reveal your total plan to just anybody) but nevertheless registering your keen interest in career advancement? Did you search conversationally for common ground with your lunch companions, looking for some future activity you could share? Did you listen carefully for clues to the other person's expertise and connections? That's good networking.

It's particularly good if at some time in the ensuing weeks you then followed up each lunch, took some kind of action based on what you learned about the other person, sent a clipping, made a phone call, or arranged for another meeting, this time with a third person included.

If, instead, you remember talking the whole time about children, dogs, houses, commuter schedules, and the high cost of lamb chops, you are again in very extensive company. Many women are reluctant to talk about themselves. A typical remark: "I don't like to brag." Few have any sense of being able to control a conversation. As a Cleveland systems analyst put it, "We talked about whatever came up, and one subject led to another, but we didn't get around to discussing our jobs." The idea that she could have brought the conversation around to good networking topics was new to her.

In contrast, consider the very organized and controlled method of networking set forth by a career counselor for her client, a young woman who started out being rather vague about her career goal and, in her own phrase, "totally mystified" about how and where networking could fit into it.

Jean was a newspaper reporter, working for a

neighborhood paper on the northwest side of Chicago. She'd been there two years, "learning a lot but not liking it much." Before that, she had put in a year as a junior writer in the advertising department of a big mail-order house, writing catalog copy; and before that she'd been editor-in-chief of her college newspaper, having worked up through three years of legwork on staff. Under questioning by the counselor, she realized that of the three jobs, the only one she really enjoyed was editor-in-chief, and what she liked most about that was not the writing—staffers did most of that anyway, under her direction—but the running of the paper. She liked being in charge. She liked making policy. What she didn't like about her job on the neighborhood paper was being told what to do and how to do it, particularly since the paper's policy was to subvert news to advertisers' interests, a policy she believed she'd have changed in a minute if she'd been in charge.

Her goal, then, was not, as she had assumed, to become a reporter on a bigger, better paper—the *Chicago Tribune*, the *Washington Post*, or *The New York Times*—but to run her own show, somehow, somewhere. Since she probably could never run any of the three papers she had considered her Mecca, there'd be no point in struggling and straining to work for them. After considerable homework and consultation with the counselor, she decided to move into public relations work, where she could use her writing skills at first, develop her management skills in a sizable agency, then finally either start her own public relations agency or become president of a going concern. ("Well, *vice*-president," she said.)

She and the counselor drew up a networking chart, mapping out a program to move her toward her goal. They decided that Jean's first networking task was to meet (1) people who use public relations agencies and (2) people who work in public relations agencies. Through the paper, she already knew about a cereal manufacturer whose P.R. agency regularly sent in recipes using breakfast flakes. Her first move was to get acquainted with the writer of the press release, which was as easy as picking up the phone and expressing journalistic interest in the recipes. Invited to visit the testing kitchens at the agency, she met other women too. She decided to do a story for her paper on what lies behind a seemingly simple recipe for cookies, which gave her an excuse to visit the client, the cereal manufacturer, as well. When the story ran in the paper—an easy sell to her editor and publisher, because he saw it as favorable to a potential advertiser—she saw to it that everyone she'd met received a copy, each with a thank-you note for his or her help in her research. She also sent it to other public relations agencies, suggesting they call her if they had similar accounts that would lend themselves to behind-the-scenes stories. They all called; she followed up with visits and interviews. Within three months she knew no fewer than sixteen women in public relations, several of whom had invited her to meetings of their professional associations (Women in Communications, the Advertising Women's Club, and the Public Relations Society). There she met women who enlarged her understanding of the ways public relations skills can be applied: one edited a university paper directed to graduates, as part of her fund-raising responsibilities in the office of a university president; another specialized in booking guests on radio and television talk shows; a third staged press-worthy events to attract volunteers to community organizations. Jean thereupon began to expand her network to include academia and government as well as business.

You could draw up a similar chart or a list for yourself to show:

1. *Your present network*—the various people you already know or know of and can readily connect with: colleagues or co-workers, present and past; your parents

and their networks; other relatives and their networks; neighbors, teachers, school friends, members of clubs you have belonged to in the past, even tradesmen, all of whom have networks of their own.

Maybe you haven't kept in touch with all those people. Chances are you never even bothered to find out who is in your parents' networks—the people they have worked with, even way back to the people they grew up with. And if your mother's best friend has a daughter who works for a designer in Paris, you never thought of the daughter as part of your network, much less the designer. But you could plug into all those networks, if you wanted to, even at this late date. They belong on your chart, or list.

2. *The network you're going to need* in order to get where you want to go. You may not know the names of these people, but you know what fields they're in and what kinds of jobs they hold. If your goal is to go into business for yourself, for instance, you're going to need information on what it takes to open up shop. You'll want to get to know women who already have done so, to learn of their experiences, to get their advice. You'll want to meet people in the financial community, assuming you're going to be needing capital. And you'll want to develop a network of potential customers or clients for your projected business. Chart or list these resources.

3. *Ideas on where and how you can meet* those members of your goal-oriented network of the future. The two most logical means of meeting new people are finding someone who already knows and can refer you to them and putting yourself in their path.

You could start on the number-one method right away, asking your own network, "Do you happen to know anyone who has gone into business for herself recently?" Following up on the first such lead you get, calling and going to see that woman business owner, you could ask her whom *she* talked to before making her move. If she then plugged you into her own network, as well she might, expecting that the good turn she does you will come back to her in time, you'd be well on your way to collecting the kind of information you want.

The number-two method requires the same move. First reach out into the community of women business owners: ask what organizations they belong to. Women Business Owners? Women Entrepreneurs? Specialized professional groups in fashion, training, real estate, consulting, whatever their business concerns? Go to the next meeting of each such group—most are open to self-invited guests who may be potential new members—where you'll meet more women to add to your growing network.

In addition to trade and professional associations, volunteer organizations provide other places where you can put yourself in the path of the kinds of people you want to meet. Many, if not most, successful people give some of their time and expertise to charities, cultural institutions, civic groups. You can target the particular people you want to meet by finding out their favorite causes and volunteering your own services.

The sort of business you have in mind to start will determine where best to look for future customers or clients. If interior decorating is your aim, you'll want to meet homeowners, architects, builders, furniture manufacturers, editors of decorating magazines, people who award contracts for decorating offices, and so on. They all belong to organizations, turn out for seminars directed to their specialties, teach courses, speak to appropriate groups, exhibit. With very little effort, you can go where they go and get acquainted with them.

Your chart or list will be altogether different if, instead of going into business for yourself, your goal is to change careers to—you know not what. (According to Richard Nelson Bolles, author of *What Color Is Your Parachute?*, four out of every five workers will seek a second career at some time or another during their work lives.) In that case you'll be listing, under "the network you're going to need," people who can tell you about opportunities and satisfactions in their various fields, career counselors, maybe instructors in continuing-education courses or graduate schools. And you'll be changing your chart or list as you go along, eliminating this possibility, pursuing that one deeper into its particular network.

Getting all this down on paper, even if only in the roughest of rough forms, will help you focus your thoughts and direct your efforts. Often a woman who is newly tuned in to networking will go off in all directions, meeting more people than she knows what to do with, spinning her wheels. That's fine if it gives her the hang of networking and helps her to feel comfortable with the technique. But networking works better when you know what you want from each new person and what you can give back in return. Having a clear goal in mind, and on paper, helps.

It also helps immensely to set yourself a schedule, a timetable of sorts, to keep yourself from falling back into old habits of "letting things happen." Networking is the process of *making* things happen; although serendipity often enters in, it's more likely to do so if you're out there where it can find you.

Jean's schedule, following up on her chart, called for making three new contacts a week, and for following up each of them at some time during the ensuing month. That is, she planned not only to meet new people in the public relations field but to keep in touch with them after she'd met them.

On her desk calendar, she blocked out three lunches a week for networking activity. As a reporter, she couldn't always count on having a lunch hour, though, so she figured on substituting drink or tea dates when necessary. She also promised herself she'd attend four evening meetings or events per month. When she fell behind, as sometimes happened, especially in the summer months, she'd redouble her efforts to maintain that average.

Another young woman gave herself a year in which to meet all the top women officers in her corporation (a multibillion, multinational one). She started by getting acquainted with their secretaries and other subordinates. It was actually two years before she completed the assignment she had given herself, but if she hadn't been following a schedule, she thinks, it would probably have taken years longer.

In your own case, suppose your networking objective is simply to start meeting and getting to know as many new people as you can, so that you can get the hang and habit of networking. Let your target be the broad one of women who work. If they happen to fit into the diagram you've drawn for yourself, fine. If not (and you can't be absolutely sure of that until after you get to know them), networking with them will be good practice for you.

In addition or instead, look for networking groups of the sort described in Part II of this book. As you've already seen, they can be vertical or horizontal, occupational or city-wide. They can also exist, sad to say, just to capitalize on the potential market value of a group of women executives. A group in the Midwest, its eye clearly on the interests of hotel owners and convention promoters rather than on women's need for equal rights, issued a press release opposing the boycott of states that have not ratified the Equal Rights Amendment to the U.S. Constitution—of which, of course, their own state was one. Members who had paid $100 to join felt they had been ripped off, not to say betrayed.

In short, don't rush to join the first network group you discover. Attend a meeting or two; talk to the officers about their personal goals and their plans for the group; read their literature and press clippings, if any. You want to be part of a mutual-assistance network, not a member of a captive "market" that a clever promoter plans to "deliver" to the many businesses eager to sell products to the working woman.

If you don't find a network that suits your needs, you could start your own. (You'll find step-by-step directions in Appendix A.)

What do you say to these people, once you've found them? You tell them who you are, what you do, and what you're looking for. You find out the same about them, and if what they do or what they're looking for fits into your own scheme of things, you add them to your network. And they add you to theirs. Then you both feel free to call on each other as the need arises. Soon or late, you get together on a project of mutual interest, helping each other, doing business together.

When using your network in the course of a job hunt, it's best to ask for sources of information rather than for leads to job interviews per se. That is, instead of saying, "I'm looking for a job. Do you know of any openings?" say something like "I'm interested in X Company. Do you happen to know anyone who's ever worked there whom I could ask—off the record—about their affirmative action plan?" or "I have an idea I'd like to present to X Company or the agency that has their account. Do you know anyone who could advise me on whom to see there?" Or like Jean, the reporter, "My experience has been with newspapers so I'm sure I could write good press releases. Do you know anybody who could tell me which public relations agencies are the fastest-growing, right now?"

That way, the person who refers you isn't in the position of recommending you for a job, only for an information interview. Equally, the person you go to see will be prepared to give you information or advice—including two other people to see—and won't have to say, "Sorry, no openings." Everyone likes to give advice; no one likes to say no. Your hope is that you will impress your interviewees with your capabilities or that they themselves will buy the idea or proposal you're supposedly asking for advice about, so that your information interviews will in fact turn into job offers. But your stance is that you're researching a particular field or industry, which you haven't yet decided to enter.

But immediate job hunting is only the least part of networking. The big payoff will come years from now, when you're putting together a big corporation and need to know who can do the legal work, who can handle the financing, who's your best bet as marketing director, and what women heading what big industries will become your most important customers. The women you meet today may not have that kind of experience and clout, but when they finally get it, wrenching it away from the "system" with the strength they're only just developing now, you'll know them. They'll be in your network, and you in theirs, because you made a point of meeting them way back when.

Meanwhile, the new women you're going to meet through networking are people you can talk to about your career. They'll be women who are caught up in their own careers, so they'll understand your concerns; they'll be knowledgeable about the work world and what it's like to be a woman in it. That's what makes them different from the women you already know, members of your social network, and different from the men in both your social and your work network. Although it's possible that your best friend from high school is also a working woman and your ex-boyfriends are also knowledgeable about the work world, that hasn't been the basis of your relationship with them. These new people you're going to meet, on the other hand, will be added to your network for strictly business reasons. You may develop more personal relationships with some of them—there's no rule against it!—but friendship is not your purpose.

Which brings us to a point that confuses many a neophyte networker: you don't have to *like* the people you network with. That's hard to swallow for some women. Men appear to be much less likely to let their personal feelings affect their business dealings. They'll work with whoever is there, with whoever's in a position to do what they want done, with pragmatic lack of regard for that person's character. Margaret Hennig and Anne Jardim, authors of *The Managerial Woman*, think this is because boys grow up playing on teams; they'd never get a nine together if everybody had to like everybody else. Whether or not that's the explanation, men do seem to be able to withhold or to set aside personal judgments in order to get what they want out of any particular situation. In my observation, they don't even drop another man who has done them dirt. They have what is to me a flabbergasting ability to move on past yesterday. Whether this is a front or not, it appears to save energy and to keep all bridges open.

So, try to set your personal and political life to one side as you build your work-related network. Include people for their jobs, their expertise, and their connections, not for their personal attractiveness or its lack.

That doesn't mean you *mustn't* like your network members, of course. You probably will. But you don't *have* to.

□4 Psyching Yourself Up

"I feel that I am a successful woman because . . ." One after another, women in the crowded meeting room stood up, gulped, and completed that sentence. For the first few, it seemed to be a struggle. They said things like "I get to work on time" and "I raised three children." But the next few spoke more distinctly, and they began to think of accomplishments more directly related to "getting ahead" in the business world: "I've had three salary jumps in two years so I guess I must be doing *something* right"; "I'm getting my degree *and* managing my department *and* looking after my family"; "I just closed a deal worth a quarter of a million dollars to my company."

By the time the exercise was over and every woman had taken her turn at the hand mike, the room had come alive with energy and hope. The women were sitting up straighter, smiling expectantly, looking a hundred times more self-confident than when they'd first drifted into the meeting.

The leader then described to them what had happened. "You were embarrassed at first, weren't you? And you, back there, you who were unlucky enough to go first, you could barely get the words out. You thought somebody would surely take you to task for calling yourself *successful?*" The woman in the back nodded vigorously. "But then you got bolder and braver, and you actually said some nice things about yourselves, and the ceiling didn't fall in, did it? And the last woman who spoke—where is she? There! Behind the column. You were actually *bragging*, weren't you? How did it feel?"

"Wonderful!" the "braggart" called out. "Terrific!" And everyone laughed comfortably. The meeting was under way.

It was a meeting about networking. The speaker presented an idea that was new to the group: when you fail to put your best self forward, frankly acknowledging your abilities, you do your listeners a disservice. With so much self-deprecating concealment to get behind, can you blame them if they don't stick around long enough to find out that you're a really good resource for them, someone they should add to their own networks? Do them a favor: announce your good points, admit you're someone worth knowing! Tell them why.

The meeting then broke into small groups for a few exercises intended to make each woman aware of her good qualities and to give her practice in talking about them. In one such exercise, each woman named something that had given her satisfaction or a sense of accomplishment in the past year. Then a partner would quiz her on the steps she had taken to achieve that feat, whatever it was, breaking it down into its components so that she could see more clearly what she did well. (The things that give us the most satisfaction are usually the things we do well.)

For example, one woman said she had gotten an A in her evening economics course. It satisfied her particularly because she'd been afraid to take the course, but it turned out to be "easy—nothing to brag about." Her partner asked questions, and together they made a list of what getting an A entailed, from turning up on time for every class (despite the difficulties of going home from work and getting the kids fed first), finding the assigned books in the library, reading and understanding unfamiliar material, asking the right questions, down to taking the final exam (*not* getting sick or having an accident in an unconscious attempt to avoid it).

The economics woman then did the same for her partner, who chose as her most satisfying accomplishment the writing of a proposal for a grant—which won $85,000 for the community center she worked for. Interestingly, her partner's questions brought out the fact that the whole program had been her own idea originally. She'd actually forgotten! She came out of that session knowing she was not only a thorough researcher and a competent writer but an innovator.

After that particular exercise, the women changed partners, with the assignment of telling the new person about the accomplishments they'd just reviewed.

"Talk as though you've just met at a networking meeting," the leader instructed. "Get the other person's name and find out what she does, just as you would in a real-life situation, but make sure you let her know what *you* do, including the accomplishment."

The low hum that had prevailed during the exercise now moved up in tone and volume as women talked to each other with new animation and conviction. A truly amazing change had come about.

The leader explained. "It's as though we have to have *permission* to think and speak well of ourselves," she said. "But once we've got it, and given ourselves permission to act on it, we are energized, supercharged." She hesitated. "I just hope these women will look and talk this way out in the real world. It's hard, really hard, for many of them. They've been 'shrinking violets' for so long!"

That's the problem, of course—taking the risk (and it *is* a risk) of being put down by others if we don't first put ourselves down. It's safer to build up another's ego—and how well we've done that, for so long, for men!—than to put our own on the line.

But some of the younger women coming into their own have never had to pull their punches for the sake of the "modest maiden" stereotype, and many of the older ones were already straining at the leash when "assertiveness training" came along to make speaking up for oneself acceptable. Probably it's only women in their thirties who need the drill of networking exercises to loosen them up.

For them, and/or for you who may be starting your own networking groups and looking for program ideas, here are some of the other exercises currently being used by facilitators:

1. List five things you don't like about yourself. Now list five things you do like.

Choose a partner and have a three-minute conversation with her, trying to show her the side you do like.

Ruth Moghadam, a management consultant and trainer in New York and California, finds that women write rapidly on the first part of this exercise. But when it comes to thinking of things they do like about themselves they often go blank. The forced conversation helps them focus on the positive.

2. What five adjectives would your boss use when describing you to a stranger?

What five adjectives would your greatest admirer use—your lover, husband, mother, whoever likes you best?

This again is an attempt to get women to see themselves as others see them, rather than to linger over their unattractive or unsatisfactory qualities.

3. Think of the one person whose good opinion of you could conceivably work instant magic on your career. Now, imagine you have five minutes in a taxi with that person. What will you say about yourself?

4. In twenty-five words or fewer, answer a stranger

from outer space who has just asked, "What do you do?" Tell what your job is. Go!

This exercise, too, is usually a round robin. The leader often interrupts, saying, "I'm from outer space, remember. I don't know what a secretary is. Tell me what a secretary *does*, not what she is." New York Women Business Owners held a special seminar on how to define a given business clearly and invitingly in twenty-five words or fewer. Anyone who was accustomed to saying, "I'm an agent," for instance, learned to say, instead, "I work with writers in developing good ideas for books and articles, then I represent them in business negotiations with editors and publishers who are interested in turning the ideas into reading matter."

Any networker is bound to be asked, "What do you do?" So it's a good idea to practice and perfect an intriguing answer.

5. Arriving at the networking meeting, everyone finds on her chair or at her place at the table a long, narrow name tag. She's asked to write in her name and job title at the top, then to fill in the blanks below. The headings are: "I am expert in . . ." and "I am interested in . . ." She then pins this tag to her left shoulder and starts circulating around the room, looking for someone whose tag says she is interested in similar things.

When everyone in the group is "bragging" this way, most women allow themselves to "admit" to their expertise, writing in everything from "keeping peace in the office" to "changing tires" to "zero-base budgeting." The idea is to be specific—to find someone else in the group who also is interested in backpacking, Doris Lessing novels, crossword puzzles, or something else set forth on the name tag.

Once this happens, the facilitator points out that this is the kind of conversation networkers will have without benefit of tags, if only they'll approach the new people they meet the same way, looking for common ground. At one meeting where those tags were used, by the way, Phyllis Cohen wrote in big letters, under "I am interested in, . . ." "GETTING A JOB!" A member who saw the tag told her about an opening at Equitable and gave her the direct phone number to call. She got the job—in training and development.

After going to a number of those practice sessions, I realized that the same questions and reservations about networking kept coming up. Here's a summary of the problem areas and the answers that were suggested by more experienced networkers. (In supportive groups, no question is too unsophisticated or "dumb" to be addressed, without put-down, by the others.)

How networking talk differs from ordinary chitchat. It's nondomestic, for the most part. Its main purpose is to get people connected on a job level. The unwritten law is to keep your husband and children out of the conversation. Appropriate small talk is of current events, particularly as they relate to women's employment. Sports, hobbies, leisure-time interests. "Woman's place" and other aspects of the women's movement. Films. And, always, the meeting you're attending—the food, the speaker, the turnout.

Students of the art prepare a few remarks ahead of network meetings, reading the papers, looking over the magazines the women they expect to meet probably read—*Business Week* and *Forbes* and the *Harvard Review* as well as *Working Woman*, *Savvy*, and *Ms*.

This method can backfire, though, if it requires the other person to say, "I've been too busy to keep up with the news" or "I haven't had time to go to a movie for the last six months." Betty K. has the best system. Instead of "What did you think of that latest release from the tobacco manufacturers?" to which the other might have to reveal ignorance by asking, "What release?" Betty puts the item out as a statement: "I was interested to see that the tobacco manufacturers are now blaming air pollution. At least they're not saying that lung cancer is good for you." The other woman can pick up on a comment like that whether she's read the news release or not.

How to introduce yourself and, if you're wearing a name tag, whether to say your name or not. Most networkers come down on the side of saying your own name clearly and often. It saves the other the effort of leaning forward and peering at your name tag, which breaks the eye contact so necessary to getting acquainted.

"I tell my clients to practice introducing themselves to their own mirrors," says Julie O'Mara, partner in Response and Associates (in California). "And if they tend to mumble, alternate saying their own names with saying, 'Hello, I'm Katharine Hepburn' or 'Hi. I'm Margaret Mead.' Or anyone else whose name they'd be proud to shout out. That's the tone I'm after—matter-of-fact but confident. First impressions count enormously, and someone who starts off by swallowing her own name is making a poor one."

Julie recommends saying your name when going up to someone you've met before, too, unless you're positive she'll remember it. "Remind her where you met. She'll be grateful, even if she then says, 'Of course!' "

Networkers usually use first names straight off, without standing on ceremony, starting with the introduction: "Hello, Sarah," to the woman who has just introduced herself, "I'm Mary Jones." But on the odd chance that Sarah prefers to be called Sally, it's safer to say, "Are you called Sarah?" and to give her a chance to tell you her nickname.

What not to talk about. The old etiquette books proscribed the three *D*'s: Death, Disease, and Domestics. The newly evolving etiquette of networking warns against three *C*'s:

Criticism—Don't bad-mouth anyone, not even your impossible boss. It's important to speak in positive terms whenever you can. Of course, when you're leveling with someone on a one-to-one basis, you must be honest, and that includes giving your honest opinion of someone who's really a black hat. But don't broadcast the negatives in ordinary conversation.

Children—And pets, and houses, and crabgrass, and recipes, unless they're job related. However, members of a network in Boston consider that the matter of finding a good baby-sitter is as business-related as salary information. And in Chicago, Erika Brown says she definitely uses her network for parenting support.

Confidences—Trading information is an important part of networking, and you get points for reporting news before it's general knowledge, but be careful not to violate personal or employer confidence in the process.

How to ask questions. An Atlanta workshop on this subject was particularly successful because the discussion leader was an experienced journalist. In sum, she said: Asking questions is a good way to draw another person out, but for two reasons it's best not to fire questions in a steady stream. The TV interviewer who sticks the mike into someone's face may get the story for her viewers, but she doesn't let us know who *she* is. That's right for her; but it's not right for you. While you're drawing information out of the other person, you want to be supplying that other person with information about yourself.

Also, a series of questions can make the other person uncomfortable. Outside the context of an interview, repeated questions can seem intrusive. In defense, people will give bland, nonrevealing answers.

Therefore, it's best to preface your questions with information about yourself. "I design training programs. What do you do?" rather than the bare "What do you do?" "I haven't been to many meetings like this, have you?" rather than "Do you go to meetings like this very often?" Particularly when you're venturing into more personal territory, reveal yourself before expecting another to reveal herself. "Have you ever been fired?" might cause an instant retreat; not so, "I was crushed when I was fired, but now I think they did me a favor. Have you ever been fired?"

One tool of the journalist's trade is well worth adapting to network conversations—the follow-up question, a second question based on hearing the answer to the first. Listen, then ask for development of the same subject. Robert MacNeil (public television) often does that with a flat-out "Could you say more about that?"

If you find yourself on the receiving end of too many questions, you can always turn them back. In answer to "Have you ever been fired?," for example, you might say, "Yes, but why do you think they did you a favor by firing you?" When overpressed, follow the example of the diplomat in that apocryphal story about guarded speech: to the question "What time is it?" he asked right back, "What does *your* watch say?"

Who pays, when networkers go out to lunch? Women had been saying they didn't know how to follow up after meeting new people they'd like to know better. Group leaders had been saying things like "Call them up. Make lunch dates" and "Invite them to go with you to the next meeting or seminar you plan to attend. *Do* something together."

But the group seemed to have some objection to making these kinds of dates with other women. When the question of who pays came up, the group came to life. "I really can't afford to be taking people out to lunch," one woman said. "We'd have to go to a nice place, not the coffee shop where I usually go, and—well, I'm broke enough already!"

It turned out that they were all assuming that the person who suggests going out to lunch is automatically the hostess. Not so. Networking is not a social arrangement; it's business. Women pay for themselves, only, or they take turns picking up the tab, just as men do. It doesn't matter who suggests the lunch. Unless she makes it clear in advance that she is entertaining, Dutch treat is understood.

In the group discussion over this issue, it was agreed that there'd be many exceptions to the rule. "I'd insist on paying if I were asking the other woman for a favor," said one. But on the whole they accepted the Dutch treat principle with alacrity.

When inviting someone to a meeting, the group decided, it would be wise to mention the entrance fee at the same time, unless you intend to pay it yourself, before your "guest" arrives. "I was thrilled to be invited to a meeting where Rosalynn Carter was going to speak," one of the women reported, "but when I got there I found out I owed my 'hostess' $35! For lunch! If I'd known it cost that much, I'd have said 'No, thanks.'"

One other caution came up: when deciding on where to go for lunch, listen for clues that the other woman might prefer a less expensive restaurant than you're accustomed to frequenting. In a small town or in an industrial park, where everybody always goes to Joe's or the company cafeteria, this nicety doesn't apply. But in big cities, where the cost of a lunch varies wildly from one restaurant to the next, it's wise to bear the price range in mind when suggesting a place. A good plan is to mention three—inexpensive, moderate, fancy—and let the other woman choose one or come up with a suggestion of her own.

Why would a busy executive want to go out to lunch with me? This query raised a legitimate, tactical question: how can a woman network *up* the success ladder? How does she suggest lunch to someone who has nothing to gain from knowing *her*, to the most important woman officer in her corporation, say?

"She doesn't," came the quick answer, but after a lot of discussion, the group developed a possible script. To a woman who belongs to a network group, which means she is theoretically interested in networking and perhaps also interested in mentoring other women, she can say, "I've been making this unofficial survey of career paths—how women like you got where they are. May I come to see you at your office some day, or could you spare the time to have lunch with me?" Or "I'm looking into business schools, and Jane Doe [naming someone who is almost at her level or at least someone she knows] said you once surveyed them all. May I come see you, or could we talk over lunch?" Or whatever is true about your specific reason for wanting to talk with her.

A script like that gives the other woman several choices. She hasn't been put on the spot about lunch. She might say, "A quick lunch would be fine. Give me a call next week," or "My work day is wild. Why don't you call me at home Monday night?" or "Why don't we talk right now? What can I tell you in the next five minutes?"

What to do about telephone screens. Discussions of this volatile subject varied widely, depending on the size of the city where networkers brought it up. In New York City it generated an amazing amount of frustration and resentment.

"Secretaries are so officious!" complained a middle manager. "They guard their bosses as though they were protecting the president of the United States!"

"I'm a secretary and it's part of my *job* to screen calls," answered another woman. "Why must people be so self-important, refusing to reveal their reason for calling to a mere secretary? You'd think they were protecting state secrets!"

Eventually, the two sides agreed on the most efficient procedure.

For screeners: Say your boss is out *before* you say anything remotely resembling "Who's calling?" or "May I tell her what it's about?" If the person turns out to be someone you think your boss will want to talk to, you can always say, "Oh, here she comes now." If and when you do find out what the call is about, include that information in the message you relay to your boss. If you weren't prepared to pass along more than name and number, you shouldn't have pressed for details in the first place.

For screenees: Instantly give your name, your affiliation or equivalent identification, and a brief account of what you're calling about—without having to be asked. If the person you're calling won't recognize your name on a message slip, also give the name of the person in your network who suggested you call, and possibly mention the name of the networking group you and/or the person you're calling belong to.

For both: Ascertain the wishes of the boss as to networking calls. She may want to take them at certain hours of the day only; she may want them referred to her home phone. If you're the boss, give your secretary definite instructions on how to handle these calls. Since they are partly personal, they may not pass muster unless your secretary realizes that you're receptive to them. If you're the caller, and the word *networking* does not evoke a knowing response from the secretary, write a letter of explanation, then call again, referring to the letter.

Usually the questions and "problems" raised at early networking meetings disappeared after women began to realize that networking wasn't very different from the socializing they'd been doing all their lives. The focus was different—business, careers, getting ahead—but the method was the same: to look alive, to be interested and interesting, to do their share of making the event, whatever it was, go.

Relaxing into that awareness of their own competence, the stiffness vanished, and it no longer seemed artificial to be getting together with other women for no greater purpose than just networking. Even the most inhibited and doubtful began to enjoy the process.

□ 5
The Mechanics

Five weeks after Gail Mandell Nissen decided she wanted to change her career, she had more than a hundred three-by-five-inch file cards on her desk, each with the name of a person who had been helpful to her job search. She also had a new job. From fund raiser for a foundation to corporate recruiter for a computer consulting firm. By intensive networking.

"I had created a mini-network, with myself as the focus," she says. "It grew so big, so fast, that I had to devise a system to keep track of it."

Her system was to make out a card on everyone she knew, when she started, and everyone she heard about or was referred to, as she proceeded. On each card she wrote name, job title and company, address, phone, plus home address and phone when she had them. Then she added a few notes as memory joggers: how she knew this person (where they met or who had referred her) and what she knew about the other's interests or nonwork activities (potential conversation pieces). In the space remaining, sometimes going over to the back of the card, she would keep track of her contacts with the subject—dates when she phoned or saw the person, what was said, and so on. If and when she ever made any kind of promise to anyone on her cards, she noted that fact in prominent red. On turning through her cards, as she did regularly, the reds would catch her eye, and she'd follow through on whatever she had promised, from "I'll let you know what happens" to "Let me send you a copy of that news story we were discussing."

Keeping in touch with people was not new to Gail; it had been a part of her modus operandi as a fund raiser. She was in the habit of checking back with her former bosses at frequent intervals, so she didn't seem to be coming from out of the blue when she called them to ask their advice on changing careers. They all saw her, offering leads that Gail promptly added to her card file. She also had connections developed when she'd been field representative for the Greater New York Blood Program, running blood programs in big corporations throughout the city, and she had friends made through a poetry quarterly for which she had done some volunteer fund raising.

From these beginnings she branched out, and from the branches branched some more. Her daily schedule was: make calls in the morning; go to lunch with a contact, "making myself highly visible"; write up cards for the people she'd heard about at lunch; go through past cards and make more calls. Somewhere along the line she heard about Alina Novak, who was doing drop-in networking seminars for NOW-NY. At NOW she met three women in the computer field. "I knew nothing about computers," she recalls, "but I was trying to be open to everything." She now recruits "OS COBOL programmers," systems analysts and other technical people in the computer field for Automated Concepts, Inc., a firm that does consulting on "the state of the art" for Fortune 100 companies. Gail is the one who staffs up for special projects as they develop. She's happy in her new work.

Actually, the card file system of keeping track of people is not original with Gail. It has long been used by politicians, prominent hostesses, public relations agents, and researchers. Anyone who needs, meets, or deals with more people than she or he can easily remember needs some such system.

Instead of cards, Regina Glenn, a bigwig in the Washington State government in Olympia, Washington, uses a loose-leaf address book, the kind with shallow pages that overlap each other, showing only the name on top of each address; these can be moved around to keep them in alphabetical order. You know how it is when you need to enter an O'Mara between O'Keefe and O'Reilly in an ordinary address book, and there's no space? With this book you simply open the ring binder and move slips to make room where it's needed. Reggie's book is six by eight inches and, when I saw it, a good three inches thick, but she carries it wherever she goes. Ask her for the name of anyone she mentions, anywhere in the United States, and she doesn't have to say, "I'll call you when I get back to my office." She's got it at her fingertips, literally.

Reggie's latest idea to improve her system is to use a Polaroid camera whenever she can. Especially at big conferences, where professional photographers are circulating anyway, so her taking pictures won't seem peculiar, she takes a picture to go with each business card she collects. (Actually, she takes two and gives one to the subject.) "Having the picture as well as the card in front of me when I call that person makes it easy for me to pick up where we left off in our face-to-face conversation," she says.

Speaking of business cards, some network groups offer their members discount prices on having their cards printed. The Career Network in Seattle, Washington, for example, said in its newsletter, "Business cards can be a vital tool in climbing the career ladder." The usual format is:

Your name, centered
(preferably without *Miss*, *Mrs.*, or *Ms.*)

Your business address and phone | **Your home address and phone (optional)**

If you have a title worth advertising, put that over your company name:

Title
Company name

If not, you might want to give the department you work in, by way of identifying the kind of work you do:

Department
Company name

Some women leave their office phone numbers off, mentioning that they'd rather be called at home. Your own job and home circumstances will help you decide.

Until your printed cards are ready, you might want to write or type the same information on small gift cards you can buy at your stationer's. Also, since not everyone you meet will have a card with her, a small notebook in which to record names and addresses will prove useful.

Business cards may be collected in plastic sleeves made for the purpose, sheets like those you store your color slides in. Also available are address-book-size pages punched for key-ring binders, and envelopes ready to add to your Rolodex. (Said "Rolly" seems to be everybody's favorite desk directory of phone numbers. When the Washington Women's Network published its *Washington Women*, a directory of women and women's organizations in the national capital, they admitted that their not-exactly-scientific research method was "We shared our Rollies.")

But the file-card system has the advantage of leaving space for comments and progress reports to yourself. The more active a networker you become, the more cards you accumulate, the more you'll need notes to help you "place" people. You may even find that you need a cross-file system, so that you can find a person's card even though you've forgotten his or her name. That is, you'd put "Nissen, Gail" under the *N*'s in your *ABC* file, but you'd also put her under *Computers* and/or "*Fund raisers*" in your file on specialties.

Here are three more mechanical aids that networkers find useful:

1. A pocket-size appointment book in which to keep track of lunch dates and other networking appointments. Some women have a separate book for networking only; others incorporate networking notes into their daily business calendar. Either way, they find it an aid in checking back over how much networking they're actually doing.

As a rule of thumb, an active networker allots three out of her five lunch hours a week to getting acquainted with new people and to firming up relatively new relationships she already has. She also tries to go out for drinks with a networking prospect at least once a week.

(Incidentally, you don't have to drink to "meet for drinks." You don't even have to say whether you drink or not—who cares? Order a Virgin Mary or club soda on the rocks or whatever without comment. The meeting is the point, not the libation you meet over. Nor is the old prohibition against unescorted women in bars relevant these days.)

2. Mailings from colleges, women's groups, Y's, professional organizations—every relevant organization in town. By getting on the mailing lists, sometimes by join-

ing or subscribing, sometimes merely by making a few phone calls, networkers find out about conferences, lectures, program meetings, and other events that the daily press seldom announces in advance. These are all great places to meet other working women. To find them, run through the yellow pages of your phone directory under "Associations," "Clubs," and "Colleges," or call the nearest Women's Resource Center for leads.

3. A file for networking materials: programs, handouts, conference attendance lists, and newspaper clippings about women with good jobs whom you may someday have an excuse to call.

But you'll probably invent a system of your own to keep track of all the new people you're going to be meeting. One thing is certain: if you keep your system active, it will more than pay you back for any time you spend developing it.

□6 Networking Dos and Don'ts

"The network is there," said an exuberant Ellen Sills-Levy. "You have only to use it!" She had been out of the country for fourteen months and had every reason to think she'd been forgotten by her former contacts when she came back to New York, but she found "an incredible network open to me. They remembered my work. People really want to help you."

She is now vice-president, manager of research and business development, for Needham, Harper & Steers, Inc., a big advertising agency, at double the salary she was making when she went to Germany for BBD&O (Batten, Barton, Durstine & Osborn), her former agency.

The way she used her network is a model for the job hunt. She called and said, "Hi, I'm back," and reported what she had been doing during her absence. The usual response was "Terrific! Let me introduce you to . . ." She made dates for breakfast and lunch, and she made office appointments. She never asked anyone for a job, only for advice, and everyone came through. "I ended up not only with a good job but with valuable new additions to my network. My personal contacts from before were the best thing I had going for me. You may be sure

I'm going to keep up with them, and keep adding to them, wherever I am."

But then she added one of the basic cautions I must emphasize, before we go into the dos and don'ts: network support is based on performance. There is no substitute for being seen as good at your job, and there are two parts to that: doing good work and letting other people know it.

This requirement makes it tough on women who haven't yet been able to establish a good work record—beginners, reentries, those whose jobs haven't let them show what they can do. But they, especially, should appreciate that the network is not magic. It can tell you whom to call for interviews, but it can't guarantee the results you want from these interviews if you haven't got what the employer is looking for. And sometimes it won't produce the interview introduction at all if what you have to offer doesn't seem to warrant it.

Such holding back is quite understandable. You'll do it yourself if you're asked for a referral by someone you don't think you can recommend, for your own credibility in your own network is at stake. Susan Berresford of the Ford Foundation puts it this way: "I have to be very careful and honest about anybody I recommend." She will frankly say, to someone who asks her for a reference she can't easily give, "I really don't think you're ready for that job. I'd rather not send you over there until you've had more experience. Even if I did, it would only be a courtesy interview, anyway." Meaning: they'd see you, but only out of courtesy to me.

Another person might not be that frank, so it's wise to bear this caveat in mind: any member of your network will help only as much as she can without diminishing her own influence. She isn't going to ask someone who owes her a favor to do her the favor of helping you unless she can be sure you'll perform up to her recommendation.

"But if I had that good a résumé," you might ask, "why would I need a network?" Because it often takes a personal referral to keep your résumé from being "filed" in a wastebasket. Because a referral gets you more attention in the right places. Because the network gives you a better chance to demonstrate that you *are* good. Because a lot of other people are good at what they do, and some of them belong to the old boys' network; you need comparable auspices. Remember the performance standard if you bump into any stone walls in your networking, as I hope you won't.

Which brings us to the second basic caution, lest you expect more than your network can deliver: what you do with your networking resources is strictly up to you. You can't sit back and wait for someone to take you in hand. The best others can do is suggest solutions. It's crucial to realize that no one is going to develop and use your network for you. You have to take responsibility for your own growth.

"Many women do not," says Martha McKay, a prominent consultant who has seen countless women in work situations. (Her Womanagement process involved all the women at American Telephone & Telegraph [AT&T], New York.) "They grow up expecting someone else to take care of them. When they carry that baggage into career training programs, they're bound to be discouraged by the results, because there won't be any unless they do something *themselves*. We try to free women to use their energies and skills in their own behalf, and they're not used to doing that."

If you recognize that you're on your own, you won't expect too much of anyone in your network, or of your network group. That's very important. Expecting too much, in fact demanding it, is a very real threat to the networking system. If too many women carry attitudes and habits of helplessness into it, this whole marvelous phenomenon of women helping women could collapse.

Women who are in a position to help will get to feeling devoured. They'll start saying, "Hey, this is not worth it." Or "I'm fifty-three years old, I've worked hard all my life, and I'm tired. Let me up!" Or, as Tomi Abbott, a magazine advertising sales manager, wryly said one day when this topic was being discussed at a meeting of Women in Communications, "I gave at the office." A legitimate reaction on the part of those who've made it could be "I want to use my strength and energies where they'll do the most good. I can't be carrying women along one by one." See them as role models, but don't cling.

Those basics agreed upon—that you have to be competent and that you have to take responsibility for your own career—here are some dos and don'ts to guide your networking.

Do try to give as much as you get from your network. The more people you can be useful to, the more will be useful to you. The give-get ratio is not exact—you may give to one, get from another—but it tends to even out. Betsy Jaffe, who advises on networking for Catalyst in New York, and Sally Livingston, of Mainstream Planning Associates in the San Francisco area, agree that a helpful, caring attitude toward those who may turn to you is like bread upon the waters. (It also brings an unfamiliar but not unwelcome feeling of power when you discover how much you *can* help others!)

Don't be afraid to ask for what you need. "That's what your network is there for," says Marilyn Moats Kennedy, who believes we don't exploit our networks enough. Trust the other person to decide for herself whether she wants to do what you ask; don't decide for her by not asking.

Do report back to anyone who ever gives you a lead, telling her what happened and repeating your thanks. This is not only plain courtesy, but it helps to keep her interested and involved in what you're doing.

Do follow up on any leads and names you're given. As you'll discover if you're on the other end of this exchange, it's irritating, to put it mildly, to have someone from your own network say, "What ever happened to X? I was expecting her to call, as you said I should, and I never heard from her."

Don't tell everything to everybody. Be selective in both your choice of listeners and the material you impart. Think of it this way: although it's flattering, in a way, to be told secrets, it's also a burden. A good rule is to tell only what the other person needs to know in order to understand and help you or your project.

For example, your network needs to know you're looking for job leads. It doesn't need to know why you want to leave your present job, especially if the reason is you think you're about to be fired or your affair with the boss is going sour or anything they might feel obligated to pass along when they refer you to their network.

Do be businesslike in your approach to your network. Keep your conversations on track and your phone calls short. The networking relationship is in most instances limited to matters of business. It's easy to forget this, particularly as you discover how really willing other women are to lend their ears and help. Because they're women, you may tend to relate to them as you do to other women in your life—your mother, your sisters, your lifelong friends. Don't. If you make this mistake, you may encounter withdrawal on their part: they'll back off so far you won't even be able to get the limited, businesslike help they were prepared to offer.

Don't pass up any opportunities to network. "Oh, I couldn't talk business at a party," a friend said to a member of her business network. Her colleague's impatient reply: "Then stay home." If you were brought up to think shoptalk was inappropriate in social situations, just listen to what the men are talking about at the next party you attend.

Network opportunities are to be found everywhere. "My city block is my network," Pat Porter said at a networking seminar at Macy's in Manhattan. Every year she runs a big Halloween party for the West 69th Street Block Association. The sixty neighbors on the steering committee are always giving each other leads. "Someone gave me the name of a person to call at *Barron's*," she recalls. Pat is an illustrator with J. Walter Thompson Advertising who also free-lances. "That editor asked, 'Do you do caricatures?' I was newly into the style of saying yes to everything, so I said yes—and the first caricature I had ever done, one of Jimmy Carter, appeared on the front page of *Barron's*."

Don't neglect traditional organizations—the American Association of University Women (AAUW), your church group, the Junior League, for example. And don't sell short the networking potential of traditional women either. Betty Allen—"not a career gal," in her phrase—brought Carol Loomis and Nancy Heckel together, just because she thought they'd enjoy knowing each other. Carol is an editor of *Fortune* magazine, Nancy a vice-president of Communispond, Inc., a New York City organization that teaches presentation skills to business executives. The result of their getting acquainted was a *Fortune* article about Nancy's company, valuable to both women: to Nancy because of the priceless publicity; to Carol because she was able to put the magazine onto an interesting subject.

And speaking of traditional organizations, don't overlook your college alumnae association as a networking source.

Do read up on the subject—do your homework—before you ask questions of your network. That's a form of respect for the other person's time: you ask for what only she can tell you, not what you could have read for yourself in an elementary book.

Do keep in touch with your old network as you move

up. You'll change; your networking needs will change; but make time for your former co-workers when you are promoted, even if you no longer go out to lunch with them. As one cynical observer says, "Some of the best contacts a person can have in terms of information are secretaries in large corporations, because it's a fact that no male over forty was ever known to look up a telephone number for himself, much less type even one line of his own stuff. Therefore, these people know everything the boss thinks and does."

Don't expect your network to function as a placement office. This is one of the mistaken expectations that many network groups are having to cope with. You may ask your network to refer you to people for job interviews. You may ask them to tell you all they know about the people they refer you to so that you can cater to their special interests (or even restyle your résumé). You may *not* ask them to make the appointment for you, much less go on the interview in your place. Sad to say, that's what some networkers seem to expect.

Nor may you hold them responsible if the interview goes badly. Maybe they'd like to know and reassess this contact accordingly, but be sure not to seem to complain. Your message must always be "Thanks for your referral. I thought you'd like to know how it went," never "Why didn't you tell me he was such a misogynist?" or, as if it were your sponsor's fault, "He kept me waiting!" or "He sent me to the personnel department!"

Do call members of your network "for no reason at all." That is, don't wait to call until you need something. "I'm getting almost paranoid about this," said a man whom I consider a member of the old boys' network (that is, Deerfield, Harvard, Wall Street, and what more does one need to qualify?). "My friends call, and after the usual pleasantries and the did-you-hear-the-one-abouts, they say, 'Oh, yes, the reason I called is . . .' and they want something."

Do bring your network into play with particular care when you're about to enter unfamiliar territory. Although you may be knowledgeable about your own field, you can't be sure your methods of operation are appropriate to another one. Ask.

Here's a sad but true example of a woman who had an extensive network but didn't think to check in with it—and got creamed.

Marcia was an experienced journalist, accustomed to submitting her ideas for articles in outline form before going ahead and writing them. If the answer was yes, the editors would then say how much they were prepared to pay for the finished article. Marcia would agree or try to get the price up first or, on rare occasion, withdraw the idea, the price being too low, and submit it to another magazine instead. The latter seldom happened, but it was always her option. In twenty years of operating this way, she had never had an idea stolen by a magazine.

One day she had what she considered a great idea for a conference. It would be just right, she thought, for the school where she was then teaching an evening course in magazine journalism. Marcia wrote up her idea, using the same format as for an article, naming the people who should be engaged to speak at the conference, lead workshops, and so forth. She mailed it to the head of the school.

The head called her a few weeks later, expressing interest and asking her to come in and talk it over. Marcia went to the meeting with visions of big bucks dancing in her head, for the school paid its teachers 10 percent of the tuition paid by the students enrolled in each class, and 10 percent of this big conference would bring her important money. The meeting went beautifully, the head man making only a few changes in Marcia's list of speakers and panelists, these so that he could bring in one or two favorites of his own. Then, leaning back in his chair, the head said, "Fine, then. We're all set. Go right ahead with the arrangements. We pay $150 for conference moderators. I assume that's agreeable?"

Weeks of work would be involved, lining up the speakers, writing the program copy, arranging for lunches, and so on. She couldn't possibly do all that for $150.

"But—" she sputtered, "my *daily* rate is $200." That was the figure set by the professional writers' association she belonged to.

"Then you're too expensive for us," he said, cheerfully. "We never pay more than $150." And, as it developed, they never paid their speakers at all. Not even an honorarium.

They agreed to disagree.

The school went ahead and put on the conference anyway. When she protested, reminding the head that it was her idea, he said, "I could have thought of it myself. The idea is in the air."

The idea, you see, was for a conference on women's networking. The first article on it had just appeared in a pilot issue of *Savvy* magazine. But if the idea was "in the air," no one had yet translated it into a conference.

The school drew four hundred women (turning more away) at $25 per person, thereby taking in some $10,000.

Marcia consulted a lawyer, who told her that ideas per se are not protected by the law. She should have had an agreement on the price before revealing the idea in the first place. In vain did she describe her usual method of submitting ideas to editors. The head of the school was not an editor. Apparently academia operates with a code of ethics different from that of publishing. Marcia had no recourse.

Ironically, since her whole idea had been based on the networking phenomenon, she had not spoken to anyone about her idea before mailing it off to the school. If she had, she could have found out that the percentage method of paying teachers did not apply to conference moderators, or that the head of the school was a man to be wary of, or simply—as the lawyer had told her, too late—that she should have an understanding about price before submitting her idea.

But, you ask, if the school was ready to steal her idea so blithely, why wouldn't some bad apple in her network have done the same? Because a savvier Marcia wouldn't have told the idea itself to anyone; she would only have checked out the method of submitting ideas, the general pay scale, and, perhaps, the character and reputation of the head of the school. She'd have talked to someone who had put on a conference for the school before, finding out about that person's experience.

But, she didn't. She didn't even talk to her literary agent, this being a nonliterary matter! But you may be sure that she'll never again rush so innocently into foreign waters. Marcia now has an idea for a game. Guess what she's going to do before she goes to see toy and game manufacturers?

Don't be discouraged if someone brushes you off. It's bound to happen. Maybe as often as three times out of ten you'll run into some kind of negative reaction to your networking. Remember this: those three times are not important; the other seven are. In short, don't take no for an answer. And don't take it personally. Try someone else, and the sooner the better, before you start magnifying the negative and internalizing it.

Do call ahead when you've given someone's name to a person in your network. Even better would be to call before giving the referral, asking if it's okay, but since that involves so many phone calls back and forth, you may be excused if you short-cut the more elaborate procedure. Just tell the person whose name you've given out, or her secretary, "You may be getting a call from X. I gave her your name as one who could advise her on graduate programs. I hope you don't mind." Consider this also a maintenance call for your own networking: you'll have reminded the other person of your continued existence!

Do refine your questions. Don't ask for the moon. I'd like to bet that no woman would go up to the male architect of a skyscraper, encountered supervising the placement of a steel beam on site, and ask, "What does it take to design a building?" But I've been asked, while in the midst of taking notes at a meeting on networking, "What does it take to write a book?" And I was present when a woman came up to a professional career counselor who is used to being paid for such advice and said, "I've decided to leave teaching. What other fields could use my teaching skills?"

Erika Brown, then head of her own executive search firm in Chicago, told me of a similar experience involving two other women: one, whom she barely knew, brought the other over during the coffee break at a lecture. Introducing the stranger, she said, "She's thinking of going back to work, but she doesn't know where the jobs are. I told her you'd know just where to look."

The career counselor said, "I don't have the schedule with me right now, but we have workshops on career change. Would you like to call my office for a brochure?" A smooth "out." But Erika Brown could only drop her jaw, staring. "I was nonplussed. I couldn't believe I was supposed to solve this woman's problem then and there. 'Going back to work'? Doing what? 'Where the jobs are'? How could I ever help anyone with that innocent kind of concept about the real world?"

The woman who was thinking of writing a book, finding herself sitting next to a professional writer, might acceptably have asked a concrete question: "Do you work from an outline?" perhaps, or "Do you ever use a tape recorder instead of taking notes?" The teacher might have asked the career counselor if she had been able to help other teachers get out of the field. But the only proper question I can imagine a housewife asking an executive searcher is "Do you handle reentry applicants?" And, if so, "May I call you for an appointment?"

Do keep expanding your network. Every time you get a

referral, ask that person for an additional name. Or two. It's as simple as asking, at the end of an interview or other conversation, "Can you suggest anyone else I might talk to about this?" People usually respond with alacrity; maybe it's just to get you off their own agendas, but the pass-along is no less valuable for that motive. Using this method, and starting with a single name, one woman got herself fifty-two interviews within three weeks in a strange city.

Another expansion method lies in your library. "Networks can leap up off the printed page," says Lillian Steinmuller, who wanted to work somewhere in the art field but didn't know where. She read art news and magazines, taking notes on individuals who wrote or were written about in them. These gave her not only names but questions to ask or comments to make when she called.

Coralee Kern created a network by phone. "Every time I saw an article about a successful woman in a magazine or newspaper, I called her and said, 'Congratulations!' Talking to these women was just what I needed—I was handicapped, homebound. We shared a lot, just talking on the phone." She was running what has become a very successful business, Maid to Order, out of the basement of her house in Chicago, but she had come to see that she was "working all the time." Her self-created network "opened new horizons." (She has gone on to organize a face-to-face, as opposed to a telephone, network, calling it WOMAN (acronym for Woman/Owner/Manger/Administrator Networking).

Do ask for only one thing at a time—information, referral, moral support. Usually you'll need separate persons for each type of help. Don't overload any one of them.

Do watch your timing. Pick a time and place where you'll be sure of the attention you want. At best, this will be in a one-to-one situation, but sometimes a network group includes problem-solving periods in its agenda, so you'll be addressing more than one person. In any case, signal your intention to ask for help: "I'd like your opinion on this . . ." or "I've got a problem I'd like to check out with you." Your listener will pay a different kind of attention if she knows in advance that she's expected to comment or advise. Get some indication of willingness to hear your problem then and there, before you launch into the whole story. If you don't hear that welcome, it's better to set up an appointment for another time.

Don't expect an instant, magic answer, and don't feel put off if, instead, your listener paraphrases what you just told her, asks probing questions about it, makes some irritating statement ("You *are* in a mess"), or offers palliatives ("Tomorrow's another day"). Even the last two may be part of her way of vamping until ready to offer advice. Wait.

Do take advice when you've asked for it. Accept it in the spirit it was intended. Do not say, even if true, "I've thought of that," or "I've tried that and it doesn't work," or "I could *never* do that," or even, doubtfully, "Do you *really* think that?" as though you're beginning to doubt the other's sanity. You'd be surprised at how many do just that. It's like stomping all over a present someone has given you, in her presence—worse, because this is a present you've explicitly asked for.

Another comment not to make, if you want this relationship to continue amicably, is "You don't understand." If that's the case, say, rather, "I forgot to mention . . ." or "I guess I didn't explain . . ." as if you're to blame for not giving enough information rather than your adviser being to blame for dull wittedness.

Do offer your help generously. Your manner will show that you're interested in seeing other women get ahead and glad to help in any way you can, but sometimes it's necessary to say so in as many words. Don't feel that you're bragging or being patronizing if you say, "I'm very comfortable with finance. If you have any problems on that score, don't hesitate to call," or, "I'm really good at proofreading if you can use another eye when you're finished with that report."

You may not need such cue cards. One of the fascinating aspects of networking is the way women are going out of their way to help each other. "It was like one-upmanship," a woman told me, describing a conversation she'd just had with another woman. "We were trying to see who could do the most for the other."

But if in doubt, offer. Don't wait to be asked: "Good luck in that enterprise. Keep me posted. I'll be glad to help in any way I can."

Don't tell anyone what to do, even if she asks you to. Above all, don't do it for her! The best you can do is help her clarify her own thinking, so that she can make her own decision, take her own action. There's a definite technique to this: ask questions, to elicit as much information as possible; ask the person what options she has considered and what she feels is right or wrong with each of them; if she's considered only two—such as quitting versus staying in a bad situation—ask her if there isn't some middle road. This kind of dialogue is really immensely valuable. You're performing more of a service when you help the other person think than when you rush right in and do her thinking for her.

Do make certain guidelines clear to your "constituency." Let women know that they can't call you at work or you can't spend an hour on the phone with them every night or whatever needs saying. Otherwise resentment will build up in you and the spirit of networking will be damaged.

Do be on the alert to hear such guidelines from others, too. Don't be offended if you hear "I can't talk now," or "I can't go into that with you on the phone just now," or the method Hunter Campbell, of Booz, Allen & Hamilton, Chicago, has decided upon, "Here are the names of three people you should talk to." (Only a fool would then ask, "Can you give me their phone numbers?" The wise networker doesn't ask an adviser for anything she can get elsewhere—from the phone book, for example, or on a separate call to the executive's secretary.)

Do deliver on your promises. If you have any trouble keeping track of them—and this is quite possible when you're in an active network—write them down. Devise a regular procedure for checking up on yourself.

Do pick the right people to ask for what you need. A woman who worked for a nonprofit agency wanted to get into the corporate world. She was actively networking, looking for entrées, but getting nowhere, when it dawned on her that she was talking almost entirely to entrepreneurs. Realizing that she needed to meet corporation women, she cooled it with her women business owners and began to go to different kinds of events and meetings.

Do take others up on their offers to help. Sometimes this is just as difficult as asking for help, and for the same reason: not wanting to "bother" anyone. When a woman offers, in this new spirit of networking, she really means it. Accepting her offer will tie her into your network even more firmly than before.

Do include all ages of women in your network. If you're riding high on the wave of new acceptance of women in business, you may think other women's "war stories" don't apply to your career, but, as Pat Carbine, editor and publisher of *Ms.* magazine, told a conference on "Women and Society" at St. Michael's College, in Vermont, not so long ago, "Backlash stalks the courts and hiring halls. Women starting careers still have to prepare for a long uphill struggle." Whatever effort it takes you to close the generation gap in your networking is bound to be worth it. Close it in both directions, including the starter-outers, too, those who have no sense of history behind their being able to get decent jobs.

Do try to circulate at network meetings. To get unstuck, simply look over the shoulder of the person you've been talking to and say, "Oh, there's someone I've been wanting to catch up with. Will you excuse me, please?"

To get unstranded, just walk up to any two people who are talking and stand there, smiling and listening, until one turns to you and says, "We were just talking about . . ." or "Hi. I'm Cindy Jones." Then you can either add your own introduction, comment on the subject under discussion, or say something like "I'm very interested in such and so myself, so when I overheard you talking about it I wanted to join you."

Most meetings have a circulating period at some time during the program—the cocktail hour, the coffee break, perhaps even networking time so announced. Take advantage of these opportunities to find out at least the name and occupation of five new women each time. Then make a point of saying hello to those same five at the next meeting, while introducing yourself to still another five. If that's at all difficult for you, get yourself on the hospitality or reception committee, so that it's part of your job to greet everyone. You can't possibly feel pushy or fragmented if you're doing what you're supposed to do.

You can continue to circulate after most of the group is seated, stopping by this table and that to say hello to familiar faces. This used to be called "table hopping" and was considered bad form, an intrusion of privacy, but networkers welcome it. They're glad you recognized them. Like you, the more greetings they get, the more comfortable they'll feel.

During the mass exodus from a meeting or network gathering, try to say a personal good-bye to the people you introduced yourself to earlier and also to those you know but didn't get a chance to talk to. Something like "I enjoyed meeting you," or "I hope I'll see you next time," will suffice. Especially if you were moving around rather briskly during the evening, it will show you weren't just chalking up contacts (even if you were!).

You might also make a few short phone calls later in the day, after a lunch meeting, or the next day after a dinner, to women you saw but didn't get a chance to speak to.

Do wake up to the "petty cash" aspects of networking over food or drinks. Many women, perhaps because they're accustomed to being taken care of by male escorts, are oblivious to the need for tipping 15 to 20 percent on any bar or restaurant bill. A network facilitator who went out with her group after meetings told me of getting stuck time after time with having to pay an extra $3 to $5 in tips for a table full of supposedly successful women. "I rely on being given a table the next time I enter the place, so I make up the difference out of my own pocket. But I resent it. More than that, I see these cheapskates as losers. Networking can't help with the kind of image they're creating for themselves wherever they go." Her last words were "In order to do big business, the little things have to fall in line."

Do be prepared for a slump following your initial excitement over learning to network. "I've spent one hundred hours in time, $1,000 in food, and it's done nothing for my career," one woman wailed. "I'm still right where I was when I started." A more knowledgeable networker might have answered, "Yes, but you've thrown out your net, increasing the odds of one day receiving that crucial phone call or of being introduced to that significant other person. What's more, you've set your image as somebody who knows people."

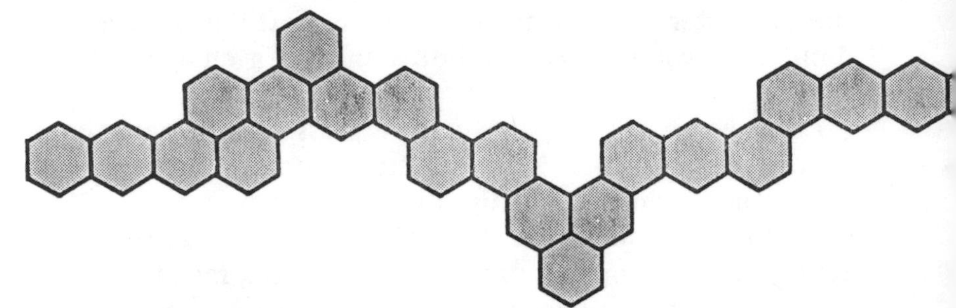

Networking

Part Two

Groups

□ 7

City-wide Networking Groups: How They Started

Networking is always personal, but all over the country, women are forming groups to facilitate it. Here are accounts of a representative number of network organizations. They're external—that is, they meet and draw their membership from outside the places where the women work. Some are horizontal, peer groups limiting membership to women who are at about the same level in their careers; some are vertical, open to all interested women, from entry level to upper management. But whatever their description, most—as you'll see—have sprung into being through the idea and the effort of a very few women, each having a core group of founders that we might almost call pioneers in this exciting movement.

If you're planning to start a group, or if you're now involved in a network that could use some of these ideas to its own advantage, watch for organizational details in these stories. (More about the nitty gritty in Part Three, and in the Appendixes of this book.)

AGOG

In Minneapolis one day in 1977, when she was "beginning to feel guilty about not doing anything about this networking idea that everyone was talking about," Katherine E. (Kati) Sasseville picked up the phone. She called five women friends for lunch the next day. They agreed it was high time Minneapolis women had a way to meet and discuss their careers and make business contacts the way men do at their lunch clubs.

They planned a follow-up lunch the following week, where their number expanded to fifteen, then they bit the bullet: they scheduled a lunch meeting to which "any good ole girl" in town was invited.

Seventy women attended that first lunch, having learned about it by grapevine—the founders made no mailing, and the press didn't announce the event. Double that number came to the second. Kati and her core group were astounded. They knew there'd be interest; they knew there was a need. But almost 150 women? With no effort to attract them?

Marcia Appel, editor of *Twin Cities Woman*, a monthly magazine, hadn't known of the first meeting but attended the second. She still remembers its impact on her. "Migod!" she thought, surveying the room where the meeting was to be held. "These are not just the usual 2 percent who turn out for women's events. Look at this mob!" The atmosphere of camaraderie was almost palpable.

The group called themselves AGOG, for Any Good Ole Girl (since changed to All the Good Old Girls), and from the first, they decided to admit any and all comers. "We wanted to hit all kinds of working women, at all levels, whether in business, professional careers, working at the university and other institutions, or in government. Our only criterion is that they have or want to have positions of responsibility in their careers," Kati says. The founders were highly placed themselves—Secretary of State Joan Growe among them—but they didn't want to restrict membership to already-successful women.

They now have two thousand members, each of whom has paid $15 to help defray the cost of mailings and other expenses. In the beginning, women came to their meetings from other cities around the state, but now those women have formed their own AGOGs: Manhato, Rochester, and Duluth have spin-off groups. There's talk of a state-wide caucus, such as the one held in 1976 to select delegates to Houston during International Women's Year.

To accommodate so many members, AGOG now has two events a month—one dinner meeting, mainly for networking, and one lunch meeting with a program. About two hundred women attend each one, probably but not necessarily a different two hundred for each type of meeting and time of day. Speakers are scheduled for the lunch and dinner meetings, but the cocktail period is for milling about only. And certain lunch and dinner attendees have been heard to wish that speeches from the front of the room didn't have to interfere with their table conversations!

The mechanics were more burdensome than anyone envisioned in the beginning. "I was getting thirty phone calls a day," Kati recalls. Although she had a secretary and staff, as befit a commissioner on the Minnesota Public Service Commission (she has since become chair of the commission, a first for a woman) she worried about this interference with her regular work. Calls were coming to her home, too, where she already had enough to do: she has six children. She soon realized the group needed paid staff, and she would advise any group now starting up to face that necessity from the outset.

Ann Peterson, hired as executive director, says, "The steering committee interviewed some twenty applicants for this 'part-time' job. Can you imagine? Twenty women were really enthusiastic about helping to run this and get things off the ground. I am supposed to be working about twenty hours a week, but of course twenty hours doesn't cover it. I spent over ninety-six hours last month. The member contact and input via mail and telephone is amazing." Ann works out of her home, but for its address AGOG uses a post office box.

The mailings are handled by Print 'n' Mail, a commercial mailing house, at lower cost than when AGOG's own person did them. The bookkeeping is something of a headache. Events are not expected to make money, but AGOG hopes not to lose money either, so it requires prepaid registration: "absolutely no reservations by phone." They learned that one the hard way, with no-shows bollixing up their arrangements with the kitchens.

Two favorite sites for the lunch meetings are the Minneapolis Athletic Club and the St. Paul Athletic Club, because they're both men-only clubs. AGOG engages private dining rooms. At a meeting I attended, men were streaming into an equivalent room across the hall, looking somewhat puzzled by the invasion of their elevators and halls by women. One time, an AGOG member remembers, the men were attending a lunch of the dental society. "We had dentists in our own meeting—all good old girls!"

Women have found jobs through AGOG, both from the bulletin board they find at every meeting and through phone call alerts, networking at its best. Although she already knew a lot of women through the women's movement and the university, Kati says AGOG has helped her more than she can say. "It's true we have a few women moving into positions of responsibility these days, but there aren't so many of us that we can feel like part of a group, the way men can. AGOG brings us together, helping us see we're not alone even if we are the only women in our particular offices." A more concrete aid to her career came about through the network when she was recommended for a job with the Federal Communications Commission. "Would the women on the committee have thought of me, and got me reported out of committee, if we hadn't been seeing each other at AGOG? I doubt it."

A few problems and how AGOG solved them:

1. In the beginning the microphone was open to anyone who had an announcement of general interest to make. Sometimes these proved not to be of general interest. Rather than get into the business of editing or approving them in advance, AGOG went to the bulletin board system. Announcements may be typed up on 4½-by-5½-inch sheets of paper, or smaller, and sent in ahead of the meetings.

2. Early on, lunch and dinner tables were laden with literature—brochures, questionnaires, whatnot. Every member, it began to seem, had a product or a cause to push this way. It got to be too much. Now a separate table for literature is provided at the entrance to the meeting room. Members may linger over it, taking whatever interests them, or not, as they choose; the lunch tables are free for what usually proves to be the main business of the day—exchanging business cards.

3. So far, the membership list has been public. The directory, which lists all paid members alphabetically and also by career identification, is distributed to all. This results in the members receiving a lot of junk mail, some complain. Whether some restrictions ought to be put on the use of the list hasn't been settled yet.

4. During the very hot election Minnesota was gearing up for, during AGOG's infancy, many of the members thought the group should invite the candidates to speak and should even endorse some of them. The membership decided against it. "Women's issues were very much a part of the campaign," one AGOGer who was disappointed by that decision recalls. "I think we

ought to have supported the good guys (who lost)." But the majority wanted to remain neutral. As one of that persuasion says, "We're a career group, not a political group. The politicos can join the League of Women Voters or the Women's Political Caucus or women's caucuses in the political parties."

Most networks of any size will have to make this decision at some time or another. Some may choose to use their developing clout, at least in support of women candidates, but AGOG feels comfortable with its decision. So far.

Other "movers and shakers"

Like Kati Sasseville in Minneapolis, other women elsewhere (1) have felt the need for a network, (2) have talked to their friends about the idea, and (3) presto! have started a network group. Here are a few examples. They don't know Kati or each other—yet!—but they've all had the same idea.

Diane Winokur felt the need to connect with other women executives. She was the only white woman at a professional level in a black-owned company, and there was only one other woman at her level there. But it was more than her personal feelings of isolation that caused her to start what has since become the Bay Area Executive Women's Forum (BAEWF). It was also a sense that she and her kind were way ahead of the printed word about women in business. She needed a dynamic data base to keep ahead in the training she herself was engaged in dispensing to women in management. "*The Managerial Woman*," she said, naming a currently popular book, "was based on the experiences and attitudes of career women two generations back. Most 'Management Skills for Women' seminars were based on what seemed to me an outdated assumption. They assumed some inherent lack of management ability in women. To my mind, management skills are management skills, the same for a woman as for a man, cat, or dog. But the organization affects women differently; that's what we need to understand and master. The skills and strategies to do that are a critical part of my management seminar."

She wanted to check out ideas like these with other women. And she had recently had personal proof that talking to another woman about a job problem can be a lifesaver: against her own impulse to quit, when a political problem began to make her job life difficult, Diane talked it over with Marilyn Taylor, a black woman who is a labor relations expert. Marilyn helped her see what was happening and what to do about it. "I drove forty minutes each time, just to talk to Marilyn," Diane recalls. "When it was all over, I had new insights into my problem; I didn't have to quit—I got to thinking how great it would be if I could meet with other women like Marilyn on a regular basis, if we could all have a forum to which we could bring our trials and tribulations, sure of meeting with like minds, similar experiences."

She sent a letter to ten or fifteen women, asking if they had felt the same need. They had. Next step was a no-host luncheon. Then a full-day seminar, in November of 1977, and BAEWF was under way. Twenty-five women, all energy and enthusiasm, attended. A year and a half later they had a mailing list of four hundred, with one hundred dues-paying members, so they had to formalize their structure, complete with bylaws, election of officers, and other systems. Despite their size, they maintain the rapport and feelings of mutual support with which they began. They have monthly luncheons: topics have included finance, stress, and networking itself; speakers have included Ruth Bader Ginsburg, the attorney expert on sex discrimination cases.

"BAEWF is not for the woman who needs to be told there's a bigger world out there," says Diane, BAEWF's first president. "We know it's there because we're in it." BAEWF is for women who are dealing with the realities, every day, unencumbered by fantasies about what it *should* be like to be a woman executive today."

Lorcy Ann Burns, vice-president and charter member of BAEWF, executive with Pacific Gas & Electric, resigned from the League of Women Voters in order to devote more time to BAEWF. "The problem we all have, of course, is being short on time. But I feel I've gained so much from this group. It has been exciting and educational to meet achievement-oriented women representing so many different professions and from such a variety of businesses," she said.

Martha Waddell is educational director, overseer of the group's seminar program. "The most exciting thing about BAEWF," she says, "is the energy and enthusiasm generated by so many bright, achieving women working together. If you look at the statistics about the numbers of women in executive positions, and the wide disparities between their salaries and those of their male counterparts, it can be very depressing. But *these women aren't crying over things. They are changing things*," Marty says.

Attorney Lee Kraft was feeling low: her fortieth birthday was coming up. It was "downhill all the way now," and what did she have to show for it?

Actually, she had plenty to show—first woman president of her state's Municipal Attorneys Association; chair of the prosecutor's board for the State Bar Association; now city counsel for her city of eighty thousand, supervising five attorneys (four of them men) while handling all the legal affairs for Bellevue, Washington; not to mention a successful family life. But there's no accounting for those fortieth-birthday blues. Lee decided to cheer herself up by having a wine and cheese party for all the women she knew and liked and worked with, women who, like her, had struggled to establish themselves in their professions. Would they, too, be looking around themselves now, questioning their success? In any case, would they like to meet at her house on that momentous fortieth birthday? They would, and did, and the end result has been a powerful force in all their lives ever since.

"I didn't tell them it was my birthday, of course," Lee now recalls, "and by the time the evening was over I'd almost forgotten that fact myself. I no longer felt over the hill. Far from it! In the company of these dynamic women, each a power in her own right, I got my second wind."

Their membership is drawn from the nineteen small cities that stretch out to the east of Seattle—Bellevue being the largest, Mercer Island perhaps the best known outside Washington—so they call themselves the East Side Network. Most of them are in politics, in one way or another: their number, which is about forty, includes six members of city councils, a state representative, judges, school board officers, doctors, and lawyers.

They meet casually once a month, usually over wine and cheese at somebody's house, from five-thirty to seven-thirty. Sometimes they have a speaker; often they invite notable guests; but their major purpose is to exchange information about what's going on.

The East Side Network has made an important difference in her life, Lee says. Remembering back to law school, when she was one of two women in her class (and considering herself lucky); remembering the client who said, on being ushered into her law office, "Are you the lawyer? I'd like to see a *real* lawyer," she finds it a great relief to be one of many—well, forty—women in positions of local power.

"The network is a terrific backup system for each of us," she says. "I can always say, 'I don't know, but let me check with my friends,' and know that at least one of the network will tell me what or whom I need to know. Among us, we know every elected official in King County, population over a million, and almost all of the influential people in the area. Somebody always knows somebody."

"*We didn't* dare *get together where we work*," Evvy K. said, "and I hope to heaven our management doesn't find out we're meeting on the outside, either. Which is exactly why we need our network so desperately—we're under watchful and suspicious eyes, every minute of the business day."

It was in that climate that Cidney B. Spillman and Sheila M. Korhammer, partners in Lifeplan, "a career and life-planning center" in Bethlehem, Pennsylvania, helped organize NEW, Network for Executive Women. "Since the intent of women organizing can be misread by male management, and might be considered a threat to the corporate status quo," Sheila told me, "the women saw Lifeplan as neutral ground. Besides, our offices afford meeting space, and we're centrally located in the Lehigh Valley." (Lehigh Valley encompasses Lehigh and Northampton counties in Pennsylvania and Warren County in New Jersey.)

NEW's goals are (1) to figure out how to get around the roadblocks the women find in their corporate paths, (2) to establish a "sister" relationship that will encourage women to share information, and (3) to develop a pool of achieving, talented women to serve as role models for younger women as they enter the work force.

"I feel better already," said Evvy after the first meeting (in the spring of 1979). "It's great to know I'm not the only one who seems to be stuck in middle management. Together, I hope, we'll get *un*stuck."

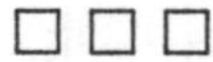

Elinor Guggenheimer had what she calls "a temper tantrum." It was 1973. She attended a NOW meeting to which all the candidates for city-wide office had come, and she found herself embarrassed. "The questions the young women on the political committee were asking were so uninformed," she remembers. Although she is a member of NOW and firmly supports their work, she thought the candidates ought to have had a more sophisticated group to appear before. "NOW was the only woman's show in town in those days," she recalls. "I thought we ought to have another one."

The first person she called with this idea was Eleanor Holmes Norton, then head of human resources for the city, now in Washington, heading up the Equal Employment Opportunities Commission (EEOC). "I asked her how she'd like to set up an elite organization. She laughed, because blacks have never been considered elitist, but she said, 'I'd love it.' Everyone I talked to about the concept was very excited about it. We could finally stand up and say, 'We're the achievers. We're important,' without being embarrassed about it."

She called Betty Friedan, Betty Furness, Barbara Walters, Muriel Siebert (the first woman to hold a seat on the New York Stock Exchange, now the first woman to serve as commissioner of banks for New York State). She had been the on-air host of a talk show for three years, so she knew "everyone in town who was not nailed down." Her friends in turn thought of others to invite, and in a very short time the Women's Forum, as they decided to call themselves, was a flourishing organization. They intended to keep the membership down to 100, but now they're 165.

Elinor became the first president in 1975. They had operated for two years without officers. Now they have Lee Lowell as an executive director, paid; she handles the meeting notices, puts out the newsletter, and does other organizational tasks. The networking the members do among themselves is constant, and the Forum is called by outsiders to supply everything from commencement speakers to fund-raising ideas.

They take no public positions on women's or other issues. When one of their number runs for office, they simply announce that fact in the newsletter, without endorsing her. But one time they did use their power—when the question of extending the time for passage of the Equal Rights Amendment was stuck in the Judiciary Committee of the House of Representatives. They got together with other women's organizations and went to Washington to lobby. Thoroughly briefed on the voting record and background of each congressman, they called on the legislators in groups of two or three. The Women's Congressional Caucus, another illustrious network, gave them staff assistance and lunch while they were there. As you know, the extension was reported out of committee and approved by both houses of Congress.

There are other Women's Forums now—in San Francisco, in Philadelphia, in Denver, in Detroit, in North Carolina, in Albany, New York. Eventually they may affiliate. Their combined membership lists might outshine *Who's Who*. But more important is all the support and the referrals the members give each other. If networking in general is limited by the paucity of women in positions of power, networking in and through the Forum suffers no such handicap.

Do they plan to expand their program for the benefit of younger women? Have they thought of initiating mentor relationships with women lower down on the career ladders? Not yet.

Sylvia Roberts, a Baton Rouge attorney—member of a comparable organization in Louisiana (called simply The Network)—wants to connect with women as they come out of college, "to keep them from becoming Queen Bees." Of the $50 dues her group collects, she says, "We do nothing with our money—nothing." Her own energy and feminism know no bounds (she has been the attorney for landmark cases in the area of discrimination in employment), so we can hope for some such development within invitational networks.

Caroline Hosken was bewildered: a new arrival in New York, a sales representative for a company headquartered in Colorado, she had run into some office politics that had her very upset. "I couldn't figure out what was going on. I was getting double messages. My boss was telling me I was underpaid but not doing anything about it, and when I tried to do something myself, he backed away. Or something like that. I still can't tell the story straight, because it never *was* straight. Anyway, I knew I needed to talk to someone, a woman who understood corporate politics, but I didn't know anyone."

Then she received from her mother, who edits and publishes *Women's International Network News*—a quarterly covering women's issues around the world—a brochure about "Executive Woman," a newsletter her mother thought Caroline might be interested in. Straight away she looked up "Executive Woman" in the phone book and said, to the unknown woman at the other end of the telephone, "I need somebody to talk to about a problem I'm having on my job. Do you know where I could find a support group?"

The voice at the other end was that of Shelley Galehouse, the new editor of "Executive Woman." "No," she said, "but I know a couple of other women who've asked the same question. I can put you in touch with them."

So began a group that now includes Caroline, Shelley, an interior decorator, a Chinese immunologist planning to start an import business, a stress consultant, an administrative assistant, an unemployed public relations woman, an insurance underwriter, a personnel recruiter, and an auctioneer. They meet at each other's houses once every two weeks or sometimes, when they're that intrigued with a problem they're working on, every week. They did that when they decided to bring in their résumés in two versions each: (1) the classical, chronological résumé, which tends to expose every gap and highlight every shortcoming, and (2) the functional résumé, which overrides gaps with its emphasis on skills and accomplishments. They have no name for their group, and no set format for their meetings, but they all say the experience is invaluable.

Sudy Blumenthal chose Houston as the place to start her life anew, after her divorce, but when she arrived there from Kansas City she was "terrified" because she didn't know any women. She went to work as an insurance agent for Connecticut Mutual, where all the other agents were men. "What you need," they told her, "is a breakfast club." It turned out that they belonged to six different clubs themselves. She could have joined one of them but decided to start her own, for women only. The result is a breakfast network called the River Oaks Breakfast Club. They meet from seven to eight-thirty every Friday morning (attendance of all forty-one members is more or less guaranteed by the fact that they pay for the breakfasts in advance, their only dues) at the posh River Oaks Country Club, a member of which lets them sign her name to the bill.

To avoid competition among themselves, they admit only one member per industry or occupation. (Three banking vice-presidents belong, it is true, but each is in a different sort of banking—commercial, personal, international.)

Getting organized took about six weeks, Sudy recalls, leading up to the first meeting in February 1976. Two spin-offs have taken form more quickly, one meeting at the Women's City Club, the other at the Warwick.

"Although our sole purpose is to exchange business information," says Sudy, "we have become friends as well, meeting socially, involving our husbands. These are really neat people. I certainly feel at home now!"

Beverly Blessing chose breakfast, too, when she decided to get a network started in Des Moines, Iowa. She asked friends to submit names of women they knew in managerial, executive, and professional occupations, with the result that the Executive Women's Breakfast Club was launched over fruit, coffee, and doughnuts in January of 1978. To keep the group loosely structured and fluid, they have no elected officers (just volunteers who keep the list, which is now of 250 women, and to make program arrangements) and their only membership fee is seventy-five cents a time, for the food. Program subjects have ranged from "Handling Frustration and Anger on the Job," a discussion led by a psychologist, to "Help! My Business Is Running My Life!" and "How to Find a Mentor." But getting to know each other is the main event, according to Beverly.

"The confidence I've gained from mixing with other ambitious women enabled me to make an important job change," she says. Formerly with an in-house advertising agency for a retail chain, she's now advertising sales promotion manager for the *Des Moines Register and Tribune*.

The network members are thirty to fifty years old, earning from $8,000 to more than $30,000. Thirty-seven percent are making over $20,000, compared with only 19 percent five years ago. Various titles reported in a membership survey include presidents of their own companies, vice-presidents of corporations, marketing representatives, claims examiner, editor, personnel supervisor, insurance agent, attorney, state senator and—a minister!

□ □ □

Nancy Korman was mad. She had done a lot of political favors for a man in the construction business, but when she called him, with an eye to showing him her portfolio and soliciting his account for her public relations and graphics firm, 706 Associates, he turned her down flat. "Oh," he said, "I give all my printing business to a man who belongs to the same men's breakfast club I do."

"While I'm doling out snap, crackle, pop," she thought, "he's making business deals."

She was still sputtering from the turndown when she ran into three other women she knew—an economist, a headhunter, and the director of a city agency. She told them the story. "We should have a breakfast club of our own," Nancy said. "If men are going to throw business to each other that way, we should be doing the same for ourselves."

It turned out to be a lunch club instead, the Women's Lunch Group in Boston. From the start, the idea was to do business. One woman had said, "I think we should bring our secretaries. It would be a good experience for them." She hadn't understood the purpose.

At the opening of each monthly meeting, each member gets up and tells what she's selling or buying. "It's like Weight Watchers, in a sense," Nancy says. "When you know you're going to be weighed in, you do better."

About eighty women belong to the Lunch Group; places for forty are reserved at the Harvard Club meetings. The only men present, as Bernice Shapiro puts it, are "the men who bring in our salad." The group tries not to have too many women from any one profession or industry—"so we're not all foraging in the same fields," says Nancy. Consequently, they've had to turn down a few women who've asked to join. Nancy advises them to start their own. "There should be thousands of these networks, with fifty or sixty women in each."

Spin-offs of their group have formed in the Boston

suburbs, as well as in Chicago and Denver, started by former members who moved away from Boston. "If I moved, I'd start a Lunch Group wherever I landed," Nancy says. "Once you've been turned on to networking with women, you wonder how you ever got along without it."

Loré Caulfield, producer-writer-director for NBC-TV, Los Angeles, interviewed some fifty women for her documentary "The Quiet Revolution of Mrs. Harris." She was struck by the fact that so many of them said they felt their lives were under the control of other people and mentioned this idea to Sallie O'Neill, continuing education specialist in the Department of Human Development, University of California, Los Angeles. The result was a seminar, "Women, Work, and Power," which Loré taught together with Linda St. Claire, Ph.D. in "nonverbal communication." (This was in 1974, before the subject of power had surfaced to the degree it has today.)

One of the nineteen ways Loré recommended for gaining power was that of forming small support groups. The idea excited the group of fifty-seven women: "The chemistry among us was fabulous, mind-blowing," Loré recalls. "Something happened to all of us! I couldn't let the idea just lie there, so I invited twelve women to my house, to start practicing what I preached."

So began Women in Business, a vital network of four hundred women entrepreneurs and professionals who continue to develop and use woman power in a mutually supportive way. After six months of organizational meetings, the founding committee launched the network with an invitational luncheon at the Beverly Crest Hotel. Seventy women paid $10 each to become charter members. They now meet monthly, in the large group, and also in small support groups at members' homes. More than that, they call each other whenever they need information, advice, or sounding boards. And the dollar value of the business they throw to each other is beyond measure.

"*I have been yearning for this*!" "This is dynamite!" "Oh yes, oh yes, oh yes!"

Such were the exuberant reactions of seventy women of Baltimore, Maryland, at the initial lunch meeting of what turned out to be two networks—the Executive Women's Network and the Executive Women's Council.

Marian (Mandy) Goetze and the other principals of New Directions for Women, a multifaceted center there, called the meeting because of what they'd been hearing from women coming to the Career Counseling Center, the Center for Displaced Homemakers, and the Women's Resource and Advocacy Center. "Many women who came to us felt dead-ended in their jobs. Wanting to make a lateral move, they asked us for answers we found we couldn't give. Women in government wanted to know about the corporate world, women in academia wanted to know about government and nonprofit agencies. Then, too, the women we were bringing into our career seminars as role models (we call them cheerleaders, because it's so cheering for women who haven't quite made it yet to see that it's possible) were telling us they had no one to talk to. They were asking us to introduce them to their peers, in other companies or agencies."

So they set up the lunch meeting. Later, after a few planning meetings, the women decided that two separate entities were needed. One would continue to use the facilities of New Directions, focusing on career development for aspiring women. The other would branch off, on its own, for the benefit of women who were already at executive level.

Thus, the Executive Women's Network was thrown open to all women. Taking out a sponsoring membership in New Directions, for $25, they were free to dip into conferences and seminars at will. Those came under such headings as "Creative Sales Careers" and "Creative Use of Personal Power." In addition, there were closed-door sessions, totally confidential, during which an individual could come to a team brought together to help her solve specific career problems.

Meanwhile, the Executive Women's Council (EWC) broke off to organize on its own. It now has seventy-two members, diverse in occupation, experience, accomplishments, and backgrounds. Forty-six percent are in business, including ten who own companies (import-export, international consulting, construction, auto dealership, moving and storage, retail store, advertising, catering); 22 percent are in education; 17 percent in government; 15 percent in nonprofit organizations. There are ten presidents (including three college presidents and one head of a nonprofit organization), six vice-presidents of corporations and banks, two deans, an assistant secretary of a state department, an assistant state superintendent and two regional superintendents, three lawyers, a CPA, a medical doctor, a psychologist, four social workers, two registered nurses, and most other members hold the title of director or manager. Four have gone from volunteer to paid management positions. One member now in corporate management is a U.S. Army lieutenant colonel (retired). The Council has seven Ph.D.'s, four candidates for Ph.D., one Ed.D., two J.D.'s, four M.S.W.'s. Twenty-three have masters degrees, twenty-two have bachelors, and eleven women achieved executive status with no formal degree to aid them. There are five recipients of honorary degrees and twelve members of national honor societies, including seven Phi Beta Kappas. There are two recipients of Fulbright Fellowships and one of a Woodrow Wilson Fellowship. A member was made a Knight of the Order of Leopold by the King of Belgium. Another was honored with the U.S. Army Legion of Merit. Many members have received Woman of the Year awards and other honors too numerous to include here. Seven Council members sit on corporate boards of directors; eighteen on boards of hospitals, academic institutions, and non-profit organizations; thirty-four are officers and board members of professional, civic, community, and religious organizations; and nearly 100 percent are members and/or former officers. Seven members are on local and state government commissions. Another sits on the Federal Reserve Board. Another is on the Board of Managers, American Bureau of Shipping.

It's no wonder, then, that Maryland Governor Harry Hughes turned to the Council for possible appointees to his administration. Ruth Adams, then president, now chair of the board of the Council, put together for him a well-documented portfolio of forty-nine outstanding women. As a result, Rita Baikauskas became the first woman member of the Board of Advisors of the Maryland Automobile Insurance Fund and Mandy Goetze was appointed to the Apprenticeship and Training Council, a policy-making body in the state Department of Labor. Says Rita, "Like many other professional women, I was suffering from an acute case of invisibility until EWC came along."

Among the many other networks that are putting together dossiers on that supposedly rare species, "qualified women," the Financial Women's Association (FWA) in New York City has suggested ten candidates for election to corporation boards of directors. They had non-FWA members make the selections and presented the women to some thirty corporate chief executives at a breakfast meeting. No less an eminence than Thomas J. Murphy, the chairman of General Motors Corporation, was their main speaker, and press coverage of the event was extensive. Susan Fischer, an executive of Wells, Rich, Greene, Inc., advertising agency, ran the show. (Other networks please copy.)

The Coalition for Women's Appointments is the

model in this area. Daisy Fields, co-founder, says the Coalition has input from fifty different women's organizations. The White House personnel office asked it for candidates for the new post of inspector general; two women were selected from the Coalition's list. Another success: appointments to the advisory committee for the metric board. Headhunters employed by government agencies often call, and an informal network of feminists within the government notifies the Coalition when vacancies occur. The Coalition holds monthly meetings in Washington to plan activities and hear speakers.

Gladys Dobelle and her husband gave a Halloween party to get back in touch with their New York friends on their return from a spell of living in San Francisco. "Just a social evening," Gladys recalls. "I had no idea of forming a group. But at about midnight we women found ourselves sitting in a circle in the middle of the floor, having a rap that left the men out. From the usual 'What do you do?' and 'Where do you work?' of the early evening—my seven friends hadn't met each other before—we were getting into job problems. When we had to break up at evening's end, we made a date to meet for lunch."

So began Dialogue, a network of twenty professional women who have been meeting once a month since Halloween of 1977. Each meeting has a specific topic, on which one of their number gives a short presentation to get the discussion started. Subjects so far have ranged from strategies for success (with a five-year plan outlined by a member who is a vice-president of Citibank at age thirty-one) to "A Baby, Maybe" (conducted so enthusiastically by the working mother of a young child that two other members have since decided to become pregnant). Dian Terry's presentation of the effect of the women's movement on women's professional life was particularly impressive to the group; some of the younger networkers hadn't been fully aware of the improvements brought about by such organizations as NOW, and Dian had been active in the movement.

In addition to getting together for discussions, Dialogue has been assembling a list of other local networks, with an eye to combining their resources or staging a city-wide conference. Another project: "Best Bets," a listing of services they've found reliable, from secretarial to domestic.

"We've had so many requests to expand our membership that we're going to set up Dialogue Two," says Gladys. "We think having more than twenty at any one meeting would restrict the discussion too much. Besides, we like the continuity: only three of our original group have dropped out (they moved away); having been together this long gives our network a special quality we'd hate to lose." Dian Terry will set up the second Dialogue, and down the road the group can see a dozen or more forming on their model. They're more than willing to help.

Meanwhile, all over the map, women have been coming together for other reasons, under other auspices, then deciding they want to keep their new relationships going by forming networks. Providing the initial contact for many have been:

Seminars, classes, or counseling groups

At the beginning of each of her very popular management courses or seminars, Susan Ogden, assistant professor of marketing and management at the School of Business, Seattle University, says, "When we finish up here, I'm going to give you a gift, a very important, wonderful gift." On the last day, throwing her arms wide, her own great enthusiasm for this concept lighting her face, she says, "My gift to you is—yourselves!"

Having worked together on management problems under Susan Ogden's direction, members of each class are bound by a common interest and a common experience. They are the nucleus of a network, and Sue has already outlined to them the matchless value to their careers of the networking process. They don't always stick together formally, meeting regularly as a network, but they always have their professor's gift—each other. Having gone away with class lists, they have phone numbers that will be useful for a long time to come. The result is what Sue calls OGDEN—Old Girls Damned Effective Network.

In the same way, Maureen Sullivan, who runs seminars on interpersonal relations for New York University, creates networks wherever she speaks to women. Three women I met at one of Maureen's seminars have since been helpful to me in my own work, and they in turn have kept in touch with others from the group.

Some seminar grads get organized more formally. Clyta (Dogi) Dillon, one notable example, started The Career Network in Seattle, with a nucleus of thirty-five members, including a few men, from twenty-one different firms in the area. As many as one hundred attend the network's monthly dinner meetings to hear successful business people speak on various aspects of career development.

A commercial counseling organization called Women's Success Teams has spawned groups in several cities. Some two thousand women have gone through this particular counseling process (as of 1979): they pay $200-plus for a twelve-hour instructional period, then go off on their own in teams of six to nine to continue to work toward the personal or career goals they worked out in the seminars. According to Elaine Weinstein, who keeps track of the teams and sometimes supplies replacements for members who drop out, the teams stay together from three months to two years, meeting weekly in each other's homes. Although put together at random, without regard to age, education, occupation, or even sex (a few men have signed up), they turn into cohesive groups with a strong feeling of camaraderie. And plugging each other into their own networks is an important part of the help they give each other.

The group to which a fabric designer belonged went so far as to lend her money when she was out of a job. She confronted her boss about a substantial raise, on the group's urgings, and on being turned down, walked out. "Wait," the team told her. "Don't take another job right away; they'll ask you back—at your price." The prediction was exactly correct. The designer's salary jumped from $175 to $500 a week.

In Tustin, California (south of Los Angeles), Mimi Grant runs an operation similar to Success Teams. It's call weCan (Women's Economic and Career Advancement Network). Also in L.A. is Women Can Win, begun by Judi Hochman. Following two-day seminars, women are placed in small groups that meet weekly.

Resources, Inc., puts pairs together, and the pairs then join with other pairs to form a network, in the management training seminars this firm runs for women in corporations. Their basic idea is to pair women who can help each other, each being strong in a skill the other needs. An assertive woman might be paired with one who's afraid to pick up the phone, for example, the shy woman being a good organizer who can help the more outgoing woman organize her papers while she herself takes coaching on reaching out. Expanded, this idea results in thirty people matching their skills and needs in a Resources seminar. They enter into an agreement for specific exchanges, continuing the mutual aid network after the program ends.

(By the way, Elaina Zuker and Joan Alevras, partners in Resources, Inc., met at a seminar, where they discovered they were both working for the same company. Their own networking has provided fertile ground for the growth of countless new networks. And they've begun a network of their own called the Consultants Consortium. "Consultants work alone, as a rule: it can be a very lonely business," Elaina says. "We really need the company of our own kind at frequent intervals.")

An internal seminar produced a small network at the General Electric Credit Corporation in Stamford, Connecticut. Twelve women, selected by their managers for their potential, participated in a three-day program directed by Paula Dym, manager of human resources (personnel). They decided to continue their connection, meeting monthly to share ideas and problems. They also go out for lunch together, which they hadn't done before.

"Corporate life can be a very lonely experience for the professional woman," Paula said. "These women no longer feel a sense of isolation. And the way they're helping each other is new to them all. Five years ago women were highly competitive with each other. I think we're now in the second phase, where women have made a place for themselves and are now willing to help one another. In this climate, I feel networking both internally and externally will grow."

And conferences

Women attracted to a big conference, particularly if it's career-oriented, can "find" each other there, then keep in touch individually or in spin-off groups. Whether or not you already belong to other groups and networks, be sure to take advantage of this method of meeting women of like interests. Just to get the names, occupations, and phone numbers of conference attendees can be worth the price of admission. And the women who lead the workshops, you can be sure, are good contacts for you; their very presence in that role proves they have good networks of their own. (How else did the conference organizers know about them?) By definition, workshops are small and informal, so it's easy to become acquainted with the leaders.

One conference that started something big, very big, a prototype for what could someday happen all over the United States, happened in November of 1978. It was the large Regional Conference for Managerial and Professional Women under the auspices of Portland State University, held in Portland, Oregon. Dr. Alice Armstrong, whose idea it was and who worked with her volunteer committee for months ahead, preparing for it, had long been aware of the need for such a conference. Women enrolled in her courses at the School of Business were avidly hungry for the contacts and the kind of information the conference was set up to provide. But even she was astonished by the turnout. For two and a half days, those lucky enough to get in soaked up guidance and instruction in everything from time management and leadership styles to mentor relationships. At the end, they were asked if they'd be willing to help organize a follow-up conference the next year. No fewer than three hundred women signed up.

Such was the seedbed for what is now the Institute for Managerial and Professional Women, which lists among its goals "to encourage network relationships for the support and advancement of women." It has supplied the conference attendees with lists of others who work in their fields. Eventually it will have a computerized career network, a cross-indexed listing of the Institute's membership, to be used as a continuing resource for job openings, referrals, and networking. It will also maintain a file of ongoing networks, so that members can tap into other appropriate groups and—down the line, as the Institute develops—networks can share materials and information through this central source. Another of the Institute's purposes is to give members "exposure to the most capable and dynamic managerial and professional women in their region."

Interestingly, women who met through one of the workshops in the 1978 conference formed what they call the Leadership Network. A test of leadership styles had shown them all to be "controllers." At their first meeting, they listed some of the things they wanted to do together:

1. *Communicate on conferences.* Not only will we share news of upcoming conferences and meetings, but those who attend meetings will relate their impressions of and knowledge gained from them. If several of us should attend the same conference, we may decide to evaluate the meeting, presenting the results to organizers of the conference.

2. *Attend special events.* There may be lectures, specialty movies, etc., that some or all of us may want to attend. These may be instead of or in addition to our regular meetings.

3. *Engage guest speakers.* We will invite to some meetings various people knowledgeable in areas that will contribute to our development.

4. *Market each other's skills.* As we learn more about one another's interests and expertise, we will be able to market them when given an opportunity.

5. *Exchange our experiences.* When we become exposed to new and unfamiliar situations in or related to our work, we'll discuss them at our meetings. Thus all of us can gain from another's experience by using each other as sounding boards or by hearing how others have handled the same situation or one of similar nature.

6. *Contribute items to our newsletter.* Anyone who has something to share with the others can send the information to the one responsible for the next meeting. This newsletter, which will probably act more as a bulletin board, will be a good way for us to keep in touch with our out-of-towners and an even better way for them to keep in touch with us Portlanders.

And so a new network got under way.

The Women Writers Satellite Conference, sponsored by the Corporation for Public Broadcasting in January of 1979, was unique in its method but the same in its effect on the women who attended. "We musn't stop here," they all said, and they set a date for a follow-up meeting on their own. During the two-day teleconference, panel discussions were broadcast by satellite to groups of women writers meeting simultaneously in four cities—Columbia, South Carolina; Dallas; Los Angeles; and New York City. Of the 125 women at the New York meeting, 35 met again to talk about their writing problems—and about starting a network. They decided to form writing workshops, their focus being their craft rather than on networking itself: drama writing, news writing, proposal writing, writing for children's theater and TV. But of course networking resulted.

The U.S. General Services Administration staged a series of regional conferences—called "Women West" in Los Angeles, "Women and Business" in New York City—during which impromptu networks formed. As a matter of fact, a form of networking that occurred before the western conference provides us with another networking success story: Kathy Reimers met Cindy Brysh at the Brentwood (California) Creative Center for Single Adults. On hearing about the government plans for a big conference, Cindy, who is assistant director of special programs at the University of Southern California, told Kathy, who is advertising director of a tabloid newspaper called *Women's Information Network*. Kathy in turn told her boss, Betsy Berkhemer. Result: *Women's Information Network* became a co-sponsor of the conference, responsible for a special feature, "The Marketplace," where women business owners sold their products and services directly to purchasing agents representing business and education. The conference drew two thousand women, all of whom became complementary members of the Network, slated to receive the paper for the following six months. Wide exposure and profits for the Network, a result of Cindy-Kathy networking!

□8 Internal Networks: Trials and Tribulations

Networking groups that form within corporation walls are up against an entirely different set of problems from those that organize across company lines.

One concerns management attitudes and the way the women in the company perceive and are influenced by those attitudes. How will management react to the idea of its employees getting together? Will a woman's being identified with such a group be good for her image in the corporation or will it, rather, bring her visibility that might prove dangerous? Will the women for whose benefit the network is organized hang back, whether because of fear of jeopardizing their tenuous relationships with their male bosses or merely because of apathy? Will either the management, hoping not, or the women, hoping so, see the group as an activist body, organized to press for change in the status quo?

Another problem concerns the political realities of working for a big corporation, which might be roughly characterized as "every man [*sic*] for himself." Is it safe for women who work for the same company to network with each other? Aren't they just as competitive as the men, just as likely to take personal advantage of any information shared with them? If so, what's the point of forming a network group?

The questions answer themselves, in the experience of women who start these groups. As one said, "You never know until you try. I know that if we had asked permission to start up, or even consulted personnel in advance, we'd have been discouraged from having, if not actually forbidden to have, our first meeting. Yet when we presented them with a fait accompli, they were cool. They even asked if they could help in any way!" On the other hand, management in another corporation, while never taking official notice of the women's group, sent spies to the meetings and had the meeting announcements torn off the mirrors in the ladies' rooms (the nearest thing to a bulletin board they had). "We hadn't known we were in a war zone," said one of the founders of that particular group. "Their attitude was a surprise, but it was also a consciousness raiser. Quite a few women decided, because of it, to make their careers elsewhere."

As for the question of competition, confirmed networkers say that they are better equipped to compete successfully when they know who's who and what's going on in their corporations—which they are not likely to know if they maintain their loner stance, talking to no one.

"Being isolated is a big part of our problem," as one woman put it. "Why do you suppose the company is so nervous about our getting together, if it's not because we'll find out things they'd rather we didn't know? Who stands to lose the most, the woman who gets into the action, taking a hand in her own career, or the one who sits quietly in her corner, waiting for the powers that be to determine her future?"

It was against such odds that Alina Novak created Networks, in what must be the archetype of corporations, the Equitable Life Assurance Society of the United States, in its New York City headquarters. Alina is now the New York City expert on networking. She's in demand for panels and workshops on the subject, has developed a networking course for the YWCA and for NOW, and *should* go out on the lecture circuit, for she is a very stirring speaker and a real enthusiast for networking. "It's the next stage in the women's movement," she says, and certainly to the degree that it puts more women in positions of power it will prove to be an important step toward equality of the sexes. Economic independence is the key to women's liberation, and networking is the key to better jobs with better pay.

Alina does all these extras for no fee, in addition to her full-time job and her work with the Equitable networks. She believes that much in spreading the word. "I feel that I have this fantastic secret," she says. "I want everyone else to have it, too."

But there's more to her ready appearance on panels and the like than goodwill alone. This activity gives her exposure in the business community. Just as everyone at Equitable knows who she is now, so do members of the Y, of NOW, of her Business and Professional Women's club (BPW), of Women in Communications. Her name was in a big Macy's ad, inviting customers to a "Women Mean Business" week that included a networking panel. She was featured in a CBS-TV documentary news item about networking, produced by Barbara Flack.

A popular test used by career counselors, to help women set their goals, asks, "Which are you going for—money, fame, or power?" Alina's instant answer to the question is "fame." Acknowledging that, she doesn't grumble about being exploited (as another person might see her free appearances).

How Alina Novak created "Networks" at Equitable

As an administrative assistant in a company that employed over fifteen thousand people, seven thousand of them in the same building where she went to work every day, Alina Novak still felt very much alone. Like many other big companies with an eye on affirmative action requirements, Equitable Life had brought in outside consultants, reportedly at great expense, to put on special programs for women. They also had frequent assemblies, orientation meetings, and the like coordinated by their large personnel department, but Alina felt as though all these were going around her somehow.

She was not a member of the women's advisory board. She managed to get to only a few of the programs; there wasn't room for everybody every time. The programs were good—a three-day seminar on career development, for example, and a rousing speech by Gloria Steinem. But there was no follow-through, no continuity. Sometimes she didn't even know about a program until it was too late to sign up for it. "It was frustrating, feeling left out and not even knowing for sure what you were being left out *of*!"

And in the back of her mind there formed the uncomfortable idea that these programs were being thrown *at* the women. Employees' needs were being assessed, more or less guessed at, by outsiders. It was all too much from on high to suit Alina. She began to think about supplementing these official programs at the grass-roots level.

Alina let her idea take form slowly. She also did not rush into executing it. What she did is particularly valuable to others, I think, not only because she was successful but because she shows how a "nobody" can operate within a huge, highly structured, extremely hierarchical corporation. What she started has become Networks—seven discussion groups that meet every two weeks—plus an umbrella group that turns out hundreds for its monthly programs. (The mailing list numbers four-hundred-plus Equitable employees, each of whom has paid $1 to be on the mailing list.) In the latest development, other Networks have sprung up in Equitable offices in other cities.

To accomplish this she first had a series of one-to-one lunches with women in the company, cautiously asking them if they'd be interested in the kind of group she was thinking of forming. Because she didn't want to be misunderstood, or seen as any kind of subversive in management's eyes if word got around what she had in mind, she wanted it to be accurate. Besides, she wanted genuine feedback on her idea. Private lunches made it possible for women to raise questions and express thoughts they wouldn't have mentioned in a larger meeting.

Along the way, Alina ran across a copy of a speech that Coy Eklund, the president of Equitable, had made several months earlier about what business could do for women. "It was definitely a feminist speech," Alina recalls. "How many other companies in the United States have top-level support for women? We'd be fools not to take him at his word." Besides, Alina is a woman with a good political sense. She realized the strategic value of using the president's speech as the focal point for a first meeting of the group she envisioned. How could the corporation object?

Next, the mechanics of setting up a meeting. Equitable has a system to accommodate employee activities and Alina knew how to use it. She lined up a room for three meetings (she had done this for a Toastmasters' group in the past) and she got a budget code number that authorized her use of the copy machines and printing facilities. (The okay came from a woman vice-president who has since retired. Another officer in another company might have made a big deal out of this request, but Mary McMahon was at once sympathetic to the idea of women needing to talk to each other and important enough to make this decision on her own. Note that personnel was not the place to go with this seemingly innocent request. They would surely have seen Alina's projected meeting as an invasion of their own turf.)

Alina distributed copies of the Eklund speech to about forty women she'd identified as possible members of a network-to-be, inviting them to a lunch-hour meeting to discuss the speech. Twenty-four came, eighteen of them the women she had lunched with over the preceding months. "I knew them all. They all knew me. That's important, especially in a big company like ours. Otherwise, they'd be afraid to come—and I'd be afraid of sabotage."

At that first meeting, talking about the speech got the discussion going, but the main topic turned out to be "Where do we go from here?" Everyone immediately sensed the importance and value of meeting again. Everyone had an idea about what to do next: "Let's send out a questionnaire," "Let's keep this small." They settled on the plan they have since followed: small groups meeting every two weeks, monthly meetings for larger assemblies.

Thus encouraged, Alina asked eight other women, most of whom had attended that first meeting, to serve with her on a steering committee. Little by little, which is probably the best way, new activities were added to a basic structure of discussion and program meetings. And Alina sent a memo to Equitable's president on the first anniversary of Networks' formation, describing all its activities. Such an unsolicited report to management is a tactic worth copying by other in-house groups.

As the groups began to expand, Alina called the head of human resources, as the personnel department is called at Equitable, requesting a fifteen-minute appointment to tell him what was happening. She went to that interview mindful that (1) every company is fearful of unionization, and (2) every personnel department wants employees to come *there* with their problems, not to turn to other employees for counsel.

Emphasizing that she was speaking for herself alone, not as the representative of any group,* Alina said the purpose of the meetings was purely educational. She expressed the hope that they would prove to be good for morale, too, for as more women got to know each other, they would feel more at home on their jobs. She left copies of the announcements distributed up until then and promised to put personnel on the mailing list for future notices. By interview's end, she felt that she had relieved any fears that management might have had about the long-run effect of her activities.

"As a matter of fact," she now says, "they had nothing to fear. We were not getting together to issue demands or confront management in any way. All we wanted was to get acquainted and to share what we knew and could learn from each other."

Alina was between two jobs while she coordinated the beginnings of Networks. During the wind-down of her previous assignment and the crank-up of her new one, she had plenty of time to devote to this side project. Besides, both her bosses were interested and supportive of what she was trying to do. Organizing always takes more time than anyone anticipates, so if you're planning to follow in Alina's footsteps, make sure your job gives you enough leeway for this work; if not, appoint someone else to receive the phone calls and handle the details of getting started—confine your own work to after-hours.

Most of the original Equitable networkers, those who attended the first meeting and subsequently helped keep the groups going, have been promoted. Whether they would have been, anyway, whether the network gave them the extra know-how and personal support they

* Important to future organizers of internal networks, assuming that they are not and do not intend to be unions.

needed to make their next move, or whether their employer simply wanted to keep them happy to avoid trouble remains a moot question. The fact remains: their careers advanced through networking.

How do Alina's bosses feel about all this? I asked Coy Eklund, chief executive officer of the Equitable. "We have never felt that women need to be in an adversarial position with management," he said. "And that viewpoint is certainly borne out by our experience. We have made facilities and support available to Networks without reservation and without surveillance by management. Our thought is that any program that helps Equitable people develop themselves—personally and professionally—is a good thing for all of us."

WCC—"with names changed to protect the 'guilty' "

Some women involved in setting up in-house networks have not wanted to be identified in this book although they've been immensely helpful in explaining their political problems and the ways they are trying to solve them. One such is Mary Joe C., a refugee from academia, who was new to the corporate world when she was hired to do training for a large firm in the Southwest. She asked if she could first spend six months as assistant to the personnel chief, a move her friends recommended against—"a woman should never be an 'assistant to' or that's all she'll ever be"—because she wanted to learn her way around before she took on the training assignment. While doing just that, she introduced herself to the four top women in the company and learned that they didn't know each other. They had similar concerns and anxieties, but they weren't talking about them. There was no one to talk to. Mary Joe got them together.

The mix was so successful that they thought other

women would profit by the same experience of meeting their peers, getting together to talk about their jobs and the corporation. They decided to form a women's group. They picked some representative women from elsewhere in the company, inviting them to meet over lunch and discuss the idea. To their surprise and disappointment, a lot of the women didn't want anything to do with it. "I don't need it," they said. Or "It's too risky."

But the original five persisted. Meeting from November 1977 through February 1978, they planned how to sell the idea to the corporation. They talked long distance with women in other companies that they'd heard had women's caucuses—notably ABC, where Marlene Sanders, the documentary producer who had been one of the founders of the women's group there, proved to be especially helpful—but they came to believe that their own idea for a group was different from the others. They weren't angry, just impatient. They liked the company, liked their jobs, and were successful in them. They decided they'd have to make their special attitudes clear to their management.

In February, after they'd drawn up a charter and firmed up their plans, they made an appointment to see the chairman of the board at nine-fifteen in the morning. They met beforehand, "for a breakfast I'll never forget as long as I live," says Mary Joe, her eyes even at this late date expressing a mixture of excitement and anxiety. Then at nine o'clock they each went to see their bosses.

"We have an appointment with the chairman in fifteen minutes," Mary Joe told the personnel chief, "to tell him we're setting up a Women's Career Council. Maybe you'd like to go with us?"

He turned white. "You've done *what*?" But once he'd recovered from his shock, Mary Joe recalls, "he was very professional about it." He went along.

The chairman was surprised, too, and he asked, "What do the women want?" in the classic manner, but in the end he bought the women's idea that the group would be a resource for him, a help to the corporation as well as to the women involved. Assured that they intended no agitation, as indeed they did not, he gave his blessing.

He went further. He engaged consultants to survey "the woman situation." They developed a series of programs for the women and even went so far as to explain it to the wives of men in the company (assuming, you see, that wives would object to their husbands working with women as colleagues!).

The seminars for women that the consultants put on turned out to be patronizing and woefully inadequate, as often happens. (An entire industry has grown up out of corporations' needs to calm the troops, it seems.)

"They set us back," says Corinne P., new president of the women's group. "It was a hard act to follow, in that women assumed we'd be giving them more of the same dumb stuff."

The first general meeting of what they named the Women's Career Council (WCC) exploded with another problem—a black-white confrontation, the blacks declaring that a group formed by white women couldn't presume to speak for them.

(This has happened in many other corporations. Where there is already a black group of both sexes in operation—and these were organized in advance of women's groups, as a rule—the black women have a difficult choice of where to put their time and their loyalties. Remembering that black Congresswoman Shirley Chisholm once said she had suffered more discrimination for her sex than for her color, many black women join the women's groups, often maintaining their membership in black caucuses as well. But others stay clear of the women's groups, considering them just one more white organization to cope with.)

Another problem the group experienced during its first year was the one that had been signaled by their first lunch: a large proportion of the eight hundred women employed there saw no need for a women's group. "I don't need anyone to speak for me," was a typical remark. "I can speak for myself." Aside from a lack of awareness as to what they were up against as women in a corporation run by men, the younger women were motivated by a wish to be accepted by men, to be seen as part of "the team." They thought being identified with a women's group would work against them.

"Most of the women I know still want the acceptance of men," says Mary Joe, who says she was a Queen Bee, without even knowing what the term meant, until her divorce. Her friends had all been men; her values had been male. "I was missing something that could have made my life richer—the understanding and support of women. Now that I have that, I wish I'd had it sooner, but I can see where some of the women in our company are coming from."

"Or *not* coming from," says Corinne, mindful of the attendance problem. As the new chair, it's her hope she'll attract holdouts to the group through her programming. WCC surveyed the women, asking for their requests and ideas on the kinds of speakers they'd like to hear. They got a 10-percent response, which they considered good. (Enthusiastic founders of in-house networks-to-be, take note.) The answers are influencing Corinne's current programs. "We're serving individual pockets within our constituency."

Thus, current programs concern personal financial planning, career paths of successful women (including some brought in from outside), laws affecting women, women in sports. I asked her why she and the other women in the Women's Career Council try so hard to involve those who seem resistant to the idea. She said, "But they *need* it so desperately! And if we can only once get through to them, through their fear and self-doubt, they'll see that they do. And once they see—don't *you* see?—we'll *all* be better off! We've simply *got* to get these women to start talking to each other!

"Until the men change, the women aren't going anywhere. But networking from within can change the women, who can start changing the men. We've got to start somewhere. I'm starting *here*."

I asked Mary Joe what advice she could pass along to women who had yet to start in-house networks.

"Think through in advance the implications of what you are doing. The corporate visibility this activity gives you can go two ways. It happens that four of our original five have been promoted, since we started the group. Maybe we would have been, anyway, but equally, we might have been seen as poor risks and been left behind.

"The time and effort required are much, much greater than you might think at first. If you're not prepared for this, you'll set up conflicts within yourself. You might begin to resent the group, even feel hostile to it. Especially if it seems thankless, as it might. Then, if you drop out, that sends messages to other women; you will have done the cause more harm than good.

"If you're prepared to stick it out, though, the rewards are considerable. For one, work life is so much easier when you can pick up the phone and ask someone you know, 'How do I do this? Who's the person to see?'"

The Women's Caucus at WGBH-Boston

An internal network that doesn't mind being identified is the Women's Caucus at public broadcasting station WGBH in Boston. The Caucus set up committees to research and draft recommendations for action on particular issues the group selects. About fifty women belong.

There's a pension committee looking into the actuarial tables of insurance companies, which use the higher life expectancy of women to skew pension rates and effectively deny women the same benefits as men. Another committee is concerned with child care opportunities; another checks out WGBH's programming for inadvertent sexism or racism.

Caroline Collins, Caucus president, says in "Equal Access, the Newsletter for Women in Public Telecommunications," "We're interested in educating ourselves and top management, so we can work together toward improvements and solutions."

That conciliatory tone is representative of many current internal networks, but their predecessors were more reform-oriented. Here are a few examples:

Inside Polaroid

Suzy Ells helped her own career when she organized a women's caucus at Polaroid Corporation in Cambridge, Massachusetts. Promotion often comes the way of women who demonstrate leadership skills this way. She became affirmative action officer for the whole corporation, and, unlike many AA officers who are stuck off in the personnel department without the power to put their programs into effect, she had a steering committee of highly placed managers, an expanding budget, and her president's ear.

It all began when Suzy was going around the plant and the offices in person, asking supervisors to release certain workers for the high school equivalency program she'd been hired to run. It struck her that most workers in the plant were women but almost all supervisors were men. "I'd look up from the factory floor to the glass-enclosed office of the boss, and there *he'd* be, feet on the desk, talking on the phone, while hundreds of women were hand-assembling *his* daily quota of cameras." In the office areas, too, women seemed to be segregated into windowless pools; the private offices were occupied almost exclusively by white males.

Suzy began talking to other women about what seemed to her an unfair ratio. "The women's movement was very much in the air in Boston that year [1971]," she remembers. "It was becoming okay to think as I did. I was getting support from everything I read." She also had what she calls "a beautiful role model": the year before, on the heels of Martin Luther King's death, blacks had made a presentation to management with the result that Polaroid had agreed to have 10 percent blacks at all levels of the corporate structure by 1975.

As Suzy and her friends began meeting, they learned of two other groups forming; one was in the plant, where the big issue was that men got clothing allowances, enabling them to buy their work clothes downtown, while women were handed blue smocks; the other was in the administrative area. "We were all three sending memos to the president," Suzy says. "It was clear we had to get ourselves together."

What they did to correct their shotgun approach was form themselves into five task forces to study the status of women at Polaroid. What their management did was assign them, as their liaison, a computer-system supervisor.

"We need good, hard data," the women told him (step one for any group working up to a confrontation with management).

"Dictate what you need," he said, "and we'll run it."

So the women's group ended up knowing more than Polaroid managers ever thought to ask about women's employment there. The statistics confirmed Suzy's original visual impression: out of 3,000 "exempt" employees (they are exempt from wage and salary regulations), only 210 were women. They dispelled the myth that women didn't stay long enough to be worth training; in the plant, the difference between male and female seniority was three months; among salaried employees, the average woman had been there seven years to her male colleagues' three.

In addition to collecting and analyzing hard data, the women studied the law. "We knew more about the EEOC guidelines than the company did." They checked Polaroid's fringe benefits against the law that neither sex may be favored over the other, discovering first of all that while the wives of male employees were covered medically, for obstetrical hospitalization, single women who worked at Polaroid were not. Also, the temporary disability of childbirth was the only disability not covered under the corporation's sickness benefits plan. (Polaroid now treats time out for childbirth the same as time out for a broken leg. And the hospitalization coverage is the same for both sexes.)

Not every woman who works for Polaroid was or will be happy with the effects achieved by the women's group, but the company now has an affirmative action plan, complete with goals and timetables for recruiting and moving women in and up in the company. Employees may see the plan, an important point in view of the secrecy that surrounds so many other companies' goals and timetables.

"We have a long, long way to go," Suzy Ells told me when I talked to her in connection with the *Redbook* article I mentioned in the introduction to this book. "Women in top management are still only 2, out of 182. We don't even have enough middle-management women waiting in the wings, prepared to move up. And we're not doing very well at moving women into skilled crafts: when men apply, they're already electricians or mechanics or whatever; women tend not to be, so we'll have to train them ourselves, and that costs big money. But women are running fork-lift trucks and highly technical manufacturing machines; they supervise production and act as security guards; they're sales representatives and financial analysts. Five years ago, all those were male-only areas."

As new groups spring up, now that Suzy's has become official, Polaroid offers facilities and invites discussion. Whether this attitude represents conscience, fear of suit (or unionization), or simply sound business practice, the results are a credit to the first women who organized themselves into an action group.

Other insiders, now going outside

Some of the women's caucuses that were formed in the early and mid-seventies no longer meet, but in many cases their disbanding is a sign of success rather than the opposite. The women's group at the Ford Foundation is a case in point. The Women's Task Force organized in 1973, focusing on maternity leave and child-care allowances for parents earning less than $20,000 a year. After winning those points, they began to push for more Foundation grants to women. They channeled Ford money to such groups as the Women's Rights Project of the American Civil Liberties Union, the NOW Legal Defense and Educational Fund, and the Women's Equity Action League Education and Legal Defense Fund. During their next stage they went official, as the Coordinating Committee on Women's Programs, but they stopped meeting along about 1977.

Now, according to Susan Berresford, program officer in the division of national affairs (working on women's grants), the Foundation consciousness has been raised high enough so that special gadflies are not needed. "The subject is understood more broadly here. It's an easy topic to bring up now; we don't need the group as a means of doing it. Also I think we all learned more about how to present our case in an effective manner. We have more confidence in our individual abilities to deal with the issues within our own areas."

But Susan and some 340 other women in foundations belong to Women and Foundations-Corporate Philanthropy, a national network; it's based in New York but has member networks in Cleveland, Chicago, San Francisco, Boston, and Minneapolis. The networking is lively. A Foundation woman can pick up the phone and talk to a colleague in another city, knowing that they're both "coming from the same place" in the work they do, so long explanations are not necessary before discussing a problem.

Susan uses the network in several ways, besides the obvious one of keeping in touch with activities in her field. One is for job information. "I must have two or three telephone conversations a week about job openings in the field," she says. "We all do a great deal of calling around." She also calls to see if other foundations will contribute to a grant she plans to propose to her board; when she can get a show of interest elsewhere it helps her to convince the officers of the project's worth.

"Big tickets"

Another example of women forming an action group inside a larger organization is what happened within the United Storeworkers Union.

Women in labor unions might be said to have a double problem: in addition to male employers, they have male leadership in their unions. No woman sits on the thirty-five-man AFL-CIO executive council, despite the fact that women constitute roughly 30 percent of the membership. Even in unions where the members are mostly women, as in the textile industry and in retailing, the major officers are men. Women's issues have not been "in the forefront of their consciousness," as one union woman delicately put it to me.

But early in 1972, with their annual stewards conference coming up for the United Storeworkers, six women who worked in the union office decided to try to change all that. They wanted their officers to do something about the inequities women storeworkers were suffering—especially their being confined to selling relatively inexpensive items, pantyhose to pottery, while men got all the "big tickets," earning larger commissions on bigger sales. Men's selling furniture, rugs, major appliances, TV's, and the like gave them two or three times the income women, who were customarily excluded from those departments, could ever earn. The group of six women persuaded the conference leaders to let them raise these issues there. They accomplished their first objective when they got a go-ahead.

"We spent about three months getting ready for the conference," Eleanor Tilson, now a vice-president of the union, remembers.

"We wanted to be absolutely certain of our facts," says Ida Torres, also since elected a vice-president, "so we could sound calm and reasonable, not whiney."

They developed handout materials, including a quiz that most of the male delegates flunked. (They were surprised to learn that their female colleagues earned only 57 percent of their own pay.) The six women prepared to lead workshops, called buzz sessions by the union.

The conference was a success but, judging by what some of the men said in the workshops, the women knew a lot of ear opening had still to be done. "Men who sell major appliances asked, 'How can a *woman* demonstrate a washer or a vacuum cleaner?' The women were hysterical with laughter," Ellie told me.

So the group's next step was to set up a series of classes in the stores, slowly developing men's awareness and also women's confidence that they could perform well in jobs traditionally held by men.

Today, women hold almost 15 percent of the "big ticket" jobs in stores organized by United. They're earning $17,000 to $18,000 compared with the $7,000 or $8,000 they'd be making now if they were still confined to their former jobs. The only department they haven't broken into, perhaps understandably, is men's suits. But those who sell women's suits and coats, who formerly made $7,000 compared to the $11,000 earned by salesmen of men's suits, are now on a par with the men.

Not least: of United's twelve officers, six are now female.

CWA

Another union women's group, much, much larger, and set up much more elaborately, is inside the Communications Workers of America. In the fall of 1978, a core group called the Concerned Women's Advancement Committee held a national conference in Minneapolis, a four-day session that brought some five hundred women from all parts of the country. They had held women's conferences at their annual union convention in the past, but this was the first time the women had met separately. The main purpose of the conference was to develop leadership skills among themselves, so that women could take a greater part in union activities. Again, although women outnumber men in the rank and file, their management is almost 100 percent male. Dina Beaumont, vice-president, is the only woman on the seventeen-member executive board. None of the nine-hundred-odd chartered locals has a woman president.

Mostly telephone company employees, but some civil service workers, the women raced from workshop to workshop at the conference in a high degree of excitement. They had never had a chance to meet so many of their counterparts from other cities, to compare notes with them, and to find out, among other things, that some contracts are better than others on matters of special interest to them (stress-related questions of production speedups and excessive monitoring, in particular).

Returning to their local unions and their own everyday jobs, the women knew how to start small support groups, and how to make themselves better heard by their union leaders. Many of the acquaintances struck up at Minneapolis are continuing, long distance.

FEW

Federally Employed Women, FEW, can be called an "in-house" network even though its "house" is the entire federal government, which employs 700,000 women. It has two principal objectives—to end sex discrimination in federal employment, and to increase opportunities for women in the federal service. It is thus more of an activist network than, say, the Equitable groups, but at the same time less adversarial than the women's caucuses that have taken such issues to the courts.

FEW has sent spokeswomen to "the Hill," to testify before Senate and House committees considering civil service reforms. It has published a handbook on filing equal employment opportunity complaints against sex discrimination. But it hasn't brought suit.

Allie B. Latimer, general counsel of the General Services Administration (GSA), tells how FEW got started: "It was the custom of the president to have winners of the Federal Women's Award over to the White House. That particular year the award winners told him that his Executive Order 11246, prohibiting employment discrimination by race, color, religion, and national origin, should have included sex. So he amended the order accordingly, with Executive Order 11375. That was in October of 1967. Later that year, the Civil Service Commission told all the agencies to set up women's programs to implement the order. So in January of 1968 the GSA appointed a committee made up of the top-ranking women.

"I was then chief counsel in the procurement division, with the highest job classification—GS-15—so I was automatically the chair. We met, but we had no idea what we were supposed to do. We were already the busiest people in the agency.

"But soon after that I went to a three-day course on management and, asking around, found that only two of the thirty women attending had even heard of the Executive Order. I stood up and asked who'd like to get together and discuss it. The response was enthusiastic.

"We met on a Saturday in April, the 'graduates' of two of those management courses, and decided to organize. We worked all summer in people's homes and in a church—it happened to be President Johnson's own church. By September we had our articles of incorporation—no problem with so many lawyers among us—and our name.

"The name was The Organization of Federally Employed Women, which made a good acronym—TOO FEW—but we soon dropped the front part. Our first project was to collect data on women in the federal service. One of our number wrote a computer program that pulled the statistics out for us. We established statistically what we already suspected: most women were concentrated in the lowest-graded, lowest-paying jobs. Fewer than 1 percent of us were in grades 16, 17, and 18. [Ten years later, according to a Civil Service Commission study, women were 2.8 percent of the GS-16's through 18's.]

"FEW has been working ever since to improve those numbers, both by pressuring the government and by helping our members qualify for promotion. We now have seven thousand members in 160 chapters, with an office and paid staff in the National Press Building in Washington. Our membership runs the gamut from entry level to agency head." Allie herself has moved up three slots to GS-18.

A state government network that grew and grew

Like FEW, the women's network in the state government in Albany, New York, had its impetus in an executive order, but it was many years later. In 1976, Governor Hugh Carey issued an order calling for affirmative action in the state government. The affirmative action officer in the state capital, Audrey Harvey, who had been in her job only two weeks at the time, engaged Cornell University's School of Industrial and Labor Relations to set up a Women's Advisors Program.

Sixty-three women from twenty-six state agencies were given two days' training on how to help other women in their departments use the affirmative action program for their advancement and how to set up separate networks in their agencies. As part of the training program, Cornell's Anne Nelson brought in a panel of top women executives in the administration, both as role models and as women who could describe the workings of the various agencies they served in. Theirs had been breakthrough appointments; they were firsts in important jobs.

The meeting ended on a high of hope and great plans for the future—and not the least inspired were the big shots, some of whom hadn't even met each other before. Including Linda Tarr-Whelan, then administrative director of the Department of Labor for the state, who has since been appointed deputy assistant to the president, at the White House (following Sarah Weddington's promotion to full assistant). "Why can't we have something like this for *us*?" they asked. And that's how it came about that, a few months later, women executives met in New

York City, under Cornell auspices, to form their own network.

They discussed the kinds of problems women face when they enter positions that were exclusively male-held in the past. Not least, they agreed, were the little things that eroded their self-confidence as they moved along, or made them super-self-conscious of their gender when, in their own view, it was irrelevant. "Like the reporter interviewing me on the phone," attorney Rosemary Pooler mentioned, "and asking me to describe my figure." Like being greeted at meetings with hearty ho-ho remarks like "What have we here? A rose among the thorns!"

Lois Gray recalled that networks have always been helpful to immigrants. "We're in foreign territory, too, trying to learn a new language and customs that at times seem very odd indeed."

They decided they had to learn more about how the civil service works—most had been appointed from other fields, Wall Street to academia. They wanted an association of women to whom they could turn instead of, as one of the women put it, "wearing myself out by bluffing." And although many were overextended already, they decided they wanted to form a continuing organization.

That was in the spring of 1977. The women executives now have not only their own lunch group but the Albany Women's Forum, a networking group of 150 to 200 women who meet once a month over a chef's salad. In Rochester, New York, where another group of state agencies has offices, a similar network has formed.

The NBC story

"Listen, Katherine, we've got to do something about this!"

They had fled to the file room, two women still quivering with rage. And that's how it began, the women's caucus that has resulted in NBC's agreement to spend more than $2 million to improve jobs and salaries for its women employees.

In other corporations, too—at *Newsweek*, at *The New York Times*, at *Reader's Digest*, at the Bank of America, at Chase Manhattan Bank—women were beginning to get together to talk about their jobs, their pay, and why nothing seemed to be happening about affirmative action in their companies. Women were still stuck in the same old low-paying slots.

Marilyn Schultz and Katherine Powers, production assistants for the "NBC Nightly News," finally balked at fetching coffee for the men on the staff. Marilyn told me, "The guys expected it only because we were women. We had a big fight in the office over what now seems a little thing."

It was December 1971. That day, after their "big fight in the office," Marilyn called a couple of women she knew, then a couple more, and Katherine did the same. They met. They sent all NBC women employees a questionnaire, uncovering extensive anger. Some was expressed anonymously; other women not only signed their names but wrote detailed accounts of their personal experiences with sex discrimination. So the core group called a general lunch-hour meeting. Seventy-five women overflowed a mini conference room, crowding into the halls, and the Women's Committee for Equal Employment Opportunity at NBC was born.

The steering committee, consisting of those willing to work at it, spent their first eight months collecting facts and devising suggestions they would later present to top management. Each woman gave at least five hours of noncompany time every week to the research, not counting meetings.

The first problem they tackled was the way secretaries

were ranked for pay purposes, not in accordance with their own work but with the titles of the men they worked for. All secretaries to vice-presidents, for example, were graded the same, whether they'd served one year or thirty. Secretaries to men not so high up on the totem pole often bore heavier workloads but were assigned lower grades. Six hundred of the nine hundred women employed by NBC were secretaries at the time. They wanted grading to be based, instead, on skills, length of experience, the work done, and its value to the company.

They also wanted a distinction made between professional secretaries (those who wanted to remain secretaries) and what they called progression secretaries (those who wanted to advance through on-the-job training). Many secretaries had been promised that the job was a stepping stone but, as Joan Martin, who had been an NBC secretary for six and a half years when the group organized, said, the reality was "once a secretary always a secretary."

In April 1972 the committee sent to their personnel department a precise proposal concerning secretaries, including an idea for reevaluating each secretary's actual job. Though personnel felt what was being asked "was impractical and impossible," according to Mary McNulty, one of the professional secretaries, the women didn't give up.

They prepared charts showing where women fit into NBC's table of organization—an initial step for any corporate women's group—each member "mapping" her own department. Sparsely placed little red dots, which they referred to among themselves as the smallpox, indicated the women in technical, managerial, and professional positions—barely one-tenth of the lot, although women were at least 30 percent of the total population at NBC. The group came up with plans to correct this situation, too: training programs, tuition benefits not then available to clerical workers, apprenticeships in the union-controlled areas, a newsletter that would publicize vacancies as they occurred.

And while they did this, they also shared their personal testimony of sex discrimination. Charlene Schunk's, for example: a programmer/systems analyst with five years in the company and seventeen years of experience in the field, she helped design and then herself maintained an important computer system. But when the job next up became available, she was told she had no future there: a new man was brought in from the outside. Or Jeanette Clark's, assistant to the supervisor of staff announcers. Her boss left; she took over his work; eight months later her job was lowered five pay grades—because she had nobody but herself to supervise.

Their information finally complete, the women petitioned for a meeting with the network president and other big shots. They rehearsed what they would say, wrote up and made copies of their suggestions to leave behind, and then, waiting for the big moment, worried a lot.

"We were determined not to sound angry or in any way militant," Joan Barberi Ward remembers, "but it was hard not to feel that way. Especially when the men we worked with found it somehow amusing, even 'cute,' that we were going to meet with the brass."

The big day came—September 27, 1972. In *the* board of directors room, before the "president's council" (all male, of course), the women made their presentation. At the end, Marilyn Schultz summed up. "What we want from you is what you have given each other and what we would give you: a chance, a choice, and respect." On October 4, Marilyn received a hand-delivered letter from the president. He said he was "impressed with the substance and style" of the women's presentation and would give it every consideration. And that seemed to be that.

"The wait was harder than the work beforehand,"

Marilyn recalls. "We made our presentation to a big meeting of the women (oddly, feeling more nervous there than in the board room), but after that we had a struggle to keep the group together—arranging for interesting speakers at our meetings, talking privately to women who came to try us out, smoothing out the difficulties that kept arising between the right wing and the left wing, the secretaries and the professionals, the blacks and the whites." (A male-female black group already existed. Black women were torn between working for racial or sexual equity. Eventually most solved the problem by attending meetings of both groups. That was the issue that had split a similar group in Washington, at NBC's station WRC. The spearhead of the network group, at least in giving the New Yorkers an idea of what could be done, the WRC group more or less fizzled out.)

Attendance at the weekly meetings was unpredictable, maybe one hundred when Barbara Walters was to speak, twenty when a lawyer was scheduled to explain the then-new Equal Employment Opportunity Act. Meanwhile, the committee kept sending notes to the president, reminding him that it had been four weeks, six, eight, since his council had taken the women's suggestions under advisement. At last, in January, the steering committee was invited back to "the summit."

"They gave us a slide show!" Charlene, now the president of the committee, remembers, still half amused, half angered by the "phony slickness" of it. The women's requests had been put on slides, one by one, followed by checklists of reasons why the network found them "infeasible."

"Don't forget what they said about the soap operas," Joan put in. The president had said that, far from ignoring the concerns of 52 percent of the population in its broadcasts, as the women had charged (while requesting that women be promoted into programming jobs), its daytime shows regularly came to grips with women's issues: adultery, abortion, rape, homosexuality, and incest.

"Women's issues! All about sex!" Joan exclaimed. "Can you believe it?"

"That's when we gave up on them," Charlene said. "We realized we'd have to take legal action before they'd take us seriously."

The decision to file a complaint with the New York City Human Rights Commission, and later to bring suit against NBC, threw into stark contrast the differences among the women whose sameness had brought them together. When it came time to sign their names as plaintiffs in the suit, and to commit themselves to unpredictable expenses to come, only sixteen were willing.

Of those sixteen, most have since left NBC—not exactly fired (which is against the law and could warrant a second suit, for retaliation), but not encouraged to stay, either. Katherine Kish, for example, who was coordinator of advertising and promotion for NBC Educational Enterprises, was told her department was to be closed down. There proved to be no place for her elsewhere, although she applied and interviewed throughout the corporation. She then devised a new job for herself, submitting detailed plans for a new department concerning community relations. NBC accepted her idea but put someone else in charge of it. She left. She's now a vice-president of Singer—landed on her feet, one might say.

Several of those who stayed at NBC have been promoted. Charlene is a manager of business systems, responsible for payroll. Marilyn Schultz moved up to become an on-the-air reporter of local news for the NBC station in Washington before she quit, "of my own free will," to go to California; now back in New York, she is an independent film producer-director.

But the best news is what they've accomplished for NBC women of the future, women they may never meet. According to the agreement worked out with NBC attorneys by the women's lawyer, Jan Goodman, NBC will spend big money to hire, train, and promote women into the mainstream of all broadcast activities. Ultimately, women will fill 15 percent of the top-graded jobs in management (short of vice-presidencies), 20 percent at the next lower level, then 27, 35, and 46.5 percent in grades going down the scale—all being above the clerical level where women have been concentrated in the past. Those numbers may seem meaningless to an outsider, but the whole secret of women's catching up lies exactly there, in being introduced to and brought along the management track.

Almost more important, because NBC programming affects us all, 30 percent of associate directors will be female. A third of the news-writing vacancies that open up will be filled by women, as will 45 percent of the news-feature assistant jobs. One woman a year will be placed in a technical position in editing, camera work, or sound.

Every time a woman is promoted, her pay will be boosted to equal that of a man at the midpoint of her new grade level (as contrasted with the former practice of paying women the minimum in each grade, then raising them by percentages of their lower salary so they never catch up with men, who are usually hired at higher rates in the first place).

A few hitches have developed, according to Charlene. For instance, management is upgrading the jobs themselves instead of promoting the women who hold them into the next level. The technical difference spares NBC from following the court order. That is, the women get raises, but not as much as if they'd been promoted.

Even so, it can be said that sixteen "Little Women," as Joan Ward called the group, succeeded in turning a billion-dollar company around. Some 2,600 past employees were affected by the agreement. The women named in the suit received $200,000 in damages; $150,000 was awarded in attorneys' fees, $75,000 for additional litigation costs, and $175,000 for monitoring the plan.

But new employees are benefiting in other ways. The steering committee of the Women's Committee for Equal Employment Opportunity is now setting up two training programs, one for exempt and one for nonexempt women, to deal with the question of how to get along in a corporation. Kosiner Associates, of Massachusetts, and Choices, of New York, will train women who can then train others—and the technique of networking will be part of the instruction.

Outside groups that help the insiders

Internal networks are not always so successful as WC=EO at NBC. Joelle Yuna, one of the organizers of a women's caucus at the Crocker Bank in San Francisco (she's now at the Bank of America, where she has doubled her salary in three and a half years), says most of the women in that group are no longer speaking to each other. "The suit changed our lives in the worst way. Even our attorney is divorcing." The bank dug in; their legal fees alone ran into millions of dollars; the women could not compete. Dragging through the years, the experience was demoralizing.

"Only my association with WOE saved me," Joelle says. "They've got guts. They're not afraid of risk taking."

WOE stands for Women Organized for Employment, which is part of another kind of network, linked with similar groups such as 9 to 5 in Boston and Cleveland Women Working in Ohio. A coalition called Working Women, National Association of Office Workers, is training leaders and setting up in additional cities—Seattle, Hartford, Dayton, Cincinnati, Baltimore, Los Angeles, and Providence, among them. Women Office

Workers (WOW), in New York City, and Women Employed (WE), in Chicago, are similarly active on behalf of clerical workers. Any one of these offices would be a great place to meet other working women—and to have some fun in the process: one of their publicity ploys is to give awards to employers. The Pettiest Office Procedure Award, in Baltimore, went to a boss who had his secretary snip the hairs growing out of his ears; in Boston, to the boss who asked his secretary to stitch up a tear in the seat of his trousers—while he was wearing them. In Chicago, the women went into offices to teach the men how to make coffee.

Outside groups like WOE can raise women's issues with company management without identifying the particular women inside who want improvements made. As Kathleen Connolly, a WOE coordinator in San Francisco, explains, "We ask to meet with management over 'something your women employees are concerned about.' They accede because we've built a good reputation in San Francisco, but generally some lower executive meets with us. We turn up in numbers, maybe twenty or thirty, which startles him, but only three of us will talk, and very carefully—no outbursts, no real confrontation. We are not the militant, flaky, 'bra burners' he expected, and we surprise him with facts he never thought we could have ferreted out."

Immediately afterward, they print what happened at the meeting. Then they "leaflet" the women who work for that company that very day as they come streaming out of the building on their way home.

"We invite them to join or to help us by supplying information. Some women telephone us—cautiously, almost suspiciously—but we assure them we'll keep their confidence. We tell them we'll fight their cause in their company if they'll help us with a campaign we're waging against some other employer. It works out very well.

"Sometimes we can introduce individual women

who've called us to others within the same company, but only very carefully. I'll set up a lunch date with Alice and ask her if she minds if Lois comes along—that sort of thing. Meanwhile WOE is going in where Alice and Lois believe they can't afford to."

Kathleen says, "In court suits, only the lawyers win." Claims become more difficult to prove without the kind of resources women employees don't have (such as computers to produce data from personnel records, and copying machines). The personal strain of bringing suit is tremendous; in the words of Betty Lehan Harragan, whose own case against her former employer (the J. Walter Thompson advertising agency) is in its seventh unsettled and unsettling year, "Companies defend themselves for firing or not promoting by saying the women concerned are neurotic crazies. If you're not that way when your suit begins, you soon will be." (But Betty went on to write the popular book *Games Mother Never Taught You: Corporate Gamesmanship for Women*, and she now speaks to network groups all over the country.)

Yet Grace Glueck, art news reporter for *The New York Times*, says, "I consider my role in *The Times*'s suit the most important thing I have done in my professional career." And the reforms achieved by women organizing inside their companies go far beyond benefits to the individuals involved. At *The Times*, "woman's lot" began to improve soon after the discrimination complaints were filed in 1972.

As a result of the suit, women will gradually fill one out of eight of the top corporate positions there, all previously male-held (president and publisher, all of the vice-presidents, the secretary and the assistant secretary, treasurer and assistant treasurer, and executives such as the directors of corporate development, industrial relations, and manufacturing). Women will also be placed in one in four of the top positions in the news and editorial departments by the end of 1982 (metropolitan editor, foreign news editor, national news editor, sports editor, financial editor, Washington bureau chief, editors of *The New York Times Magazine*, the *Book Review*, and of every major section of the newspaper, plus the posts of executive editor and managing editor).

But, more than that, and more than the back pay awarded the 550 women covered by the suit, is the effect the changes will have on *The Times*'s coverage of the news. Betsy Wade put it this way: "The broader significance of this agreement is that we now expect the top management levels of the paper to open to all the previously excluded groups in our society, and we expect this will affect the attitudes in our society."

At Chase Manhattan, the settlement provisions included a three-year career development program for women in clerical-secretarial positions—women not directly involved in the suit brought by the caucus. Ten Chase women professionals started that. In contrast to the NBC group, which openly invited all women in the company to committee meetings, they met in utmost secrecy, having read the weather signals in their bank as "hazardous."

9 to 5, the Boston equivalent of WOE, went after the banks in that city, first collecting such statistics as: half of all male bank tellers were earning more than $7,000 but only 5 percent of female tellers; the median wage for full-time bank employees was $9,000 for men and $4,900 for women; only 628 of the 14,160 women employed in Boston banks were black. 9 to 5 testified before the U.S. Senate Banking Committee, enlisted the aid of the Massachusetts State Banking Commission, and filed suit against New England Merchants Bank.

Getting started

If you should decide to organize an action-oriented group within your company, here are some pointers:

1. Focus at first on an easily definable, relatively small

problem. At *The New York Times*, it was the paper's rule against using *Ms.* in place of *Miss* or *Mrs.* They failed to change that one, but as a rule, working on something that simple will be good practice. Getting the rest rooms cleaned up will be a lot easier than having all jobs evaluated; having job evaluations explained and reviewed openly will be much, much easier than proving and changing a systematic pattern of sex discrimination. A series of successes, however small, will relieve frustration, generate a positive attitude, and keep the group from falling apart when tougher battles loom.

2. Make sure that members of your core group are beyond reproach on job performance. It is against the law to fire anyone for union-organizing activities. Any "concerted activity" by employees to improve their working conditions, even if it's only better parking that they're after, is protected by the National Labor Relations Act. It is against the law to fire a woman who files a sex discrimination complaint, too. But there's always a period before the union is actually on record as such, or before the complaint is formalized, during which time a hostile management could start picking off activists, one by one, by subtle discouragements that could cause an unsupported individual to leave. Proving that such events are in any way connected with organizing is difficult, at best, but it's more possible if the victim's work record is impeccable.

3. Get legal advice right away. Even if you don't sue or even file a complaint with your appropriate city, state, or federal commission, you should know at the outset what kind of evidence to begin collecting. The Chase women kept careful diaries, recording by date everything from sexual innuendo to broken promises, and extracting from executives written replies to their requests for promotion.

4. Talk to other women elsewhere who have been through the same experience. In short, network.

5. Start collecting money as soon as possible. Most women's groups can manage small, regular contributions better than lump sums. And women who back off from joining your group nevertheless may be glad to chip in anonymously. A suit can take two to five years and cost $5,000 a year just in out-of-pocket expenses.

Feminist lawyers may risk their time, and when the suit is won their fees will be paid by the corporation, by court order. But lawyers are not permitted to pay for copying, investigating, filing legal papers, or phoning. The group they are representing is responsible for that.

The Chase women each contributed $20 a month before they retained their attorney, and $500 a year thereafter. Cost to individuals would have been smaller, of course, had their group been larger. They were only ten.

6. Be patient with visitors and with potential new members. Give them a chance to voice their gripes; tell them the history of the group; involve them by offering some small assignment on a very optional basis. Follow up personally.

7. Rotate essential jobs, sharing control with as many others as possible. These jobs may be chairing meetings or serving as liaison to the personnel department or, in Chase's case, to their attorney. Rotation sidesteps both takeover by the most energetic and determined, and the opposite hazard, burn-out of the originators.

8. Reach at least one decision per meeting (even if it's only to set the time and place for the next meeting). Covering old ground and seemingly getting nowhere can decimate the group fast.

9. Keep in touch, no matter what. And keep your sense of humor.

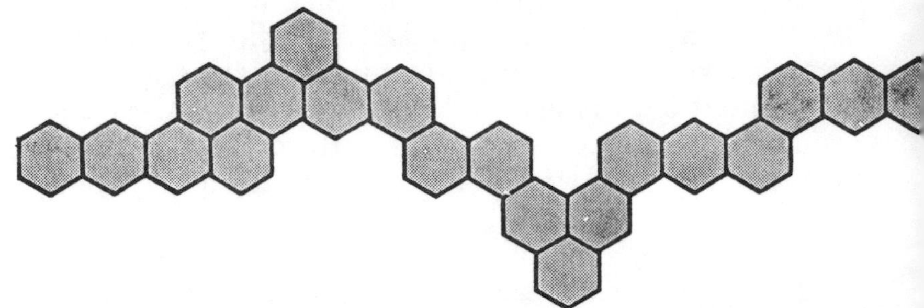

Getting

Part Three

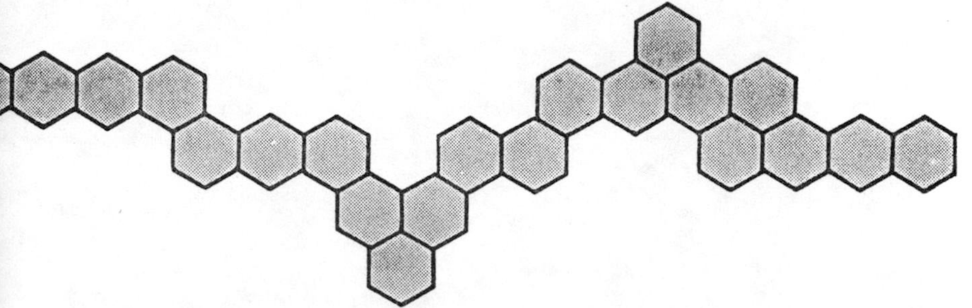

Organized

9

Fourteen Knotty Questions

But suppose none of the foregoing catalysts is now operating in your work life and you haven't found a ready-made network group that suits you. Suppose you decide to start one yourself.

As you've seen, it can be done, *has* been done, by a single woman getting the idea and lining up a few friends who share her enthusiasm for it. The mechanics are fairly simple, the procedures logical and, in many cases, self-evolving. It's not difficult. Says Barbara Keck, who instigated the group that's now called Women in Management in Stamford, Connecticut, and environs, "I was so surprised at how easy it was to do this." She was also pleased at the helpfulness of other women. "I've never been turned down by anyone I've asked to help. Everyone has been very supportive."

So that you won't have to reinvent the wheel, a detailed, step-by-step plan for starting a group is included in Appendix A of this book, with sample bylaws, membership criteria, and other documents from going networks, reprinted with their permission in Appendix B.

But typically, a new group has to work out for itself the answers to fourteen knotty questions. Some of the pioneers didn't anticipate these, so they had to fight them through one by one as they arose. A new group might well benefit by their experience, raising and discussing the questions in advance.

1. Shall we have a purpose beyond networking?

Most networks are limiting their purpose to career issues, on the theory that plenty of activist, issue-oriented groups already exist. They may develop mentoring programs for younger women or sponsor sensitivity sessions for men in hopes of raising consciousness of women's problems in business, but most are strictly apolitical. They don't even endorse their own members running in election campaigns.

The logic is: issues split women and general issues are not relevant to business dealings. If you need information on writing a grant proposal or advice on asking for a raise, your informant could be a "total woman" type or a feminist—it wouldn't matter so long as she was willing to share what she knew about your question.

The Women's Lunch Group in Boston has no purpose beyond networking. At each monthly lunch meeting, held at the Harvard Club, each attendee tells what she does, what she's interested in finding, and what current leads she can offer to the group. The women talk informally over lunch; some stay on afterward for individual networking. They have no speakers, no programs.

In contrast, as you've seen, the Financial Women's Association in New York has taken on the issue of how few women serve on corporation boards of directors, and groups like WOE in San Francisco and 9 to 5 in Boston are definitely issue-oriented.

Most groups end up with a statement of purpose, even if the purpose is to remain purposeless. Having it written down helps avoid a problem that Hunter Campbell has articulated. She's an executive with Booz, Allen & Hamilton, management consultants, in Chicago, and has put together a women's group that meets at her house. "Women know they want something," she says, "but they don't know what. When their expectations aren't spelled out and acknowledged, they're bound to be disappointed."

A New York group devoted an entire meeting, during its organizational phase, to discussing each woman's needs—how they might be met by this new group, how they were not already being met by other groups she belonged to. The network formed by New Directions for Women in Baltimore realized early on that members had conflicting needs, so they split into two groups. Another network split over the basic question of size: some of the members wanted a peer group, small and intimate enough to develop trust; they wanted to be able to lay out their problems in confidence; others wanted to get to know as many women in as many different jobs as possible. Obviously, the same group couldn't meet both needs.

Here's how two different external groups, on opposite coasts, have stated their purpose:

The *Washington Women's Network* says it is

an informal "old girls' network" of women leaders inside and outside of government in Washington, D.C. The Network was formed in 1978 with the following goals:

- to facilitate communications among women leaders and executives
- to share support, information, and technical assistance
- to utilize and enhance the activities of women's organizations
- to increase the visibility of women leaders
- to assist in recruiting women executives for government jobs
- to stimulate special training opportunities . . .

The Career Network, Seattle, Washington, says:

The basic purpose of the club shall be that of encouraging its members to become more competent in their jobs and more confident in themselves so that they might achieve their career goals. The Career Network shall provide members with a vehicle through which they can offer support of each other regarding career plans and get feedback both positive and constructive. Through a consolidation of effort it shall afford its members a significantly greater opportunity to hear well-known lecturers and local authorities than would be the case were they to act alone.

And here's how a representative in-house group stated its purpose.

The Women's Resource Group, Penn Mutual Life Insurance Company, Philadelphia, Pennsylvania, states:

I. *Statement of Purpose*
   A. To reinforce the positive perception and image of women as equal partners in the work force, both for themselves and for others.
   B. To serve as a support system for women and to provide a forum in which women may serve as resources to each other by sharing experiences and insight.
   C. To provide an educational vehicle for women to learn from other women.

II. *Goals*
   A. To become more knowledgeable about the corporation, the inner workings of its various departments and its political structure.
   B. To offer skills training which women can utilize in their own personal development.
   C. To expose women to presentations on major business functions and personal growth topics.
   D. To facilitate the ongoing communication of our Affirmative Action program.
   E. To act as a resource for inputs to our corporate Affirmative Action program.

2. *Shall we be selective about membership?*

Women with a strong sense of sisterhood tend to shy away from anything that smacks of elitism. No one wants to be a Queen Bee. She's the woman, you'll recall, who made it on her own, the hard way, and wanted everyone else to suffer and struggle just as hard. Today the opposite attitude prevails. Most women executives want more and more women at their own levels, to establish the normalcy of being a woman in business and eventually to rid the marketplace of gender considerations altogether.

As a practical matter, however, a woman executive wants to talk to someone who knows at least as much as she does, one who is experiencing the same kind of work problems or, better, one who has put such problems behind her. That someone is not likely to be a file clerk, or a newly minted M.B.A.

What the woman executive wants is a network of other executives, her peers, a horizontal network. But the file clerk doesn't want to talk to *her* peers in a network group. She does that enough in the office. She wants to talk to women way up the career ladder, women who can tell her how to get out of the file room. So the network she wants is a vertical one.

Obviously, these opposing needs cannot be fulfilled by the same organization, at least not at the same time. Here's what some of the going networks advise:

a. Go ahead and be elitist; let the chips fall where they may.

The Women's Forum has done this, in New York. At the outset it was decided that only women who had "arrived" were to be asked to join, women who were at the top in their various fields, and that the membership should be limited to 125. They have had some predictable difficulties with sour grapes, as you might imagine, and now even some of the founders believe they could use an infusion of younger blood.

Still, to belong to such an organization is considered an honor, akin to being listed in *Who's Who*, and its networking possibilities are superior. As one member said, surveying the room before one of the monthly Forum meetings, "I'll bet I could get an introduction to anyone in the world, starting right here." Another member, one of the few female senior vice-presidents in her billion-dollar company, had the occasion to use this network for job-hunting purposes. She had been "terminated" in a corporation-wide reorganization. "The network really functioned. Forum members began calling me—I didn't even have to call them—the minute the 'purge' news hit the *Wall Street Journal*. They've been opening doors for me ever since." (She is now a vice-president in charge of international personnel for a bank of worldwide influence.)

Women's Forum-West in San Francisco has comparable criteria. Deciding whether an applicant qualifies is the task of the membership committee, which numbers three (to avoid tie votes), who hold no other office (to keep this function free of whatever politics might conceivably move the board of directors). The board must approve the membership committee's recommendations, however—another form of balance. As a further precaution, the group's bylaws specify that anyone whose application has been turned down by the board may appear before the full membership, according to preset procedures. (It hasn't happened.)

The Philadelphia Women's Network wanted a peer group but did not want to be as exclusionary as the Forum there. They set as their criteria a bachelor's degree plus five years' experience; a master's degree plus three years'; or no degree with seven years' experience. But they haven't really enforced it. Says Diane Freaney, one of its founders, "We really go by whether we think the person will contribute or not. We haven't turned anyone down."

One of the most selective groups I know about has no name, no written membership criteria, doesn't even meet at a preannounced time and place (meaning that a would-be member couldn't just turn up at a meeting as a self-invited guest, as is the case in many large groups).

"Unless you know a member," a founder told me, "you don't even know this network exists." Prospects are invited by members but must come to three meetings before they're considered as permanent additions. If the group doesn't take to a candidate, they just don't tell her when or where the next meeting will be held. ("It has happened.")

But they're only about forty women, eighteen to twenty of whom always turn up. A larger number probably couldn't operate in the same way.

One group I met with during its formative stages spent several meetings trying to describe the woman they wanted as a member. They realized neither salary, title, nor even experience alone could really identify her. In the end, they decided to select their members one by one, on the basis of full information about her particular job level.

b. Limit membership to a particular field.

Melinda Lloyd, president of the Financial Women's Association in New York, says their great strength lies in the fact that their members have a common ground. They have not allowed the membership criteria to be diluted; everyone is in finance in some capacity or other. Most members (65 percent) are in the investment business, in brokerage firms, banks, and so on. Fifteen percent are in the corporate world; the others are in law, government, consulting; but they're all actively involved with "the bottom line." In addition, they have three years' experience in the field (or an M.B.A. with one year's experience).

Their method of handling new memberships helps them keep control of applications. A candidate must attend at least three functions before she can apply, and she must be sponsored by two members. (Sponsors can be counted on not to put forward anyone who doesn't meet the standards.)

Women in Business, Los Angeles, and the breakfast

network in Houston take the opposite tack, limiting the number of members who come from any one field. They have representatives of industry, the media, advertising, retailing, finance, and other fields. But if another insurance broker applies, she may find that the insurance quota is already filled.

A group in Connecticut started out with the idea of limiting itself to women executives in industrial corporations but found a much wider constituency. "Women from consumer companies, women business owners—they were all so eager, so hungry for this exchange that we changed our concept." Industrial Women Executives' Association became Women in Management.

"We want to be inclusive, not exclusive," said Barbara Keck, the founder. "We have membership criteria covering the candidate's current position, which has to impact on profit, strategy, or policy; her education, with a B.A. as a minimum; and her work experience, two or more years in a nonclerical position. But I'm insisting that we weigh heavily the community or volunteer experience of the reentry woman. She learned a lot during her years at home, and we need her perspective on careers today. She remembers how it used to be. Our twenty-two-year-olds need to hear about that; they have no idea what the forty-two-year-olds faced."

c. Let members self-select.

That is, name the group to define it; design the programs to attract a particular work level; or set the membership fee high enough to discourage the levels you don't want.

Groups like New York Women Business Owners, Women Entrepreneurs (San Francisco), the Congressional Wives Task Force and Women in Government Relations (Washington, D.C.), Women in the Humanities and Social Sciences (Chicago), and Women's Economic Round Table (New York) are defined by their names. Washington Women's Network is open to all, but the average office worker is not going to be interested in a program featuring a talk on the federal budget. Women in Management (Connecticut) dues are $75 a year. The average clerical worker won't rush to plunk that amount down.

Another form of self-selection is built into the criteria for membership of the Executive Women's Council, Greater Pittsburgh, which says, "A potential member of EWC must (1) exhibit active support of the purposes and objectives of the organization; (2) indicate a commitment to feminism where feminism is defined as the belief and practice that women should have political, economic, and social rights equal to those of men. . . ." Any Pittsburgh executives who go around saying, "I'm not a women's libber . . ." would self-select themselves out of the admirable EWC.

Cornell's Anne Nelson points up another form of self-selection, as applied to membership in the Albany Women's Forum (Albany, New York): "It's everyone who can take two hours for lunch!" says Anne.

For a last word, here's what Kati Sasseville, one of the founders of AGOG (in Minneapolis), said on the subject when representatives of a dozen other networks met to discuss the formation of a network of networks: "Our group made the conscious decision to be nonexclusive on the theory that smaller networks would form within the large one. In an exclusive group, your problem is, for example, one day you need to hire a junior graphics designer, and your network doesn't reach down that far. In our group it does.

"It also reaches up, so it can help if your problem is that the governor just cut your budget $20,000 for a very important project and you need to talk to him.

"At our steering committee meeting last week, we were discussing our experiences and how successful we felt the group had been, and we decided it's *primarily* because of our nonexclusivity. I think the parallel is the

American experience—that the reason that America as an idea is unique and successful in this world is its concept of nonexclusivity, nonlimitation, that with egalitarian ideas you encourage the best in everyone, you do not limit, you bring people up. This is a very strong commitment of the leadership of our organization."

3. *How shall we add new members?*

The answers to this question vary from that of the network that lies low and hopes no one will hear about it to the one that arranges for a big newspaper story to attract every woman in town.

Women in Management wrote to the personnel directors of the eighty-five companies in their area, as listed in Dun and Bradstreet, suggesting that it would be beneficial to the corporation to have their women attend the first big meeting. "We asked them to circulate our notice and to post the letter," Barbara Keck told me, adding wryly, "I don't think a lot of that happened." What did happen was newspaper and radio publicity for their scheduled speaker, Janet Jones, a partner in a New York executive search firm, who was to speak on career paths for women in industrial companies. As a result, almost ninety women turned up, at a Stamford club room that held sixty. Women in Management was an instant success.

The Philadelphia Women's Network wrote letters, too, but they addressed potential members, inviting them to attend their first dinner meeting. Since the letter is so well written and so complete it could serve as a model for other groups, it's reprinted in Appendix B.

Friends of NOW-NY, planning a similar mailing, went through a directory of corporations that lists corporate officers, looking for female names. "That in itself was a consciousness-raising exercise," says Jane Pendergast, chair of the organizing committee. "I was prepared for tokens. I wasn't prepared for page after page listing no women at all!" NOW's plan was to ask the women officers to suggest which middle-management and upper-management women from their companies might be most interested in joining the network.

Inviting new members one at a time, recruiting them in person, has been the method most favored by horizontal networks.

Personal solicitation has also worked well for in-house groups, for some women are afraid to incur the disapproval of management by joining any kind of employee group. The recruiter should always make clear that the network has no plans to agitate. Organizers of in-house groups should be "establishment" women who are known to the prospects, by reputation if not in person.

Getting started in a big company, with eighteen floors and acres of desks, one group drew up a table of organization for the company, identifying each department and division, then studying the personnel telephone directory to locate representative women in each area. It was not the kind of place where employees could move around freely—part of the reason why these women needed a network group; they seldom knew anybody outside their own small territory—so they recruited by telephone. Usually they made the first call to a candidate's office phone, but then asked for the home phone number so that they could have a more leisurely conversation later. Once they got the first woman in any particular department, they asked her to call the people she knew personally. Their advice: Don't be discouraged if your wonderful idea falls on a lot of deaf ears at first, and don't waste time trying to convince anyone who isn't ready and waiting for this idea to come along. The members you want are out there, somewhere. You'll find them.

4. *What kind of structure do we need?*

According to one school of thought, organized structure is death to networking. More than one woman I talked to said, "The minute you start with the constitution and the election of officers, what you've got is not networking but Mickey Mouse."

On the other hand, as a character in a novel by Malcolm Bradbury says, "If you want to have something that is genuinely unstructured, you have to plan it carefully."

The most successful small groups I've observed had no leaders, by deliberate choice. The caucus at ABC-TV in New York has a rotating chair; it wouldn't have any at all if it weren't necessary for one person to take the responsibility for keeping the meeting on track each time.

Deliberately leaderless groups make a point of guarding against the assumption of power by "natural" leaders, however helpful they may be. Everyone takes her turn, leader type or not.

But leaderless groups are notoriously inefficient. They can and often do go round and round, never reaching any conclusions, seldom moving discussion on. A member of one told me her group never decided anything. "Never," she said. "The whole year, the only decision we ever made was to meet again."

The first step away from leaderlessness is to have a steering committee that sets policy and makes all the decisions as the necessity arises. Usually a core group of six or eight, but sometimes larger, this can be a leaderless group in itself, no one person responsible for any particular function and decisions taken by consensus, or it can be set up in a task force fashion. In the latter case, each member of the core group takes charge of a specific area—membership, programs, publicity, whatever. Each recruits her own committee from the general membership. There may be an overall coordinator of the task forces, in effect a chair of the steering committee, but there is no president, vice-president, board of directors, or other office, and the general membership is never asked to vote on anything.

But when any group grows large—or starts out with that intention—it usually finds that it needs formal organization. Despite the "Mickey Mouse" charge, meetings run according to *Robert's Rules of Order* and the like have their positive side: they provide good experience for the women who take on these jobs. As Heather Booth, director of Midwest Academy (Chicago), says, "Women have been the backbone of most organizations, but usually as stamp lickers, telephone callers, and doorbell ringers. They haven't had the chance to play major roles in strategy mapping and decision making." Network groups give them that chance; they can develop leadership skills in a setting where amateurism will be readily forgiven.

Once decided to tool up in the traditional structure, a group usually goes the way of Network in Portland, Oregon, whose bylaws are reprinted in Appendix B with the permission of their first president, Lillian Skinner.

Having the duties and privileges of the officers carefully spelled out, as this group does, avoids a problem that Dr. Judith M. Bardwick, an associate professor of psychology at the University of Michigan, has addressed. She says that when natural leaders take charge, simply because they're the strongest and most forceful members of the group, not because they've been elected, their leadership becomes personalized. The weaker members of the group then try to ingratiate themselves with the person, not the office; in so doing, they undercut the power of the strong, because when the stronger woman responds to the emotional needs of the weaker, she is muting her own effect.

The dynamics of such a group are immensely complicated. Chances are, the women involved don't see what's happening, but as Dr. Bardwick spells out in "Some Notes about Power Relationships between Women," a chapter in *Beyond Sex Roles* by Alice Sargent, the end result is clear: "Those who emerge in dominant positions are subtly attacked for taking on the leader role. The tyranny of the weak triumphs, as the emotionally demanding, weaker women dominate what occurs, thereby becoming the strongest members of a group that is now focused not on coping skills but emotional needs."

If it takes an election of officers to prevent all that, one wonders, why not?

5. *What format shall we follow for our meetings?*

Groups that let this question fall where it may usually end up with a kaffeeklatsch. Without some agreed-upon rules and procedures, meetings almost invariably turn into gripe sessions.

A typical group developed its rules of the road by using the big-sheet-of-paper method, brainstorming the subject of how to run their meetings. Following the rules of brainstorming—no evaluations, no discussion, just ideas, all of them recorded no matter how outrageous (without comment)—they wound up with six big sheets full of suggestions. Discussing them, then, they arrived at a consensus. They decided:

To start on time, no matter who's late. Save socializing for after the meeting.

To start with boasting. Give each person five minutes to say what great things she did since the last meeting, what she accomplished, what a good job she's doing at whatever she does.

Follow with discussion. Take turns in presenting a topic, perhaps an article or a book, to talk about.

Then do problem solving. Any member with a work problem can ask for ten to twenty minutes to lay it before the group for ideas on what to do about it. Emotional problems are not appropriate unless work-related. (If the same people dominate this period, and some don't ever bring in problems, we'll set more definite standards later.)

General rules: No interruptions, no put-downs, no judgments; no flip remarks; be honest and trusting; listen, really listen; keep what you hear confidential.

Have a news period. Go around the room, each person contributing a lead, tip, item of interest.

Do a closing exercise. Have each person say something positive. "I'm glad I was here because . . ." "What I liked about this meeting was . . ." "I really appreciated it when . . ."

They decided to put the sheets up on the wall each time, as reminders.

Another group posted a sign saying, "No guilt accepted here—everyone's responsible for her own feelings." Another decided, "We are not a therapy group."

In a larger group, a common pattern is to start with self-identifications, passing a hand mike around the room so that each person can say her name, her job, and (a possibility) what she can give to or take from the group. "I'm looking for information about trade advertising." "I've heard of an opening in my company's foreign office." Where the group is too big for everyone to be covered, the mike goes to new members, guests, and anyone who has a news item to relay.

That kind of group usually has a scheduled speaker or some such program, as the focal point of the meeting, but their agenda includes networking before and after. When the format calls for discussion of the speaker's subject, they break into small groups. But then, so that the body as a whole can benefit from the small group discussions, one member of each group is appointed to report to the membership on what went on in her group. The report is either given verbally, then and there, or written and submitted to the newsletter editor for publication.

6. How often shall we meet?

In the beginning, most networks meet every week or two, getting organized. They then go to monthly meetings, with subgroups and committees meeting as needed in between. Eventually some come to the point reached by the Women's Round Table at Pacific Gas & Electric, in San Francisco. A group of executives looked up one day and said, "Hey, we don't need to get together anymore, except maybe quarterly, because this network is working: we're all calling each other." In member Lorcy Ann Burns's judgment, that's a sign of success.

If a support group gets past the frequent meetings stage, any member could call a meeting for help with any problem, as it arose. Women in Foundations, New York, uses that system, if it may be called a system, for its program meetings; one member calls another and says, "We really ought to have another meeting." Then it's up to whoever has the time and the energy to set up a panel, send out the notice, and handle the acceptances for the brown-bag lunch meeting.

Executive Women's Council, Greater Baltimore, has an interesting approach to the meetings question: instead of scheduling their dinner meetings on the same night of the week, every month, they meet Tuesday one month, Wednesday the next, Thursday the next. That way, if a particular night of the week is in conflict with other standing commitments for some of the women, they're bound to find at least one date agreeable.

As a general rule, meetings (if interesting and productive) serve to keep people involved and provide a vehicle for introducing new members to the group. Also, running them is good practice for the volunteers; they are training grounds for the next generation of leaders. Current leaders should always be trying to build the next team, preparing for the "burn-out" that happens to even the most enthusiastic volunteer after a time of heavy involvement.

7. *Should we affiliate?*

As the network idea spreads and groups proliferate all over the country, the idea of joining forces is emerging. At this writing, several efforts to bring the groups together are under way: with the help of a small grant, the Washington Women's Network arranged a meeting to be attended by two representatives from each of the various network groups they had identified, coast to coast. Among other topics, they discussed the feasibility of forming a "network of networks." The idea met with such enthusiasm that they have since assigned task forces to cover membership, long-range plans, communications, funding/financing, and the preparation of a national directory. Jody Johns, manager of human resources development for Martin Marietta Aerospace and a member of the Executive Women's Council, in Baltimore, will coordinate the work of the task forces. Ann Peterson, executive director of All the Good Old Girls in Minneapolis, will serve in that same function for what they are calling the Alliance, handling communications and acting as a clearinghouse for information regarding other networks.

At about the same time, New York Women Business Owners sponsored a meeting of other such local organizations, to see if a loose federation would be useful. The Women's Forum in New York was getting together with Forum leaders from Denver, Philadelphia, and San Francisco, the Women's Forum of North Carolina being present in spirit only. And Alina Novak was forming Networks Unlimited, a nonprofit organization to provide services for network groups. The National Association of Female Executives was planning to offer programs and other materials to local networks begun by their members across the country.

One advantage of affiliation, for a newly forming group, would of course be the saving of time and energy that would otherwise go into writing bylaws and working out, from scratch, problems that have already been addressed and solved by others of the same mind. Start-up time would be reduced to almost nothing. The new group could focus on attracting the desired members without having to bother with legal and mechanical details. This has already happened for core groups in other cities consulting with the Women's Forum in New York City.

Latest candidates for affiliation with this impressive roster have been networks in Detroit, Atlanta, and Toronto. Lee Lowell, executive director of the Women's Forum in New York, "walks them through" the procedures, bylaws, membership criteria, monetary requirements, and other structures that have proved workable. As she says, "The networking here works so well, it has to work nationally as well. When any Forum member, anywhere, needs an expert on this or that, she knows whom to call."

Another advantage, seen particularly by women who travel in their work, or who might conceivably be transferred to other cities at some point in their careers, is the prospect of being able to find friends and useful contacts in other locales. "You don't have to leave your home office to see the value of a national membership list," said an executive at one of the meetings where affiliation was being discussed. "I do most of my 'traveling' by phone. I'd *love* to know whom to call in Dallas or Boston or Atlanta when I'm planning a promotion or product test."

Access to a national job bank and referral system would be another plus. Matching members with job openings could be done by computer, but any cross-referencing on such an ambitious scale would be beyond the means of the average small group. Large groups also do better than small in setting up credit unions, insurance plans, discount privileges, and other such side services to members. Equally, if networks intend to become a power source for women, an entity that the corporate world may eventually turn to as a resource or that government might consult as a constituency, sheer numbers will count!

An alternate way for one network to plug into others would be by means of coalition. A coalition is usually formed around a single issue, as in the case of the Coalition for Women's Appointments described earlier. But the word is sometimes used loosely—the Coalition of Labor Union Women, for example, consists of individual members. The women don't purport to represent the other women in their particular unions. The Coalition of 100 Black Women, too, is made up of individuals, not organizations. Some coalitions don't use the word at all. The International Exchange Committee in the Oakland, California, area, for example, is a coalition of the Junior League, the AAUW, and the League of Women Voters. They meet "to share information and to promote activities of common interest as approved by the member organizations."

But the term itself is less important than the purpose it usually achieves, that of bringing representatives of separate organizations together to share information resources and to work together on projects that might be too big for any one of the organizations to handle alone.

In Los Angeles, the Women's Presidents' Council accomplishes this end, joining eight organizations there, including Women in Business, the Organization of Women Executives, Women in Management, Women in Film, and Women in Advertising.

The disadvantages of affiliating with a larger organization include the relative impersonality of a distant headquarters, the loss of local control, the worry that size may be counterproductive when the object is to get to know other women *well*, and the cost of supporting a national headquarters.

"We're good at fund raising," said a member of one group. "Our events are financially successful. We don't see why we should turn over a portion of what we earn to a national headquarters. What would we get out of it?" Her assessment of the trade-off was "Thank you, but no thanks." But sometimes it works the other way.

Old-time women's groups already have national organizations—the AAUW and Business and Professional Women (BPW), for example. So does not-so-old NOW. While your network is considering affiliation, you might like to network with members of those organizations, finding out what they feel they lose and gain by being part of a national organization.

The Feminist Writers' Guild began straight off as a national network. For the first year, 1977, supporters sent in membership fees ($10) with the understanding that they would not receive any services in return "for quite a while." The temporary national steering committee worked on organizing; the national structure committee drew up a constitution, "an awesome task"; and 1978 saw the publication of their first newsletter, the vehicle for a national network. A member can write the Guild and receive the name of a contact person in her area or else a list of local members. By 1979 they had almost a thousand members and chapters in seventeen states. "We have all acted to end our isolation and form a visible, vocal network that continues to grow." With the election of the first national steering committee, in January, "we now move into the second phase of our existence—as the patriarchal publishing-reviewing establishment trembles with awe at our growing power!"

Chapters initiate their own projects: the San Francisco group has created a publishing collective—they plan to take a class in printing, then go into publishing their own works; Boston held a panel meeting on the politics of reviewing—who gets reviewed and why; many chapters are working to get more feminist books into bookstores, libraries, and schools.

The national organization hopes one day to own and operate a feminist writers' retreat, with child-care facilities. They are investigating writing grants, which are disproportionately given to male writers, and college writing classes, where female students often encounter sexist attitudes. A handbook on writing, publishing, and jobs related to writing is in the works.

8. What about men?

Women worry about seeming to discriminate, by sex, when their down-the-road mission is to eliminate the sex discrimination that cripples members of their own sex. It's a legitimate worry, and the long-term answer to being excluded from men's clubs and the old boys' network is certainly not to exclude them from ours; the answer is integration of equals in both. But the most thoughtful of networkers are coming down on the side of separatism, for now. As one of them put it, "Until we *feel* equal and equally skillful, and until we are universally perceived as such and we don't have to be proving the point at every turn, we need a place and a mechanism to develop ourselves."

"Let's not kid ourselves," a woman in Kansas City said. "We're going to be griping about men here. We're going to be developing strategies that will work with them. We're going to be trying to figure out how to outfox them. We can't possibly do that if they're here, listening and watching. Bring one man in and we'll all shut up—doesn't everybody *see* that?"

Some networks have proceeded on the assumption that men wouldn't want to join in any case, so they don't have to spell out their preference for women only; men won't apply. A luncheon club for business and professional women in Boston, which meets in the dining room of a once men-only luncheon club, is open to men; but so far no man has asked to join.

"If you can be comfortable in a room full of women," an officer of New York Women Business Owners answered a male member of the press on this point, "we'd be glad to have you." In Philadelphia, a senator asked to come to the network's cocktail hour. "His motives were political, of course," said Diane Freaney, "but I'm glad to have any man who's willing to reach out in that way to *my* network."

The Washington Women's Network invited spouses and other men to one of its bigger, more important meetings (held to welcome Sarah Weddington when she was appointed a special assistant to President Carter, replacing Midge Costanza). Only four men came, for a score of four to four hundred.

Dr. Alice Armstrong and her network in Portland are handling the man question in an interesting way, inviting men to come talk about subjects on which they and only they are experts, such as why men feel threatened by the rapid advancement of women into the executive ranks, and what difficulties they have in accepting women. They're not being asked to tell women what women are doing wrong, as they so often like to do, but what perhaps they themselves are doing wrong *in re* women. In effect, this is sensitivity training for both sexes.

The most prevalent way of handling the question is to keep men in the position of invited guests or speakers rather than members or participants. The new Women's Economic Round Table of New York and Washington has a notable concept. "We have a men's auxiliary," says Maria Rolfe, its founder, tongue only slightly in cheek. It includes the president of the men's Economic Club in New York, which until recently excluded women; five now belong.

The River Oaks Breakfast Club in Houston has a men's auxiliary, too—the husbands who eat at the corner drugstore while their wives are breakfast-meeting at the River Oaks Country Club. In the government, the Interagency Task Force on Women is 40 percent male, Sarah Weddington told me, "because they are the policy makers." Men may pay the $10 membership fee that supports the Woman's Salon, a two-hundred-member group of women writers in New York City, but they may not attend.

"It's ridiculous to leave men out," Judy Tisdale said, as a group of us talked about networking in San Francisco. "We have to work with business." The advisory board of the Women's Resource Center, which she helped organize in Palo Alto, California, includes important men.

A few men are among the 170 members of the Chicago Society of Women CPA's. "They tend to be from personnel or are otherwise concerned with women's advancement in their firms," says Marjorie June, one of the founders of the group.

The men of New York and New Jersey's Port Authority, the agency in charge of bridges and tunnels, have formed their own groups. In answer to Women's Equity (WE), they have started ME and IT—ME stands for Men's Equity, IT for Italian Talent. And take note of the name under consideration by the men related to Women in Film, a group formed in 1979 by Ginny Durrin, who works with her husband in Durrin Films in Washington, D.C. Says Ginny, "We are WIF. The guys are threatening to form PIF—Pigs in Film."

9. *What shall we call our group?*

The hot topic, surprisingly enough, is whether or not to include *women* in the name. "We spent three hours on that," said a member of a new group that finally decided not to. "Three *heated* hours. We lost a few feminists then and there, but the majority seemed to think that any *women's* anything will be automatically perceived as strictly second-class."

"But *women* is who we are," said another, "and the whole idea is that *women* are now networking, doing what men have always done but doing it in our own unique way. I think we should brag about being women, not hide behind some name that could mean anything *but* a women's network."

With or without *women*, some of the most popular names now being used include these words:

Network—and sometimes that alone, as in Baton Rouge, Indianapolis, and Portland, Oregon. Or, as in another small group in Portland, the Women's Network Group.

Resource—the Resource Network in New York is so named because the members consider that each woman is a resource for the others. They live up to the name by providing each member with not only the usual contact list of names, titles, and phone numbers but a loose-leaf notebook of detailed bios. Job functions are described in the bios, as well as past positions, education, other organizations the women belong to, and hobbies-interests. The bios shorten the time it usually takes to find out all that about another networker, and having the information in written form, for handy reference, helps a member decide whom to call with what question.

Council—used by Baltimore, Pittsburgh, and several in-house networks.

Lunch or *Luncheon*—the Friday for Lunch Bunch, in Olympia, Washington, and two Boston groups with the name of the meal included. *Breakfast*, too, as you've seen, in Des Moines and Houston.

Consortium—a group of consultants uses this rather impressive term. Although it has a financial meaning in the first definition in the dictionary ("an international business or banking agreement or combination"), definition two is: "association, fellowship, club, society."

Forum—with definition three in Webster's, right on: "An organization that holds public meetings for the discussion of subjects of current interest."

Round Table—suggesting discussion at a *round* table so there's no head of the table.

Counterparts—a group of affirmative action officers uses this.

One of the first networks, made up of wives of the "Washington establishment" men, and meeting in Arvonne Fraser's living room, back in 1969, called itself the Nameless Sisterhood. That name reflected not an inability to decide on a name for their group, but the women's feeling that they had no names of their own. They had always been seen as wives. The media always wanted to know who their husbands were. "This is the first time in fifteen years that I've been asked who *I* am," said one.

Then again, consider the secret society type of name such as MAD, in Washington, D.C., of which Dee (deWolf) Smith says, "I don't feel compelled to tell what it means." (What it means is Men Are Dumb, but the occasional men who attend as guests at the regular Wednesday-night meetings at this or that bar, in downtown Washington or at the Washington Press Club, don't necessarily know that.) MAD is a vertical network in the best sense of that term; women at all levels in public broadcasting, radio, and television belong, the producers and writers and executives having known all along that the secretaries are as well educated and as highly motivated as they, having taken such jobs as a means of getting into the system. MAD is an "easily mixing group," according to one of their number, and "one of the best in town for really making contacts"—that is, networking.

If you plan to file incorporation papers, and many networks take this step, your lawyer will want a choice of three names to submit, on the chance that your first and second choice may already be taken.

You might try playing around with variations on the words *web*, *mesh*, *connections*, *links*. Whatever you decide, please send name and address to Mary Scott Welch, 333 E. 30th Street, New York, NY 10016, for inclusion in the next edition of this book.

10. Shall we have elections?

In San Francisco, Lorraine Legg, vice-president and general manager of Boise Cascade Credit Corporation, was drafted. "We decided you should be president of Women's Forum-West," the others in the group said. And that was that.

In Washington, Dorothy Gevinson, assistant for legislative research, national government relations, for Procter & Gamble, got her company's permission, since election would no doubt cut into her working time; campaigned, appearing before the nominating committee, the board, and the membership; and was elected president of Women in Government Relations.

In between, the pattern is more or less casual: the founders fill the jobs for the first six months to a year, gradually involving new members in committee posts and on task forces of one kind or another, then whoever's ready and has the time volunteers to take over.

Whatever its style, though, a group is wise to spread the responsibilities as widely as possible, so it won't run down if and when the organizers fade out. A good plan is to have a vice-president who is elected for that post *plus* the presidency in the following term. She learns the ropes as vice-president; there's no awkward in-between period.

11. How visible do we want to be?

Within a company, the visibility of women's groups has ranged from official, complete with budget and full use of the company facilities, to completely secret, so much so that even a candidate for membership can't find out about meetings.

The group at Pacific Gas & Electric in San Francisco decided on a middle ground. "We went to personnel," recalls Lorcy Ann Burns, "to the affirmative action officer. We said, 'Come tell us about AA. Tell us how we can move up in this company.' We took that approach instead of challenging the program, instead of confronting the management with its shortcomings in terms of women's jobs. But we decided not to ask for financial support, and not to use the interoffice mail. Anyone can pay dues and get the newsletter sent home, and I've no doubt the newsletter reaches the top office, somehow, but we're not inhibited in what we say in it, as we would be if production and distribution were going through official channels at their expense."

The reason for operating independently is the greater freedom it affords. The reason for being official is, of course, the ease; also the chance to involve women who would be afraid of joining a group that didn't have the bosses' blessing.

Deciding which route is most appropriate where you work is a matter of assessing the climate there: How friendly or hostile is it? How supportive of women? How sophisticated in its personnel and public relations approach to affirmative action? A good women's group can be seen as a plus by one management, proof of its liberal policies and also a welcome vehicle for working with women. But the same kind of group can rankle and scare another kind of management, seeming to pose the same kinds of threats that unionization poses.

Before you organize, it might be a good idea to get a reading on the company from an outside observer. An executive search firm would be a good source, and/or any union that deals with the company. Even if there's no union involved, any union organizer could tell you what signs to look for to predict company reaction to group formation. But you can't ask your questions cold, at least not if you want less than equivocal answers, so use your personal network to find someone who can introduce you to the headhunter or the union organizer.

External groups are usually open, visible, and public, and they welcome the publicity the local press gives them. This not only attracts new members but gives the women involved exposure to the establishment. Becoming an entity in the minds of employers has its advantages. "I saw your name on the meeting board at the club," an important corporate executive said to Diane Winokur, sounding surprised but also impressed. "What's this BAWEF you're president of?" As Diane says, "Male attention can't hurt."

But sometimes the members prefer not to be identified with any kind of women's group. They don't want their companies to doubt their dedication and loyalty. If they're office holders, they don't want that part of the public that uses *women's libbers* as a pejorative term to think of them in that connection. Besides, if the group gives them a good strategy or a little more backbone, they don't want anyone to be able to say, "They put you up to this."

Also, being invisible makes it easier for a group to be selective about who may join. If you're undecided about which way to go, you might start out quietly, without announcing your presence to the general public, and see what happens. You can always go public, but once you do, you can't go back.

That generalization is not entirely true; witness the women's group at Avon, the cosmetic company in New York. Originally called Concerned Women of Avon (CWA), and organized to press management for change in practice and policy toward women employees, it dwindled away. "It was co-opted," said a woman who no longer works there. "Management promoted or transferred the gutsier women, making them too busy or too far away to keep the group going, and tranquilized the rest of us. I mean, they managed somehow to convince us that they were doing what we'd organized to persuade them to do. We lost our momentum and our purpose. Not that we should have, mind you; just that we did."

So now, instead of the public CWA, there is a private (that is, external) women's networking group that meets once a month outside the office. Secretly.

12. *What about confidentiality?*

Although it should go without saying, networking groups have found it necessary to keep reminding each other that what's said in meetings must go no farther (not the public, program meetings, of course, but the discussion meetings where women are encouraged to air their problems and share their job experiences). Without a belief that the rule of confidentiality will be faithfully adhered to, women won't express their true feelings or talk in personal enough terms about the problems they're having to make it possible for the support group to help them. Even at best, it takes a while for members to develop trust in the group, so the least little leak, early on, can kill all chances of getting beyond superficial exchange. It's not going too far to open each meeting with "Don't forget—what we say here is not to go out of this room, even if it seems inconsequential." In addition, when you yourself have a touchy problem to discuss or an original idea to try out, restate your assumption that your confidence will be respected. Members of one group tested their number by putting out some misinformation and seeing if or how it came back. Others I've talked to find that very idea offensive, but it's a device not uncommon to office politics, so you might remember it in case of need.

If you keep minutes of your meetings—and most

groups find that it *is* desirable to have a record to refer to—let them contain only the group decisions reached, not the arguments pro and con or the topics discussed or the personal aspects of same. A list of those attending can be valuable. Also, a note on who took on what assignment, with what due date. But according to those who are what they themselves call "paranoid" on the subject of confidentiality, bare bones, always.

13. *Could we use professional help?*

Often a member who can use her secretary and her office facilities handles the mailings, with the tacit approval of her management. Susan Berresford, of the Ford Foundation, does the job for Women in Foundations, "but it's time-consuming. Just keeping the list up-to-date is a chore."

The solution is to hire a professional mailing house. And/or an executive director. The Women's Forum in Denver set a $75 membership fee so that it could afford a director; its members don't have to volunteer for clerical jobs.

Betty Dooley, staff for the Congresswomen's Caucus Corporation, is paid partly out of the clerk-hire system of the Congress: members can contribute from their budgets. But she suggests—and many others agree, wishing with hindsight they hadn't struggled with the paperwork as volunteers—hire with the expectation of more money coming in.

The Washington Women's Network has the professional help of the National Women's Education Fund, using that already intact organization (complete with offices and staff) as what it calls its secretariat. Although the fourteen- or fifteen-member steering committee that is the heart and mind of this network is entirely volunteer, the hands are paid.

The Detroit Women's Forum uses somewhat the same

system. The secretariat is the American Jewish Committee, which started the Forum in keeping with its policy of establishing coalitions with other ethnic, racial, and religious groups. Unique in that union leadership played a part in its development—such United Auto Workers notables as Dorothy Haener serving as a bridge between blue-collar and white-collar workers—the Forum charges only token dues of its two hundred members: $10. For its first four years it charged no dues at all, the American Jewish Committee picking up the tab, including the salary of coordinator Ruth Driker Kroll.

For more help still, consider what the National Women's Political Caucus did when it wanted to start a monthly meeting for women in New York; it retained the firm of Arts Letters & Politics, Inc., run by three women with long experience in staging events and raising funds, both as volunteers and as public relations experts. The result was Thursday Caucus, which has become something of an "in" place to go in Manhattan for lunch on the third Thursday of every month. "The $12.50 lunch isn't much—cold quiche and salad or grape leaves on pita bread or the like, self-served on paper plates, with jug wine or coffee—but the networking," as one attendee says, "is terrific: I never fail to run into at least three women I've been meaning to call and to make the new acquaintance of someone I've heard about." Besides which, the speakers are invariably knowledgeable on a newsworthy topic of interest to women.

Here's how the pros went about getting it under way, as related by Sarah Kovner, Barbara Handman, and Allyn Urbahn of Arts Letters & Politics:

1. "We staged a fund raiser for the ERA several months beforehand. This identified our audience for the Caucus."

The fund raiser itself was a big production: one could attend a Sunday brunch or late supper, Monday lunch, cocktail buffet, or dinner at six famous restaurants, with big-name hosts receiving at each. You could pay $35 to join Lauren Bacall and Marlo Thomas, among others, at Tavern on the Green, or pay $25 to lunch at Summer House with Viveca Lindfors and Phyllis George, or $175 for a two-day pass to everything.

The restaurant proprietors donated their places *and* the food and service, in exchange for the publicity and goodwill they knew the event would generate. The restaurant fund raiser drew fifteen hundred participants and produced a lively mailing list for use in starting the Thursday Caucus. These were people who could be counted on to open the next mailing with interest and with the expectation of meeting a congenial, even notable, group at future gatherings.

2. As most of us know from volunteer work, a profound letdown sets in after any event that has taken as much of our time and energies as this caucus fund raiser did (which is another argument for using professionals if possible). In this case, Barbara lined up the space for regular meetings (the American Place Theatre), the others lined up a speaker whose name would attract this now-identified audience (feminist author-critic Susan Sontag). A member of the Caucus, who works for an advertising agency, designed a handsome letterhead, and the first mailing for the new Thursday Caucus went out.

Each letter included a return envelope (unstamped) and a card with a place for the recipient to check this clue to future interest: "I cannot attend but wish to be kept on your mailing list for notice of the next meeting."

These mailings now go to seven hundred people each month. About 20 percent attend; another 20 to 30 percent send in the reply card. (Those who don't reply are dropped from the list after four such silences.)

"It takes two days to get the mailing out," Allyn Urbahn says. "While doing other things, answering the phone, et cetera, two aides address, stuff, and stamp the envelopes. Another couple of days are required for handling the returns, answering inquiries, and the like. Add one day for lining up the speaker, the day of the event itself, and about half a day afterward for bookkeeping. The lunch is catered—it's the least of the attractions—but we've had a few complaints about it." Actually, the $12.50 charge is a break-even price—this despite the fact that the speakers are not paid and the space is donated. That's New York for you, but it's also the cost of professional handling.

If you'd like to copy this method, just set your membership dues high enough to pay for this kind of help; it runs about $1,000 a month at New York City prices. It will be a relief to all concerned not to have to work volunteer duties in an overcrowded schedule, and the effect will be classier.

The Professional Women's Alliance, a network in San Francisco, engaged a professional firm to organize its luncheon for Sarah Weddington. According to Roxanne Mankin, the firm charged $1,000, for which it took care of the invitation mailing (to assembled lists of all the networks in town), issued the $25 tickets, and made all the physical arrangements for the event. (The networkers themselves made the White House contact and handled the publicity on a volunteer basis.) As Roxanne said, "We're all busy people. We don't have time to do this ourselves. Besides, the pros are experienced in running this very kind of event: they know what to do, and they do it efficiently and well."

14. *What about expenses?*

Kathleen M. Graf, an insurance and investments counselor in Portland, Oregon, recommends that core members of new groups put in $100 each at the outset to cover expenses. "Otherwise you'll be nickel-and-dimed to death. Costs mount up. Lillian Skinner, the first president of the Network, bankrolled us and, knowing it was her money, we economized where we shouldn't have. As membership chair, I wish our mailings had looked more professional."

When the National Commission on Working Women was organized, Kathy Bonk, among others, decided their materials should look good. She was tired of the tacky, amateurish appearance of mailings for women's groups. The group spent $600 to have a handsome logo designed; it probably makes a million-dollar difference in the way they're perceived by the public. They're not exactly a network, in the sense this book uses the term, but their lead is worth following by network groups everywhere—particularly those that want to attract supersuccessful women.

Particularly good-looking graphics are used by Dimensions in Kansas City, the Network of Women in Business in Indianapolis, and the Executive Women's Council in Baltimore. When complimented, one of the women said, "Professional-looking? But of course! That's what we're about!"

Another money note from the Indianapolis network: "To get extra money for speakers, we call on bankers and ask for support," says Joretta White, vice-president. "We promise to mention them on our brochures and at the luncheon. We also invite them to our receptions the night before the luncheons, along with our sustaining members."

In Chicago, after investing almost $1,000 of her own money to get a network started, Coralee Kern went to the Playboy Foundation for help. They agreed to underwrite completely the June 1979 meeting on women and finance, printing and mailing the notices to a list of five hundred, and picking up on the other expenses of Woman/Owner/Manager/Administrator Networking (WOMAN).

□ 10 Holding on to the "High"

"I had to peel myself off the ceiling after every meeting," Carol Royce said, describing the "high" produced by networking with other businesswomen in Portland, Oregon. An account executive for Binder Products, Inc., which makes custom-designed loose-leaf binders, Carol was a charter member of Network there. Just meeting each other, and realizing that they shared feelings and experiences as women trying to make it in a male-dominated world—that was enough to keep any network group going in the early stages of its development. Having lunch or dinner or drinks, the barest excuse for getting together, was all any network needed at first. But after a while—after the organizational tasks had been completed, with bylaws and incorporation accomplished, with officers elected or some other system for running the meetings agreed upon—most groups felt the need for some additional attraction to keep the members coming, some extra *oomph* to maintain the original high.

They have answered that need in one or all of these ways:

1. Program meetings, presenting a drawing-card speaker or an expert on a subject of great interest to the

members, or both—that is, both a "name" speaker and a compelling subject.

2. Workshops, usually in the nature of craft sessions, members sharing or outsiders bringing in nuts-and-bolts information and skills to aid the professional development of those attending.

3. Action, such as mounting a campaign to get more women on corporation boards, to upgrade secretarial jobs, to expose sexual harassment on the job, to study the equal pay issue.

4. New blood, expanding their membership to include a wider variety of careers, ages, and types of working women.

Some get at those solutions, make those plans, through a concentrated, brainstorming meeting of the founders and current officers.

The Bay Area Women's Executive Forum took its nine-member board on an all-day retreat, with the help of the Coro Foundation, which provided a facilitator for their sessions. The object was to consider where they'd been and plan where they were going. "We dreamed large dreams," Diane Winokur, a founder, says, "all the way to building club facilities where we could dine and swim and drop in any time." Their membership had gone from 30, in the creative stage, to 120. They talked out the problems of size, finally deciding they were equal to them: intimate networking could still go forward in a larger group; new members would bring new energies to continue the work.

(The Women's Forum of North Carolina, that prestigious network that includes former Secretary of Commerce Juanita Kreps, has a retreat, too, a weekend at a "really nice place," but according to Martha McKay, it's "strictly R and R [rest and rehabilitation]," with no agenda. "We get to relate to each other on a different level.")

On the assumption that you're either in a network already or planning to start one, I've gathered the following pointers on the four methods above from networks across the country. Here's how to maintain the "high."

Programs and workshops

The most important, most crucial aspect of running a speaker program—according to those who have learned this the hard way, its necessity cannot be overstressed—is making sure the speaker understands the sophistication and the career level of the audience. A network group of gung-ho women executives, or even women who are only, so far, in the aspiring stage of executivedom, are insulted by speakers who may mean well but talk down to them.

This poses a very real problem for the program committee. How does one tell the chief executive officer of a big corporation that he mustn't say to the group that he's eminently qualified to understand women because he has a wife, three daughters, and a female dog (sometimes called, ho-ho, a bitch)? At least one man has said exactly that to assembled women. How to prevent such a disaster? Two ways:

Review the speaker before inviting him. Hear him talk to other groups or read the past speeches his public relations person will be glad to show you. If he's too far off base, just don't ask him. If his title is all he's got as an attraction for your membership, realize that's just not enough.

Last spring, program chairs of a number of network groups in New York City reviewed a talk on power that Dr. Alice Armstrong gives in the Northwest. Alice happened to be in New York for another purpose. The group got together on a volunteer basis—networking in action—for the "cause" of future network programming. Groups in other areas could do the same.

When plans for a network of networks are realized,

speakers can be reviewed quite easily. The first network group to hear someone will send an evaluation to the others on the speaker's circuit. Or one program chair will be able to call others, in several other cities, to get a line on a speaker she's considering. Jean Donohue, founder of Women's Network in Seattle, already does this.

Even then, the differences in the memberships will have to be taken into account. If some networks have members who have never heard, read, or thought about their socialization as women, and how it now interferes with their ambitions in the workplace, they really need a series of speakers carrying, say, the Hennig-Jardim* message; the first time one hears these ideas, they are exciting, eye-opening. But don't present that kind of program to a network of bank or other corporate vice-presidents who have long ago said to themselves, "Okay, okay, but *now* what?"

Brief the speaker ahead of time. The easiest, most direct way to do this is to present him or her with a profile of your membership. You should know your network members' titles, responsibilities, salaries, and ambitions for the future. Describe the kind of programs the membership has most applauded in the past.

Another good ploy is to introduce the speaker the night before or earlier to some of your most articulate and dynamic members. As I've mentioned, the Network in Indianapolis does this by way of a reception the night before the monthly luncheon program, also inviting prominent women of the community who don't yet belong to the Network to this cocktail hour. A speaker who had underestimated his audience would have to be unusually dense not to change a standard presentation after talking to these alive and achieving women.

You might also ask for a written speech ahead of time, on the pretext of giving it to the press at a premeeting

* Margaret Hennig and Anne Jardim, *The Managerial Woman*, published by Anchor Press (Doubleday) in 1977, based on work done in 1970 and 1973.

conference. You probably will have the press conference, in any case, and having the speech in advance will allow you to suggest to the speaker changes that might seem necessary. Speakers will thank you—not to mention the membership.

All is not lost, however, when a program bombs, as Katherine Nash, career counselor and author of *Get the Best of Yourself*, demonstrated at a Chicago conference. The keynote speaker, a hotel executive, made such outrageous statements as "Women should go into the hotel business because they're naturally good hostesses." A woman in the audience, unable to contain herself, stood up and said what everybody else in the room was thinking: that he was insultingly patronizing of a group whose intelligence and professionalism deserved more respect.

During a workshop later in the conference, Katherine Nash tore up her prepared script and said, "Let's examine that experience. Was that a constructive way to confront the speaker? Was that impulsive reply the best expression of the group's anger and resentment? If not, let's see if we can come up with alternative behavior."

The workshop group came up with three other levels of response: (1) a private meeting with the speaker, attempting to educate him by explaining why his audience responded as it did, citing specific passages in his speech so he'd understand exactly what was being objected to, and why; (2) a letter, with the same mission, signed by all the others at the table where the woman was sitting before her outburst; (3) a meeting of the whole conference, or however many of the attendees were interested, to discuss what had happened and to decide on a collective action. A note tacked to the message board could have gotten this going.

At the end of the workshop they thought of a fourth action—organizing a sensitivity training course for male executives, with the now-educated hotel executive as one of the leaders.

In short, the disastrous keynote speech brought the women together for a livelier discussion than they might have had following a more appropriate talk.

The most successful program topics networks have told me about fall into these broad categories:

Job content, job function. Internal networks bring in department and division heads to explain what they do and how their output fits into the corporation's overall purpose. The more members learn about the inner workings of the company, the better they understand where their own jobs fit in and where they might go from here. Addressing the Women's Advisory Committee of the network group at Philip Morris headquarters in New York City, for example, Ellen Merlow explained what a brand manager does, bringing in samples of her work and other "show-and-tell" materials of interest. But, no less importantly, she was an encouraging role model for the women.

External networks are more likely to invite speakers who can survey an entire field or discipline, not only explaining what the work is like but predicting its place in the members' future work lives.

For example, a computer expert predicts astounding new capacities and uses for computers within the foreseeable future. Network members picture themselves with computer terminals on their desks and conclude that they'd better start learning more about what they can and can't ask computers to do in their particular businesses.

The news is not always good, but it's useful in any case. For instance, women who might otherwise have been cheered to learn that more and more of their sex were getting into nontraditional jobs with the phone company—such as becoming linesmen—were shocked to learn that these were exactly the jobs that would be phased out or deskilled by future technology. (Sally Hacker, of the University of Oregon, suggested that women were being moved into those jobs for exactly that reason: they would resist less than men, or less effectively, when the crunch came.) Thinking about women's employment in general, and keeping up with the facts to aid that thinking, can be an important part of every woman's understanding of the marketplace.

Job behavior. Calling on psychologists, career counselors, organization and development experts, authors of books that examine corporate politics (Rosabeth Moss Kanter's *Men and Women of the Corporation*, for instance, and Betty Lehan Harragan's *Games Mother Never Taught You*), program coordinators try to add to members' knowledge of the human foible side of working.

Under this heading come such promising program titles as "How to Manage Men," "What's with Women Bosses?" "Are You Assertive Enough?" "Coping with Office Politics," and, the title of Theodora Wells's latest book, *Keeping Your Cool under Fire*. "Silent Power Games," about nonverbal communication, was a hit at the Institute for Managerial and Professional Women in Portland, Oregon.

The Resource Network, a small group in Manhattan, took up assertiveness in an interesting way, issuing a one-page discussion paper that described particular situations and asked the members what they would do. The presentation reminded everyone of comparable problems and experiences, adding to the group's store of information and examples. "It helps a lot to get other women's ideas about your problems, not in the abstract but in the very specific terms of a real-life situation," says Maggi Cowlan, a founder of the group. "We plan to use this case study method as often as we can."

□ □ □

Career paths. Endlessly fascinating is the story of "How I Got Here," as told by successful women. Along with the personal, anecdotal material, speakers can be asked to discuss such topics as strategies for promotion, the need for formal credentials, or the role of the mentor.

Job skills. The skills specific to each different kind of career belong in small workshops rather than in programs for the entire membership, but networks have found that everybody needs to know more about management principles and techniques, business writing (reports, memos, proposals), time management (and getting organized), presentation skills, and budgeting (and other bottom-line matters).

The skill of decision making is a popular and useful topic. One network used a book of that title, *Decision Making, a Psychological Analysis of Conflict, Choice, and Commitment*, by Dr. Irving L. Janis and Dr. Leon Mann, as the focal point of a discussion program. Each member was asked, in advance, to bring in pro and con data on a decision she was about to be required to make or a similar story about a decision she had made in the past so that the group could practice the techniques and share their ideas on the subject.

By the way, authors of current books can often be persuaded to speak for low fees, or none at all, in order to publicize their books. When a publisher sends a writer on a tour of radio and television stations, the public relations people are glad to know of club dates that can be added to the schedule. So it would be a good move to let the publicity departments of the major publishers know of your network's existence; or when you read of a pertinent book, write and ask if the author is available for speaking engagements. (But read the book first, to make sure this writer's message is what your group wants to hear!)

Risk taking is another subject that can be taken up in a

membership-participation manner, like decision making. Or, you can buy ready-made games to use with your group. For example, Ruth Moghadam told me about "The Desert Survival Situation, a group decision-making experience for examining and increasing individual and team effectiveness in risk taking," which is available from Human Synergistics, 39819 Plymouth Road, Plymouth, Mich. 48170.

As for the mini seminars, as some networks call them, dealing with specific careers and skills that might not interest the whole membership, a model is the series started by two members of NET (the Peninsula Professional Women's Network of Palo Alto, California). Both assistant vice-presidents and corporate bankers at Bank of America in San Francisco, they led off with "Financing a Small Business."

The members of Women in Business, Los Angeles, have run small-group discussions on time management, team building in corporations, entrepreneurial skills. Although announced to the general membership, the mini meetings are held in members' homes and therefore limited to the first ten or twelve women who call in.

Women in Government Relations in Washington, D.C., has a unique approach to providing its members with the information that lobbyists need. They have a task force for each of the legislative areas they follow: agriculture, antitrust, corporate, energy, environment, health and nutrition, international trade, labor, tax, transportation, wage and price control. The task forces are responsible for watching the happenings on "the Hill," as they refer to the Capitol. Any of the 168 members can call any task force chair any time for information or advice. Or they can attend the task force meetings, which are akin to mini seminars themselves.

A skills area that many women feel themselves to be weak in is math. Programs built around the question "Who's Afraid of Math?" have succeeded in many networks. Often professors from local colleges are brought in as resource persons. Luckiest networks are those near Mills College, in Oakland, California, where the Math/Science Network has been set up to promote the participation of women in this area. Their activities include providing speakers.

Personal, coping matters. These program topics range from "Using Physical Exercise to Alleviate Stress" and "Handling Frustration and Anger on the Job"—two recent hits in the Des Moines (Iowa) Executive Women's Breakfast Club program series—to "How to Become Rich and Stay That Way," which brought out 94 of the 170 members of the Chicago Society of Women CPA's.

The coping part of this general topic area includes handling marriage and motherhood along with the paying kind of career. Emanuel Women in Management, an internal network at the Emanuel Hospital in Portland, Oregon, got good response with "Exploring Myths: Can Women Be Effective at Home and on the Job?" But in networks where the question is already answered (Yes!), groups take up such practical matters as options in arranging for child care, how to handle school requests for daytime volunteer work, and services available to working mothers.

The subject of stress provided one of the most successful programs that Dimensions (Kansas City, Missouri) ever put on. A woman psychologist talked about the drip-drip, Chinese-torture effects of sexism, which create the last straw for women who have been otherwise self-contained. Suddenly they blow up over some minor irritant, the last straw. Talking about how to understand and anticipate these breaks, possibly to avoid them, makes for a very good consciousness-raising discussion.

Personal topics are sometimes used to draw in women who are not sure they want to belong to a network, internal or external. Those women can be lured in with deliberately lightweight subjects such as—at the Embarcadero Center Forum in San Francisco—"How to Park in San Francisco and Get Away with It." The Equitable Networks (New York) have presented "Body and Soul," with a former dancer and a psychologist demonstrating dance movement and exercise as part of self-awareness, and "A Vitality Special," with a half-hour of actual exercise preceding a forty-five-minute rap group on developing the proper image at work.

Community affairs, or: what's going on around here? A woman in business has to understand her environment, her city, so here and there network groups bring in speakers who talk about subjects of local interest that have nothing, really, to do with the members' work. Thus the River Oaks Breakfast Club in Houston heard from a defense attorney and a couple who had started a halfway house for former prisoners and drug addicts. In Minneapolis, AGOG brought in managers of a nonprofit theater company.

These topics, let it be said, can dilute the purpose and excitement of networking. What has the local sewage plant to do with your members getting ahead in the corporate world? How will knowing about the city planning association serve them? As one network programmer said about speaker ideas, "I always ask, what has this got to do with getting ahead? Many are shocked by that forthright statement of our purpose, but—what the heck?—they should talk to the PTA or the AAUW or anybody but us about these things. We are definitely business-oriented, career-oriented, what's-in-it-for-us-oriented."

The big picture on women's employment is often at least a part of a program, and in some cases it is the whole. The Women's Media Group in New York City, for example—a hundred-plus women from print and broadcast media—had one of its best programs when Harriet Rabb, the attorney in a number of important

Title VII cases (*The New York Times*, *Reader's Digest*, for instance) spoke. "We usually don't have a speaker," Sally Artiseros, of Doubleday publishers, told me. "Our major aim is networking. But when Harriet spoke we were all transfixed. Inspired."

Sylvia Roberts, Judith Vladeck, Ruth Bader Ginsburg, and Jan Goodman are other feminist lawyers who can talk about their cases concerned with sex discrimination on the job. The Women's Bureau and other government offices might have speakers you could call upon. (If you could get the director, Alexis Herman, herself, you'd have a dynamite program.)

Some networks are going for the big picture on inflation and the economy as well. Those concerns, of course, play a part in women's employment.

But we always have to come back to—who are the members? What are their interests and problems? What will bring them out? One of the principals of a going network confessed, when she asked me to speak to her group about what my research for this book had been teaching me about networking as a national phenomenon, "These women have to know they're a part of something big, not just a little lunch club we're getting together here. The boredom threshold is very low around here. So come, give us the national picture, please."

Once brought out, the members reap the rewards of the main purpose of the organization—networking. Time- and energy-demanding though the paid and unpaid jobs of women certainly are, they must be looked beyond. Networking provides the look beyond, but not if the members of a networking group cannot be kept coming to the meetings.

Apart from the program categories, the way you present your chosen speaker and program topic may determine its success. Jean Donohue and the Women's Network in Seattle grouped three programs together and publicized the events as a "Celebrity Series," thus bestowing added importance on the speakers (who happened to be Rosabeth Moss Kanter, Caroline Bird, and I!).

Sad to say, although the material presented may be exactly the same, "A Talk about Finances" will not bring out as many members as "How to Get Rich and Stay That Way." The Women's Network of St. Bart's (St. Bartholomew's Church, New York City), for example, got 38 percent interest from its membership on what they called "Personal Marketing." Suppose they'd labeled the program instead "How to Sell Yourself, on Paper and in Person." I suspect that the 38 percent would have zoomed to 98. Luckily, most networks now include skilled public relations women, whom the program chair does well to seek out.

News "hooks" can help—that is, plugging your topic into the daily news. Thus, "How to Get a Raise" would be announced to your members and introduced by your speaker with the latest statistics on the gap between men's and women's earnings, or with news about a member who doubled her salary by getting herself written up in the local press.

Even if your programs were set far ahead of time, you can always layer a news item on top of the subject at hand. As you brief your speaker or send out notices of the meeting to your network, you can usually say something like "The story behind . . ." or "What *really* happened when . . ."

Let the audience participate during or after the program, or give them some action to take. "I always put paper and pencil at each place," said a program coordinator for a network in the Northeast. "And give them some kind of game to play before or after." She gave me this example: the speaker was to report on new labor statistics; the program chair asked the group to guess what percentage of managers are women, and how many women make over $20,000 a year. "I didn't require them to expose their guesses," she said, "and I think they listened better."

And do follow up the program in some fashion. The savvy program director always has a sign-up sheet handy, for those who want to have some further information mailed to them, or a petition they can sign, or a committee they can join, or at least a notice of where this speaker may be heard next.

Actions and projects

In addition to good programs and workshops, as suggested above, networks keep their members at a high level of involvement by means of a variety of actions and projects. I've heard of campaigns against sex harassment on the job, support for women involved in Title VII cases, and surveys of employers' policies on part-time and flex-time work. Holding a "speak-out" on sex harassment serves the double purpose of involving the members and interesting the press. (Not an ego trip; a good write-up of any network's activities adds to its credibility with the other sex; it also helps attract new blood to the group. Working Women United Institute, 595 Park Avenue, New York, N.Y. 10021, will supply information and possible speakers. Alliance Against Sexual Coercion, P.O. Box 1, Cambridge, Mass. 02139, offers direct service to women in the Boston area.)

Group projects have a cohesive effect on the membership. Starting a mentoring program, bringing in younger women to profit by the more experienced members' savvy, proves good for both women thus paired. Staging a student night, an event for women who are not yet out in the "real world," also works well for both the members and the students. It's one way to find out what kind of job counseling the students are getting, which information could lead to a campaign by the network to educate guidance counselors who are still discouraging young women from going into nontraditional fields.

Also, as attorney Sylvia Roberts told a networking meeting of Friends of NOW-NYC last fall ('79), prevention rather than attempted cure through litigation is probably the best way to proceed against sex discrimination in the eighties. Suing has become too costly, in time and energy as well as in dollars that women don't have—especially if they lose and are required to pay the exorbitant attorneys' fees run up by corporations opposing them! So Sylvia's recommendation is that women who've learned job savvy the hard way impart it to neophytes, step by step, to prevent their getting caught in the classic switches of corporate politics—and also to prevent their becoming Queen Bees when and if they *do* succeed in their careers. This kind of ongoing project could make a network truly *important* in its community.

An effective project taken on by the Federation of Organizations for Professional Women, in Washington, D.C., was publication of the directory I've mentioned before. Julia Graham Lear, who coordinated the project, calls the directory "a networking tool."

Another directory in the works at this writing is a directory of networks! I've given my list (as reproduced in Appendix C of this book) to AGOG, the network in Minneapolis, which is involved in setting up what will probably be called the National Alliance of Women's Networks. As with the Washington directory, the first one will have to be published before the omissions can be corrected, but eventually, with everyone working together—*networking*—the list will be up-to-date.

Organizing a job-listing service is a project that American Women in Radio and Television (AWRT) has found effective. A national organization, they have a toll-free number that members can call for a recorded message carrying information about job openings all over the country. They call it CareerLine. The recording is updated every two weeks, but an employer or a networker can insert a message on twenty-four-hour notice. A local organization could copy this idea, using a member's telephone answering machine to tape the latest news from the grapevine. Local employers could be notified of the project, in hopes they'd list openings with the network on a regular basis.

Good luck with all these ideas—and with all your networking!

Appendix A

How to Start a Network Group

During a discussion of this topic, over a Chinese lunch, two fortune cookies set the tone for what follows. The fortunes were, believe it or not:

> "Choose a direction before you start."
> "Have faith in what you are doing."

Provided in that spirit, here's a step-by-step program to get you through the start-up phase of a new network organization.

1. Start with a core of two or three women who agree with you about the general need for a new group. Together, work up a list of, say, twenty other women you'd like to include. You don't necessarily have to know those twenty; in fact, it might be better if you didn't. List them by description: maybe "a middle manager from each department of the company," if you're forming an in-house group and want to be sure you get initial representation in each part of the organization; or "someone with media contacts"; or "someone high up in the financial community."

What you're after, frankly, are successful women with whom others will want to network, women who are qualified to become unofficial mentors, if they so choose. You hope they'll attract others at their own level as well.

These women will be the hardest to interest in the first place, even if you already have a personal relationship with them, so your core group should plan carefully how to approach each of them and should rehearse what you're going to say. Be prepared for such objections as:

"I haven't time to participate, and I don't believe in joining just to be joining."

"I'm afraid I wouldn't be much use to you. My views are hopelessly 'establishment,' my interest and loyalty are with management here."

"Not now—but let me know how it all works out. Maybe later I'll be out from under enough to consider joining you."

"I belong to too many organizations already."

In reply you'll probably emphasize that no real time commitment is involved—you plan to do the work yourself—but you really need their advice in these critical formative days. Their experience and knowledge are invaluable at this stage. Depending on the women, an appeal to their sense of duty to the women's movement may also be effective. Can they really resist the invitation to become advisers-on-pedestals while at the same time doing a good deed for the sisterhood? If so—if they really can't spare the time to come to even the first meeting—ask if you can at least consult them from time to time as plans develop. If the answer is yes or even "I suppose so," you have the beginnings of an advisory board. Eventually the names of women like these on your letterhead will give your group credibility.

And maybe it won't be such a hard sell after all. Upper-level women need networking, too, and some of them are keenly aware of their need.

Also, among the first twenty, in addition to stars, try to have at least three who are known doers. You've seen them get things going in other organizations, so you know they can be counted on to work or to motivate others to work.

Here again, since these are probably the busiest people around, be prepared to hear that they are "overcommitted." Again, be satisfied if you can get them to come to just the first meeting, if only to lend their advice in the initial stages. You and your two friends are probably doers yourselves, or you wouldn't be starting a new group, but you don't want to do it all.

Also include women who you hope will fill (or advise you on) various predictable functions as plans proceed. Ideally, you'll have among you a lawyer, a public relations-publicity-media woman, a financial woman, and someone who understands computers.

2. Set the date, time, and place for the first three meetings, first checking to make sure there's no conflicting event scheduled at the same time. You can't know about all the conflicts, but you can at least avoid choosing the known meeting times of the Women's Political Caucus, say, or the opening night of the ballet.

The reason for setting the meeting time yourself, instead of first finding out who can come when, is that otherwise you'll spend hours and endless phone calls negotiating a time when everyone can come. If your first three candidates cannot make the time you set, adjust, of course, but by the time you reach the tenth potential member, at the latest, you should be immovable.

The reason for setting up three meetings (and it might be four) is: that's how long it's going to take you to iron out the start-up questions. Knowing that ahead of time will keep the women from thinking you're not getting anywhere in the first two meetings. And having decided that you'll get those matters settled before proceeding will keep you from rushing into action before you're ready.

To those who want to join you but can't make the first meeting, promise a report.

Depending on your estimate of the busyness of your candidates, the three meetings can be separated by one week, two, or a month. (After having been in on the formative stages of one group that met monthly, with much flipping of calendars to agree on the dates, and even then unable to turn out everyone every time, I think closer is better.)

An office conference room might seem ideal, but one of the questions you're going to discuss is whether to be visible to your companies' management, so an off-site place would be better, at least at first.

If you decide on somebody's home for the first meeting, prepare written directions for getting there and see that every woman has a copy.

3. Consider drawing up an agenda for the first meeting and writing out a tentative statement of purpose for the group. If

you go this route, supply each woman with a copy in advance—perhaps distributed along with the directions a few days before the meeting, thus serving as a reminder of the time and place.

The agenda might be as simple as: self-introductions of those attending; deciding whether we want to form a group; listing questions to take up at next meeting (membership qualifications, organizational structure, and other basics). Having an agenda will help keep the meeting focused. Knowing in advance what's expected of them will help the participants contribute to the discussion. But—a big but—your assuming the leadership in this fashion may not go down too well. You may prefer to stay looser than a written agenda suggests. Just invite people to "come talk about the possibility of forming a network group."

4. At the first meeting, have on hand either a blackboard or an easel holding a newsprint pad on which one of you will write in big letters, for all participants to see, the key words of ideas and suggestions that come out of the meeting. If you haven't seen this technique in action—workshop facilitators use it widely—know that it helps keep meetings focused. It also saves a lot of time by avoiding repetitious suggestions—when a person can *see* what's been said before, she usually won't say it again. And it provides a record.

Have ready also:

- A list of those attending, giving each person's name, identification, address, and phone numbers—a copy for each person. (Include the stars who expressed an interest, even if you know they're not coming. You can explain at the meeting.)
- A copy of the agenda, if any, for each person.
- Name tags or, better, if you'll be sitting around a table, large, blank fold-over place cards on which each person can write her name, and felt-tip markers to use on these.
- Self-help refreshments.
- A tape recorder, if it won't inhibit your group. One problem all groups share is that of filling in one member who misses a meeting, wasting the group's time to do so. If a cassette recording of the missed meeting were available to that person, a lot of backtracking could be prevented. This

is inadvisable if the material is in any way confidential, of course.

5. At the meeting, you'll probably start with introductions. Start yourselves, including a few words on what prompted you to call this meeting, then move to each person, going around the group in order of seating.

If you have not drawn up an agenda in advance, try to elicit one from the group first thing. Write it on the board or paper, assign A-B-C priorities to the items, and then decide how long to spend on each in order to finish at an agreed-upon time. Knowing you're going to finish in two hours, the endurance limit of most networkers, will get the meeting off to a happy start.

One more preamble: announce the date and time for the next meetings, explaining why you have taken that initiative. This information too will have a positive effect on the group. They'll know they don't have to settle everything in this one evening. If discussion bogs down or goes on too long on any one topic, you can move along by suggesting that this item be held over to the next meeting. Someone can be keeping track of those topics, for a future agenda.

Assuming that the group decides to go ahead with plans for a network, these people become the network's steering committee. It can operate as a committee-as-a-whole, for now, but eventually you will hope for volunteers to take over the various tasks of getting started. If that happens at the first meeting, so much the better, for if everyone goes out the door with a specific task to perform, you can be sure they'll all be back next time. The open secret of success in keeping groups together is getting everyone involved as a participant. Mere observers drop out.

Tasks to delegate, if possible, are:

- Sending out a summary of this meeting, along with a reminder of the next, to the whole list.
- Talking to those on the list who didn't make this meeting, to tell them what happened and/or to tell them about the cassette.
- Writing a statement of purpose, based on this meeting's discussion, to have ready for the next meeting.
- Generating a list of questions that have to be decided

before enlarging the group. (Maybe this list can be brainstormed at the end of the first meeting. Otherwise, one member could list the basics, get a few additional ideas from others, and circulate the list as a starting point next time.)

6. In the first few days after the meeting, talk to each attendee in person or on the phone to get her reaction. Any reservations, questions, ideas thought of too late to bring before the group? If any have volunteered for the tasks above, check up on how they're doing. Remind everyone of the next meeting. Whip up enthusiasm for it.

If you haven't time to talk to each person, use the telephone tree method. Ask one person to call two or three others, each of whom is then asked to call two or three others, and so on. (This further involves the callers.)

7. Arrange with someone else to chair the next meeting, as you did the first. The idea of a rotating chair may come up naturally, or you'll be deciding on some other structure as the planning progresses, so it's important that you sit back as soon as possible. You want the others to see this as *their* group, not yours. You'll still have to put in the most time and effort to get the organization going, but work through others as much as you can. Don't be out front all the time.

8. Once the basic questions are settled, as they probably will be in the next several meetings, you will want to open up the membership, set a format for regular meetings, and develop a long-range plan.

You may want to consider a plan that has worked for others: decide to have two types of meetings, one to hash out the policy questions and to discuss the business of the network, the other to get going on actual networking—that is, personal problem solving, rap sessions, whatever you envisioned when you had this idea in the first place. Otherwise, the business of getting organized could get really boring, not to say frustrating to those of you who want to use the network for specific career advancement purposes.

9. Formalize two things you're probably going to need, before you need them: a way for the group to evaluate itself from time to time; and a suggestion box or some such device to receive anonymous suggestions or complaints. People will

sometimes drop out rather than say in open meeting what bothers them. But they'll write an anonymous memo, which the steering committee can then take under advisement. Maybe an occasional meeting should be devoted in part to discussing the contents of the suggestion box. In any case, it's important to acknowledge and, where possible, to defuse disgruntlements, lest they grow out of all proportion to their merits.

Appendix B
How Other Networks Started

Lehigh Valley Corporate and Professional Women: Preliminary plan

April 22, 1979
7:30–9:30

A group of ten women met at LIFEPLAN to discuss the formation of a support system network for Lehigh Valley corporate and professional women.

The general consensus was:

- that networking:
  - *was both appropriate and needed
  - *would provide a forum for corporate and professional women to give and seek help in the advancement of their careers
  - *would help younger women find career paths
  - *would provide for job-related support
  - *would facilitate implementation of the mentoring process
  - *would provide for an information base on what other companies are doing for their women employees, in training, education, day care, etc.
  - *would offer an avenue through which professional women could share companionship

- that the meeting structure format be varied:
  - *informal group discussions
  - *occasional speakers
  - *occasional cocktail meetings
  - *gripe sessions/moral support sessions
  - *possible alternation of program and social meetings
- that the Allentown/Bethlehem/Easton Standard Metropolitan Statistical Area (SMSA) be considered for membership parameters
- that effort be made to involve women from as many corporations and businesses as possible

Two diverse problems were mentioned:

- that of women feeling under-utilized in terms of their skills and abilities
- the difficulty of finding women for highly specialized jobs, such as in engineering and computers

Specific Identified Needs Were for:

1. Rap sessions regarding road blocks that impede upward mobility within the corporate system.
2. Sharing of information regarding career opportunities.
3. Environment for making contacts (women serving as resources for each other).
4. Development of a pool of knowledgeable, successful women to serve as role models in the mentoring process.
5. Social opportunities to meet with other professional women.
6. Time management information to facilitate dual role of women: businesswoman/homemaker.
7. Information bank regarding corporate policies, procedures, and educational programs, as they relate to women.

Other areas for consideration at future meetings [drawing in part from the typescript of this book]:

- What shall we call our group?
- What format shall we follow for our meetings?
  - *officers/elections?
  - *rotating chair?

*committee of the whole?
*no structure?

- Should we affiliate?
- How visible do we want to be?
  *go public?
  *confidentiality?
- Shall we be selective about membership? How selective?
- What about men?
- Should we have a purpose beyond networking?
- What would be our financial needs? How would they be funded?
- Should we promote (or provide) special skills training opportunities? Assertiveness/self-esteem training opportunities?
- Should we facilitate a sharing of technical assistance?
- Should we offer lecture programs by well-known lecturers and local authorities?
- Should we monitor affirmative action progress in the Lehigh Valley SMSA?
  *to keep track of?
  *to help shape?
- Should we actively promote increased participation by qualified women on Corporate Boards of Directors?

Women in Management of Southern Connecticut: Plan of organization

Objectives (Preliminary)

- To develop a fuller understanding of business and its function.
- To provide opportunities for members to enhance one another's professional advancement by providing a strong network of professional contacts, mutual education, and mutual encouragement.
- To offer opportunities for increased professional development by means of timely and pertinent seminars, workshops, panels, and speakers devoted to serving the needs of our membership.
- To achieve recognition of the contribution of women to the southern Connecticut business community.
- To encourage other women to seek professional positions within the business community.

Membership

- The organization has initially been aimed at women in middle and upper level management in companies located in southern Connecticut.
- Membership qualifications will be decided during the next 3–4 months by the membership committee working with the policy committee.
- Guests will always be welcome at educational meetings.

Our goal will be to form an organization, the nature of which will make all fees and dues tax deductible and payable as a professional expense by your employer (where applicable).

Interim Officers and Committee Members Needed

POLICY COMMITTEE:
- Chairman of Membership Committee
- Chairman of Opportunity Committee
- Chairman of Program Committee
- Director of Administration
- Director of Communications
- President (Chairman)
- Secretary
- Treasurer

President
Secretary
Treasurer
Director of Administration
Director of Communications

Committees: Membership Committee (at least 5)
Opportunity Committee (at least 3)
Program Committee (at least 4)

Functions (Interim)

Policy Committee:
- determines objectives and direction of the organization.
- has ultimate decision-making responsibility to resolve issues relating to functioning of the organization (i.e., membership qualifications, dues structure, etc.).
- will work with the secretary to shape the charter.
- will develop mechanisms enabling it to be responsive to the membership.

President:
- chairman of policy committee; aids in giving direction to the organization.
- maintains constant liaison with other officers and committee members.
- establishes contact with other organizations to find out about charters, organizational structures.

Secretary:
- responsible for putting organization on a legal, nonprofit, corporation basis.

- main coordinator for writing of the charter.

Treasurer:
- responsible for establishing a banking relationship.
- examine dues structure of other organizations; suggest appropriate dues structure to us.
- contact other organizations to learn about ways to obtain corporate sponsorship.

Director of Administration:
- develops relationships with services vendors to provide necessary administrative support. In interim, develops volunteer services.
- works with treasurer to develop the organization's budget.

Director of Communications:
- responsibility to write (and work with administration for dissemination of) meeting and other announcements to the membership.
- editor of newsletter (monthly publication).
- public relations coordinator with the press.

Membership Committee (5 or more)
- before next meeting (2nd or 3rd week of January) each committee member will meet with approximately 10 participants at tonight's meeting:
    *to discuss the objectives of the organization, to hear suggestions on membership qualifications, etc.
    *to work with participants to increase the network.
- will be responsible for recommending membership policy.
- new member cultivation will be an ongoing responsibility.
- will develop application form, selection procedures; contact with other professional women's organizations to get input.
- answer inquiries from prospective members.

Opportunity Committee (3 or more)
- keep membership current with legislation affecting women executives' working lives.
- develop the apparatus and act as a clearinghouse for job opportunities for the members of the association; notify the members of these opportunities through the newsletter.

- develop liaison and coordinate with other women executives' organizations.

Program Committee (4 or more)
- choose meeting topics and engage speakers for monthly association meetings.
- develop meeting ideas, responding to needs of membership.
- develop list of meeting places.
- provide hospitality for speakers and perform other functions of arranging rooms and menus.

Philadelphia Women's Network: Membership letter

Philadelphia Women's Network
1405 Locust Street, Room 1111
Philadelphia, Pa. 19102
(215) PE 5-3520

October 6, 1978

Dear

Earlier this year, eight Philadelphia business and professional women met to discuss the formation of a group that would meet a need they all had felt. The need was the opportunity to get to know other Philadelphia career women working in a variety of fields. We all agreed that our contacts were usually limited to others in our own professions and that what we needed was a *network of friends* from different areas of expertise to contact when we wanted advice and support for our daily career concerns. We were also excited by the opportunity to expand our understanding of new issues and ideas through our contact with speakers of achievement and energy.

We continued to meet through the summer to shape this group. We are calling it the *Philadelphia Women's Network*. Our purpose is

> to promote a spirit of cooperation and understanding among our members; to enhance one another's professional advancement by providing a strong network of professional contacts, mutual education, and mutual encouragement; to achieve recognition of the contribution of women to the Philadelphia community; and encourage other women to seek professional positions within the Philadelphia community.

We are incorporated as a non-profit Pennsylvania Corporation. We have drafted bylaws. Our dues in this first year are

$50. We have developed a program concept and the first year's schedule of dinner meetings. And, most importantly, we have each identified from our personal and professional contacts other women who could be interested in joining a group of this kind.

That's why we're writing to you. In this first year, we are aiming at attracting a Charter Membership of approximately 100 Philadelphia business and professional women. We hope that you will decide to join our membership at this very exciting stage in our Network's formation. We expect this group to make a substantial contribution to the Philadelphia business and professional community by providing our members with a unique opportunity to share ideas, skills, and experiences.

We invite you to join us at our first meeting, November 8, 1978, to learn more about our group, to meet other business and professional women, and to hear our speaker, Judge Lynne Abraham. You will have an opportunity to discuss the objectives of the Philadelphia Women's Network with us and to see how they fit in with yours.

If you find our idea interesting, please join us at our first dinner meeting. A description is enclosed with this letter along with a reservation form. If you are not able to attend this meeting but would like to be notified about future meetings and developments, please note that on the reservation form and return it to us.

For a long time, Philadelphia has needed an organization that brings together the leading business and professional women in an effective network. We think that the Philadelphia Women's Network will fill that need now.

We look forward to meeting you.

Cordially,

For the Steering Committee

Women's Forum-West: Articles of incorporation

One: The name of this Corporation is: WOMEN'S FORUM-WEST.

Two: (a) The specific and primary purpose for which this Corporation is formed is to bring together Northern California women of diverse accomplishment and experience.

(b) The general purpose of the organization shall be to promote the interests, conditions and position of women in the professions, science, the arts, education, industry, commerce and public service, in a manner consistent with the provisions of section 501(c)(4) of the Internal Revenue Code of 1954, or any successor thereto.

(c) This Corporation shall have and exercise all rights and powers conferred on corporations under the laws of the State of California provided, however, that this Corporation is not empowered to engage in any activity which in itself is not in furtherance of its purposes as set forth in subparagraphs (a) and (b) of this second Article.

(d) No part of the net earnings, properties or assets of this Corporation, on dissolution or otherwise, shall inure to the benefit of any private person or individual or any member or director of this Corporation, and on liquidation or dissolution all properties and assets of this Corporation remaining after paying or providing for all debts and obligations shall be distributed and paid over to such fund, foundation or corporation organized and operated for charitable or religious purposes as the Board of Directors shall determine.

Three: This Corporation is organized pursuant to the General Nonprofit Corporation Law of the State of California.*

Four: The county in the State of California where the princi-

**Important:* Laws concerning incorporation vary from state to state, so this model is for an example only.

pal office for the transaction of the business of this Corporation is to be located is the County of Santa Clara.

Five: The powers of this Corporation shall be exercised, its properties controlled, and its affairs conducted by a Board of Directors. The number of this Corporation's directors is three (3) and the names and addresses of the persons who are to act in the capacity of members and directors until the selection of their successors are:

NAME	ADDRESS
Barbara B. Creed	225 Bush Street San Francisco, CA 94104
Susan W. Bird	225 Bush Street San Francisco, CA 94104
Beverly Willis	545 Mission Street San Francisco, CA 94105

The number of directors herein provided for may be changed by a by-law duly adopted by the members.

Six: The authorized number and qualifications of members of this Corporation, the different classes of membership, the property, voting and other rights and privileges of members, and the liability of members to dues and the method of collection thereof, shall be as set forth in the By-Laws of this Corporation.

IN WITNESS WHEREOF, for the purpose of forming this nonprofit corporation under the laws of the State of California, we, the undersigned, constituting the incorporators of this Corporation, and including all the persons named herein as the first directors, have executed these Articles of Incorporation this ____ day of ______________, 1978.

____

____

____

STATE OF CALIFORNIA

City and County of San Francisco

) SS.

On this 10th day of January, 1978, before me, ______________________________, a Notary Public, State of California, duly commissioned and sworn, personally appeared Barbara B. Creed, Susan W. Bird and Beverly Willis, known to me to be the persons whose names are subscribed to and who executed the within instrument, and acknowledged to me that they executed the same.

IN WITNESS WHEREOF, I have hereunto set my hand and affixed my official seal in the City and County of San Francisco the day and year in this certificate first above written.

____

Notary Public
State of California

Network, Portland, Oregon: Partial bylaws

ARTICLE III

ELECTED OFFICIALS

Composition

Section I

The elected officials of Network shall be a President; a First Vice-President; a Second Vice-President; a Third Vice-President; a Secretary; a Treasurer; and four (4) Members-at-Large. No person may hold more than one office at the same time.

Terms of Office

Section II

The elected officials shall be elected by the active and life members of Network for a term of one year, or until their successors are elected, and shall serve for no more than three (3) consecutive terms in the same office.

Vacancy

Section III

A vacancy among the elected officials other than that of President, shall be filled by the Board until the next elections at the annual meeting. In the event of a permanent vacancy, as determined by the Board, in the office of the President, the Vice-Presidents will succeed in order of rank until the next annual meeting.

Duties

Section IV

The duties of the elected officers are as follows:

President

The President shall be the chief corporate officer of Network and shall preside at all regular meetings of Network, the Board of Directors, and the Executive Committee Meetings; shall implement actions of the Board and directions given by the Network membership; shall be an ex officio member of all committees established by the Board (except the nominating and membership committee); shall, with the Treasurer, sign all written contracts and obligations as directed by the Board; shall appoint committee directors subject to ratification by the Board; and finally shall serve as a member of the Board for one year following the conclusion of her term as president.

First Vice-President

The First Vice-President shall be responsible for the administrative functions of the Board of Directors; act as President in the temporary or permanent absence of the President; and carry out the duties assigned by the Board of Directors.

Second Vice-President

The Second Vice-President shall be responsible for the direction of all committees assigned by the Board; act as President in the temporary or permanent absence of the First Vice-President and President; and carry out the duties assigned by the Board.

Third Vice-President

The Third Vice-President shall be responsible for the direction of the membership committee; act as President in the temporary or permanent absence of the Second Vice-President, First Vice-President and President; and carry out the duties assigned by the Board.

Secretary

The Secretary shall be responsible for seeing that all notices of all meetings of Network (annual, special, and executive) are issued and shall see that minutes of such meetings are prepared and distributed within two weeks following the meeting.

The Secretary shall be responsible for the custody of corporate books, records, and files, shall exercise the powers and perform such other duties usually incident to the office of Secretary or designated by the President or Board. The Secretary shall also prepare a yearly summary of Board action for the annual meeting.

Treasurer The Treasurer shall be responsible for the receipt and custody of all moneys of Network and for the disbursement thereof, for the keeping of accurate accounts of moneys received and paid out, and for the execution of contracts, or other documents as authorized by the Board; and for the preparation and issuance of financial statements and reports. The Treasurer shall prepare a financial statement for the annual meeting. The Treasurer shall perform such other duties usually incident to the office of Treasurer or designated by the President or the Board.

Members-at-Large All members-at-large shall become the liaison between general members and the Board.

Removal An officer of Network may be removed, with or without cause, by vote of two-thirds of the total membership of the Board.

ARTICLE IV

COMMITTEES

Membership A membership committee of at least three members shall be appointed by the Third Vice-President. The membership committee's duty shall be to interview qualified persons with a view to having them apply for membership in Network; to review and monitor the job status of the active members; to seek out new members in job categories that are not represented by the membership; and to plan, activate and maintain programs for acquiring new members. The membership committee is responsible for submitting names of new members to the Board for approval.

□ □ □

Establishment of Other Committees

Section III

The Board shall establish such committees and/or task groups as it deems necessary. Such committees shall have such name, responsibilities, and existence as may be determined, from time to time, by the Board. All committees (except the nominating, and membership) will come under the direction of the Second Vice-President.

Directors

Directors of committees shall be named by the President and confirmed by the Board. Such directors shall serve until the new President is elected, or until their successor has been appointed. Members of a committee shall be selected by the committee director.

Authority

Each committee director becomes a member of the Board of Directors. The director shall make committee recommendations to the Board and take such action as the Board deems necessary. The Second Vice-President is responsible for reporting committee recommendations to the Board if the committee director is absent.

Executive Committee

Section IV

The executive committee will be established to carry out normal Network business in the interim between Board meetings.

Composition The executive committee shall consist of the elected officers of Network and not less than 4 nor more than 8 members as recommended by the President, and approved by the Board at its first meeting following the annual meeting. The President shall be director of the executive committee.

Duties The executive committee shall have and may exercise the powers of the Board in the interim between Board meetings, except that the executive committee SHALL NOT: have the power to adopt the budget; take any action which is contrary to or a substantial departure from the direction established by the Board; amend, alter or repeal the bylaws; elect, appoint, or remove any member of the executive committee or any director or elected officer of Network; amend the constitution; adopt a plan of merger or consolidation with another group; amend, alter or repeal any resolution of the Board. The executive committee shall submit to the Board reports on action taken.

Meetings Meetings of the executive committee shall be held as deemed necessary by the President or a majority of the executive committee. Notice of the time, place and purpose of the meeting shall be given not less than 5 days prior to such a meeting.

ARTICLE V

BOARD OF DIRECTORS

Responsibilities Section I

The affairs of Network shall be managed and guided by the Board.

Composition Section II

The Board of Directors shall consist of all elected officials, the immediate past President, and all committee directors. There shall be no less than 14 nor more than 30 Board members.

Duration of Term Section III

The Board members shall serve 1-year terms, or until their successors have been elected or assume office. Terms shall begin as soon as possible after the annual meeting.

Vacancies Section IV

Vacancies on the Board shall be filled by the Board.

Quorum Section V

One half or more of the members of the Board shall constitute a quorum.

Meetings Section VI

The Board shall meet on the third Wednesday of the month. They must meet at least twice a year. Special meetings may be called by the President or a majority of the Board members.

Removal Section VII

Any officer or committee director who is absent from 3 regular meetings may be dropped and the vacancy filled by a majority vote of the Board members.

Appendix C

Network Directory

This directory includes all networking groups listed in the author's files, with the exception of in-house organizations. It is of necessity incomplete, since new networking groups are being formed all the time. Any suitable organization wishing to be included should send the name and address of the group to the author so that she can add it to future editions of the book.

Arizona

Executive Women's Council of Southern Arizona
c/o Carolyn Lucz
2700 E. Speedway
Tucson, Ariz. 85716

Women Emerging (WE)
7244 E. Indian School Road, #102
Scottsdale, Ariz. 85251
Phone: (602) 994-1811

California

Advocates for Women
256 Sutter St.
San Francisco, Calif. 94108
Phone: (415) 391-4870

The American Society for Public Administration
Committee on Women in Public Administration
c/o Sally Gutierrez
University of California
311 S. Spring St.
Los Angeles, Calif. 90013
Phone: (213) 741-6081

Bay Area Executive Women's Forum
356 Urbano
San Francisco, Calif. 94127
Phone: (415) 421-5848

Bay Area Professional Women's Network
55 Sutter St. #329
San Francisco, Calif. 94101

California Elected Women's Association for Education and Research (CEWAER)
c/o Assemblywoman Marilyn Ryan
P.O. Box 7000, Room 242
Redondo Beach, Calif. 90277
Phone: (213) 485-3357

California Women in Government
1334 Idlewood Rd.
Glendale, Calif. 91202
Phone: (213) 795-4068

Embarcadero Center Forum
P.O. Box 2902
San Francisco, Calif. 94126
Phone: (415) 362-3212

Feminist Writers Guild
P.O. Box 9396
Berkeley, Calif. 94709
Phone: (415) 524-3692

Friends of the San Francisco Commission on the Status of Women
P.O. Box 2331
San Francisco, Calif. 94126
Phone: (415) 558-3653

Math/Science Network
Math/Science Resource Center
Mills College
Oakland, Calif. 94613
Phone: (415) 635-5074

The Peninsula Professional Women's Network
701 Welch Rd., Suite 1119
Palo Alto, Calif. 94303
Phone: (415) 328-2040

Professional Women's Alliance
2020 Union St.
San Francisco, Calif. 94123
Phone: (415) 775-3137

San Francisco Financial Women's Club
808A Spring St.
Sausalito, Calif. 94965

Women Entrepreneurs (W.E.)
P.O. Box 26738
San Francisco, Calif. 94126
Phone: (415) 788-4430

Women in Business, Inc.
5000 Wilshire Blvd., Suite 1402
Los Angeles, Calif. 90036
Phone: (213) 933-7330

Women in Film
8489 W. 3rd St., Suite 49
Los Angeles, Calif. 90048
Phone: (213) 651-3680

Women in Theatre
P.O. Box 3718
Hollywood, Calif. 90028
Phone: (213) 466-7126

Women Organized for Employment
127 Montgomery St., #304
San Francisco, Calif. 94104
Phone: (415) 566-0849

Women's Forum, West
c/o Lorraine Legg
Boise Cascade Credit Corp.
P.O. Box 10100
Palo Alto, Calif. 94303
Phone: (415) 328-7500

Women's Resource Exchange
35282 Farnham Drive
Newark, Calif. 94560

Colorado

Colorado Network of Women's Resource Centers
Better Jobs for Women
1038 Bannock St.
Denver, Colo. 80204
Phone: (303) 893-3534

The Open Network
P.O. Box 18666
Denver, Colo. 80218
Phone: (303) 832-9764

Professional Secretarial Services Association
10650 Irma Dr., Bldg. 17
Northglenn, Colo. 80233
Phone: (303) 451-5766

Women's Forum of Colorado, Inc.
6051 East Dorado Ave.
Englewood, Colo. 80111
Phone: (303) 779-4070

Connecticut

Counterparts
c/o Joyce Lawson
Personnel Dept., General Electric
3135 Easton Tpk.
Fairfield, Conn. 06431

Hartford Women's Network
Hartford Region YWCA
135 Broad St.
Hartford, Conn. 06105
Phone: (203) 525-1163

Mid-Day Club
c/o Patricia Kane, Atty.
45 E. Putname Ave.
Greenwich, Conn. 06830
Phone: (203) 661-3434

Women in Management
P.O. Box 691
Stamford, Conn. 06904

District of Columbia

American Association of University Women
2401 Virginia Ave. NW
Washington, D.C. 20006
Phone: (202) 785-7750

American Women in Radio and Television (AWRT)
1321 Connecticut Ave. NW
Washington, D.C. 20026
Phone: (202) 296-0009

Associates Network of Women's Institute for Freedom of the Press
3306 Ross Place NW
Washington, D.C. 20008
Phone: (202) 966-7783

Association of Flight Attendants
1625 Massachusetts Ave. NW
Washington, D.C. 20036
Phone: (202) 797-4015

Concerned Women's Advancement Committee
Communications Workers of America
c/o Patsy Fryman
1925 K St. NW
Washington, D.C. 20006
Phone: (202) 785-6700

Congressional Wives Task Force
P.O. Box 1978
U.S. House of Representatives
Washington, D.C. 20515

Executive Women's Division
National Savings and Loan League
1101 15th St. NW
Washington, D.C. 20005

Federally Employed Women
Suite 481
National Press Bldg.
Washington, D.C. 20045
Phone: (202) 638-4404

Federation of Organizations for Professional Women
2000 P St. NW
Washington, D.C. 20036
Phone: (202) 466-3547

Mexican-American Women's National Association
L'Enfant Plaza Station SW
P.O. Box 23656
Washington, D.C. 20024
Phone: (703) 521-0097

National Association of Women Business Owners
2000 P St. NW, Suite 410
Washington, D.C. 20036
Phone: (202) 388-8966

National Association of Women Deans, Administrators and Counselors
1028 Connecticut Ave. NW
Washington, D.C. 20036
Phone: (202) 659-9330

National Commission on Working Women
1211 Connecticut Ave. NW, #400
Washington, D.C. 20036
Phone: (202) 466-6770

National Council of Negro Women
1346 Connecticut Ave. NW
Washington, D.C. 20036
Phone: (202) 223-2363

National Council of Puerto Rican Women
Cleveland Park Station
P.O. Box 4804
Washington, D.C. 20008

National Federation of Business and Professional Women's Clubs
2012 Massachusetts Ave. NW
Washington, D.C. 20036
Phone: (202) 293-1100

National Women's Health Network
2025 I St. NW, Suite 105
Washington, D.C. 20006
Phone: (202) 223-6886

National Women's Political Caucus
1411 K St. NW, #1110
Washington, D.C. 20005
Phone: (202) 347-4456

The Network
c/o Lynne D. Finney
Federal Home Loan Bank Board
1700 G St. NW
Washington, D.C. 20552

Organization of Chinese-American Women
3214 Quesada St. NW
Washington, D.C. 20015
Phone: (202) 227-1967

"*60 Words Per Minute*"
1346 Connecticut Ave. NW
Washington, D.C. 20017

Washington Women Economists
c/o Tanya Roberts
1719 S St. NW, Apt. 5
Washington, D.C. 20009

Washington Women's Network
c/o National Women's Education Fund
1410 Q St. NW
Washington, D.C. 20009
Phone: (202) 462-8606

Women in Film
P.O. Box 39049
Friendship Station
Washington, D.C. 20016

Women in Government Relations
1801 K St. NW, Suite 230
Washington, D.C. 20006
Phone: (202) 833-9500

Women's Equity Action League (WEAL)
805 15th St. NW, #822
Washington, D.C. 20005
Phone: (202) 638-4560

Florida

The Florida Women's Network
P.O. Box 18981
Tampa, Fla. 33679
Phone: (813) 251-9172

National Association of Insurance Women
Furlong Insurance Agency
280 NW 42nd Ave.
Miami, Fla. 33126
Phone: (305) 446-0832

Georgia

Georgia Executive Women's Network
4131 N. Gloucester Pl.
Atlanta, Ga. 30341
Phone: (404) 455-7590

Women in Film, Inc., Atlanta
P.O. Box 52726
Atlanta, Ga. 30355
Phone: (404) 523-6200

Women in Network (WIN)
P.O. Box 1309
Albany, Ga. 31702
Phone: (912) 432-4114

Hawaii

Network of Marketing Women
P.O. Box 27513
Honolulu, Hawaii 96827

Illinois

Chicago Society of Women Certified Public Accountants
2337 Commonwealth Ave., #1F
Chicago, Ill. 60614
Phone: (312) 525-8887

Chicago Women in Publishing
P.O. Box 11837
Chicago, Ill. 60611

Coalition for Women in the Humanities and Social Sciences
Newberry Library, Family and Community History Center
60 W. Walton St.
Chicago, Ill. 60601
Phone: (312) 943-9090

Council on Women's Programs
c/o Elaine Sullivan
Oakton Community College, Room 328
7900 N. Nagle Ave.
Morton Grove, Ill. 60053

International Federation of Women's Travel Organizations
c/o Linnea Smith Jessup
2416 Prudential Plaza
Chicago, Ill. 60601
Phone: (312) 861-0432

International Organization of Women Executives
1800 N. 78th Ct.
Elmwood Park, Ill. 60635
Phone: (312) 456-1852
(312) 296-7011

National Association of Bank Women
111 E. Wacker Dr.
Chicago, Ill. 60601
Phone: (312) 565-4100

The Network of McLean County
1311 Holiday La.
Bloomington, Ill. 61701
Phone: (309) 662-5506

Woman/Owner/Manager/Administrator Networking (WOMAN)
2520 N. Lincoln Ave., #60
Chicago, Ill. 60614
Phone: (312) 472-8116

Women Employed
37 S. Wabash
Chicago, Ill. 60603
Phone: (312) 372-7822

Women in Management
c/o Career Strategies
2762 Eastwood St.
Evanston, Ill. 60201
Phone: (312) 869-0553

The Women's Advertising Club of Chicago
c/o Judith Schmuesser
McKnight Medical Communications, Inc.
550 Frontage Rd.
Northfield, Ill. 60093
Phone: (312) 446-1622

Indiana

The Network of Women in Business
9331 N. Washington Blvd.
Indianapolis, Ind. 46240
Phone: (317) 844-8503

Iowa

Executive Women's Breakfast Club
P.O. 5262
Des Moines, Iowa 50306
Phone: (515) 276-7706

Women's Resource and Action Center
University of Iowa
130 N. Madison
Iowa City, Iowa 52242
Phone: (319) 353-6265

Louisiana

Library Administration & Management Association
Women Administrator's Discussion Group
University Library
Loyola University
6363 St. Charles Ave.
New Orleans, La. 70118

Network
P.O. Box 3081
Baton Rouge, La. 70821

Maryland

Executive Women's Council, Greater Baltimore
c/o Eastford Professional Services
304 W. Chesapeake Ave.
Towson, Md. 21204
Phone: (301) 825-7841

Executive Women's Network
Baltimore New Directions
12 E. 25th St.
Baltimore, Md. 21218
Phone: (301) 889-6677

Massachusetts

Boston Luncheon Club
c/o Deane C. Laycock, Trust Officer
Fiduciary Trust
P.O. Box 1647
Boston, Mass. 02105
Phone: (617) 482-5270

9 to 5
140 Clarendon St.
Boston, Mass. 02116
Phone: (617) 536-6003

Massachusetts (*cont.*)

West Suburban Area Women's Network Group
Middlesex Community College
P.O. Box T
Bedford, Mass. 01730

Women Elected Municipal Officials
Massachusetts Municipal Association
131 Tremont St.
Boston, Mass. 02135

Women Entrepreneurs
18 Brattle St.
Cambridge, Mass. 02138
Phone: (617) 492-0999

Women's Lunch Group
35 Wykeham Rd.
West Newton, Mass. 02165
Phone: (617) 969-3678

Michigan

Detroit Network
c/o Phyllis Kozlowski, Atty.
1756 Penobscot Bldg.
Detroit, Mich. 48226
Phone: (313) 961-5010

Detroit Women's Forum
c/o American Jewish Committee
163 Madison
Detroit, Mich. 48226
Phone: (313) 965-3353

Detroit Women Writers
Detroit Public Library
5201 Woodward Ave.
Detroit, Mich. 48202

Women in State Government
Michigan State University
College of Communication, Arts & Sciences
East Lansing, Mich. 48824

Minnesota

All the Good Old Girls
YWCA
603 S. Second St.
Mankato, Minn. 56001
Phone: (507) 345-4629

All the Good Old Girls
Rochester Community College
Consortium Office, Rm. 1028
Rochester, Minn. 55901
Phone: (507) 285-7275

All the Good Old Girls, Inc.
P.O. Box 20121
Minneapolis, Minn. 55420
Phone: (612) 888-6234

Professional Women's Group
Minneapolis YWCA
1130 Nicollet Ave.
Minneapolis, Minn. 55403
Phone: (612) 332-0501

Missouri

Dimensions Unlimited
P.O. Box 19531
Kansas City, Mo. 64141
Phone: (816) 436-5277

Women in Business Network
Ralston Purina Co.
Checkerboard Sq. 6T
St. Louis, Mo. 63188

Women into Public Leadership
Allendale
14601 Holmes
Kansas City, Mo. 64145
Phone: (816) 942-3960

Nebraska

Omaha Network
c/o Marlene Hansen
Hansen & Hansen
1905 Harney
Omaha, Nebr. 68102
Phone: (402) 345-2122

New Jersey

Princeton Women's Resource Network
c/o Mary Ellen Capek
Princeton University, Continuing Education
South Ivy La.
Princeton, N.J. 08540

New Mexico

The Association
c/o Lewis Limited
Box 3009
Las Cruces, N.Mex. 88003
Phone: (505) 522-8032

Lewis Limited
Box 3009
Las Cruces, N.Mex. 88003
Phone: (505) 522-8032

New York

Advertising Women of New York
153 E. 57th St.
New York, N.Y. 10022

Albany Women's Forum
c/o Jan Beesmeyer
Executive Director, Albany YWCA
28 Colvin Ave.
Albany, N.Y. 12205
Phone: (518) 438-6608

American Women's Economic Development Corp.
1270 Ave. of the Americas
New York, N.Y. 10020
Phone: (212) 397-0880

Catalyst
14 E. 60th St.
New York, N.Y. 10022
Phone: (212) 759-9700

Coalition of Labor Union Women
15 Union Sq.
New York, N.Y. 10003
Phone: (212) 255-7800

Coalition of 100 Black Women
60 E. 86th St.
New York, N.Y. 10028
Phone: (212) 794-0252

Council on Women in Ministry & Women's Ecumenical Consulting Group
475 Riverside Dr.
New York, N.Y. 10027
Phone: (212) 870-2347

Dialogue
c/o Gladys Dobelle
20 W. 64th St.
New York, N.Y. 10023
Phone: (212) 580-8800

The Fashion Group, Inc.
9 Rockefeller Plaza
New York, N.Y. 10022

Financial Women's Association
P.O. Box 5303
Grand Central Station
New York, N.Y. 10017

Fifth Avenue Forum
Marble Collegiate Church
29th St. and Fifth Ave.
New York, N.Y. 10001

New York *(cont.)*

Friends of NOW-NY
84 Fifth Ave.
New York, N.Y. 10011
Phone: (212) 989-7230

International Association for Personnel Women
P.O. Box 3057
Grand Central Station
New York, N.Y. 10017
Phone: (212) 734-8160

The Long Island Women's Network
2261 Helene Ave.
Merrick, N.Y. 11566
Phone: (516) 378-3441

National Association of Media Women
157 W. 126th St.
New York, N.Y. 10027
Phone: (212) 666-1320

National Association of Women Artists
41 Union Square W.
New York, N.Y. 10003
Phone: (212) 675-1616

National Home Fashions League
41 Madison Ave.
New York, N.Y. 10010
Phone: (212) 685-4664

The Network—Women Managers in Government
Center for Women in Government
Draper Hill, Rm. 302
1400 Washington Ave.
Albany, N.Y. 12222

Networks Unlimited
c/o Alina Novak
142 W. 49th St.
New York, N.Y. 10019
Phone: (212) 921-0005

New York Association of Women Business Owners
525 West End Ave.
New York, N.Y. 10024
Phone: (212) 787-6974

The New York Women's Bar Association
c/o Linda Lamel
New York State Insurance Dept.
2 World Trade Center
New York, N.Y. 10047
Phone: (212) 488-4122

New York Women in Film, Inc.
P.O. Box 108
Ansonia Station
New York, N.Y. 10023
Phone: (212) 988-6884

Public Relations Society of America
845 Third Ave.
New York, N.Y. 10022
Phone: (212) 826-1750

The Resource Network
c/o Maggi Cowlan
204 E. 20th St.
New York, N.Y. 10003
Phone: (212) 983-5162

Rochester Women's Network
c/o Women's Career Center, Inc.
121 N. Fitzhugh St.
Rochester, N.Y. 14614
Phone: (716) 325-6165

Society of Photographers and Artists Representatives (SPAR)
P.O. Box 845
New York, N.Y. 10022
Phone: (212) 832-3123

University and College Labor Educators Association
c/o Anne Nelson
Cornell University
3 E. 43rd St.
New York, N.Y. 10017
Phone: (212) 599-4550

Woman's Salon
463 West St., Apt. 933B
New York, N.Y. 10014
Phone: (212) 691-0539

Women and Foundations/ Corporate Philanthropy
866 United Nations Plaza, #435
New York, N.Y. 10017
Phone: (212) 759-7712

Women Executives in Public Relations
127 E. 80th St.
New York, N.Y. 10021

Women Office Workers
680 Lexington Ave.
New York, N.Y. 10022
Phone: (212) 688-4160
(212) 688-5837

Women's Action Alliance
370 Lexington Ave.
New York, N.Y. 10017
Phone: (212) 532-8330

Women's Direct Response Group
P.O. Box 5134
FDR Station
New York, N.Y. 10022

Women's Medical Association of New York
Box 108
1300 York Ave.
New York, N.Y. 10021
Phone (Dr. Gilder): (212) 472-5436

Women's National Book Association
P.O. Box 237
FDR Station
New York, N.Y. 10022
Phone: (212) 757-5546

Women's Council of Long Island Association
c/o Huntington Center, Adelphi University
Pidgeon Hill Rd.
Huntington, N.Y. 11746
Phone: (516) 423-1585

Women's Economic Round Table
860 United Nations Plaza
New York, N.Y. 10017
Phone: (212) 759-4360

Women's Forum, Inc.
221 E. 71st St.
New York, N.Y. 10021
Phone: (212) 535-9840

Women's Media Group
Box 2119
Grand Central Station
New York, N.Y. 10017

Women's Network of St. Batholomew's
St. Bartholomew Community Club
109 E. 50th St.
New York, N.Y. 10022
Phone: (212) 751-1616

North Carolina

New Girls' Network
Director of Continuing Education
Salem College
Winston-Salem, N.C. 27108

Women Executives
5842 McNair Rd.
Charlotte, N.C. 28212

Women's Forum of North Carolina
P.O. Box 2514
Chapel Hill, N.C. 27514
Phone: (919) 929-7139

Women's Professional Forum of Greensboro, N.C.
c/o Edith Conrad
1609 Hobbs Rd.
Greensboro, N.C. 27410
Phone: (919) 288-7453

Ohio

Career Advancement Network
3805 N. High St., Suite 310
Columbus, Ohio 43214
Phone: (614) 267-0958

Cleveland Women Working
3201 Euclid Ave.
Cleveland, Ohio 44115
Phone: (216) 432-3675

Dayton Women's Network
c/o Pat Falke
2230 S. Patterson Blvd.
Dayton, Ohio 45409
Phone: (513) 294-2244

Dayton Women Working
c/o YWCA
141 W. 3rd St.
Dayton, Ohio 45402
Phone: (513) 228-8587

The Women's Network
People's Federal Savings
39 E. Market St.
Akron, Ohio 44308

Womonways
P.O. Box 20145
Cincinnati, Ohio 45220
Phone: (513) 221-0579

Working Women
National Association of Office Workers
1258 Euclid Ave., Room 206
Cleveland, Ohio 44115
Phone: (216) 586-8511

Oklahoma

American Business Women's Association
c/o Alnoma E. Dinger
Southwestern Bell
P.O. Box 1380
Tulsa, Okla. 74121
Phone: (918) 585-6250

Oregon

Institute for Managerial and Professional Women
P.O. Box 93
Portland, Ore. 97207
Phone: (503) 244-1006

International Network of Business and Professional Women
6424 N.E. Mallory
Portland, Ore. 97211
Phone: (503) 289-0400

The Leadership Style Network
11751 E. Burnside, #37
Portland, Ore. 97216
Phone: (503) 255-5219

The Network Group
P.O. Box 500
Beaverton, Ore. 97005

Women in Public Management
c/o Jane Hartline
Route 1, Box 526
Portland, Ore. 97231
Phone: (503) 621-3357

The Women's Network Group
8585 S.W. Bohmann Pkwy.
Portland, Ore. 97223
Phone: (503) 246-3409

Pennsylvania

Executive Women's Council, Greater Pittsburgh
4120 Jenkins Arcade
Pittsburgh, Pa. 15222
Phone: (412) 261-2028

Forum for Executive Women
c/o Norma Tither
Rohm & Haas Co.
Independence Mall West
Philadelphia, Pa. 19105
Phone: (215) 592-3000

HERS, Mid-Atlantic
3601 Locust Walk
University of Pennsylvania
Philadelphia, Pa. 19104

Network of Executive Women
c/o Lifeplan
40 E. Broad St.
Bethlehem, Pa. 18018
Phone: (215) 866-8888

New Girl Network
2347 Columbia Ave.
Lancaster, Pa. 17603
Phone: (717) 392-4252

Philadelphia Women's Network
1707 Spruce St.
Philadelphia, Pa. 19103
Phone: (215) 667-2629

The Woman's Network
325 West Ave.
Wayne, Pa. 19087
Phone: (215) 687-9485

Texas

Architectural Secretaries Association
Dallas Chapter
1004 Business Parkway
Richardson, Tex. 75081
Phone: (214) 234-3254

Executive Women of Dallas
1507 Pacific, Third Floor
Dallas, Tex. 75201
Phone: (214) 655-1311

National Association of Women in Construction
2800 W. Lancaster
Fort Worth, Tex. 76107
Phone: (817) 335-9711

River Oaks Breakfast Club
520 S. Post Oak Rd., Suite 100
Houston, Tex. 77027
Phone: (713) 621-1660

Women in Communications
National Headquarters
Box 9561
Austin, Tex. 78766
Phone: (512) 345-8922

Utah

Military Spouse Network
1584 N. 400 West
Sunset, Utah 84015

Virginia

The Forum of Williamsburg
c/o Jean C. Wyer
The School of Business Administration
The College of William and Mary
Williamsburg, Va. 23185
Phone: (804) 253-4610

Home Economists in Business
301 Tower Suite
301 Maple Ave. West
Vienna, Va. 22180
Phone: (703) 938-3666

Peninsula Women's Network
Christopher Newport College
P.O. Box 6070
Newport News, Va. 23606
Phone: (804) 599-7153

Washington

The Career Network
P.O. Box 3081
Everett, Wash. 98203
Phone: (206) 258-5900

Seattle Women in Advertising
c/o Rosalie Sayyak
P.O. Box 4295
Seattle, Wash. 98104
Phone: (206) 223-4042

Women's Professional and Managerial Network
1107 E. Olive St.
Seattle, Wash. 98122
Phone: (206) 323-6490

Wisconsin

Women in Self-Employment
c/o 317 W. Johnson St.
Madison, Wis. 53703
Phone: (608) 257-7888

Canada

Vancouver Women's Network
Centre for Continuing Education
The University of British Columbia
Vancouver, Canada V6T 1W5
Phone: (604) 228-2181

For the names and addresses of professional associations that have women's caucuses—additional grounds for networking—look under "Women" in the national trade directory entitled *Associations of the United States and Canada*, published by Columbia Books, Inc., 734 15th St. NW, Washington, D.C. 20005. Your library probably has a copy.

The National Association for Female Executives, 421 Fourth St., Annapolis, Md. 21403, has amassed a list of more than 800 network directors (and/or women interested in starting networks) all across the country. For a copy of the list, send $2 to that address.

Also, the Federation of Organizations for Professional Women, 2000 P St. NW, Suite 403, Washington, D.C. 20036, lists over one hundred affiliates.

Appendix D

Reading List

Books mentioned in the text

Bolles, Richard Nelson. *What Color Is Your Parachute?* Berkeley, Calif.: Ten Speed Press, 1972.

Booth, Heather. *Direct Action Organizing: A Handbook for Women.* Chicago: Midwest Academy (600 West Fullerton, Chicago, Ill. 60614), 1976.

Friedan, Betty. *The Feminine Mystique.* New York: W. W. Norton & Co., 1963.

Harragan, Betty Lehan. *Games Mother Never Taught You: Corporate Gamesmanship for Women.* New York: Rawson Associates, 1977.

Hennig, Margaret, and Jardim, Anne. *The Managerial Woman.* Garden City, N.Y.: Anchor Press/Doubleday, 1977.

Janis, Irving L., M.D., and Mann, Leon, M.D. *Decision Making.* New York: Free Press/Macmillan, 1977.

Miller, Jean Baker, M.D. *Toward a New Psychology of Women.* Boston: Beacon Press, 1976.

Nash, Katherine. *Get the Best of Yourself.* New York: Grosset & Dunlap, 1976.

Sargent, Alice G. *Beyond Sex Roles.* St. Paul, Minn.: West Publishing Co., 1977.

Wells, Theodora. *Keeping Your Cool under Fire.* New York: McGraw-Hill, 1980.

Other books to look into

Albrecht, Maryann; Burack, Elmer; and Seitler, Helene. *Growing: A Woman's Guide to Career Satisfaction.* Belmont, Calif.: Lifetime Learning Publications, 1980.

Baxandall, Rosalyn; Gordon, Linda; and Reverby, Susan, comps. and eds. *America's Working Women: A Documentary History—1600 to the Present.* New York: Vintage Books, 1976.

Bird, Caroline, *Everything a Woman Needs to Know to Get Paid What She's Worth.* New York: Bantam Books, 1974.

———. *The Two-Paycheck Marriage—How Women at Work are Changing Life in America.* New York: Rawson, Wade Publishers, 1979.

Blaxall, Martha, and Regan, Barbara, eds. *Women and the Workplace: The Implications of Occupational Segregation*. Chicago: University of Chicago Press, 1976.

Davidson, Kenneth M.; Ginsburg, Ruth Bader; and Kay, Herma H. *Sex-Based Discrimination: Text Cases and Materials*. St. Paul, Minn.: West Publishing Co., 1974.

Fenn, Margaret. *Making It in Management: A Behavioral Approach for Women Executives*. Englewood Cliffs, N.J.: Prentice-Hall, 1978.

Gordon, Thomas, M.D. *Leader Effectiveness Training—L.E.T.—The No-Lose Way to Release the Productive Potential of People*. New York: Wyden Books, 1971.

Gornick, Vivian, and Moran, Barbara K., eds. *Woman in Sexist Society—Studies in Power and Powerlessness*. New York: Basic Books, Inc., 1971.

Janeway, Elizabeth. *Man's World, Woman's Place: A Study in Social Mythology*. New York: William Morrow & Co., Inc., 1971.

Kirschenbaum, Howard, and Glaser, Barbara. *Developing Support Groups*. University Associates, Inc., 7596 Eads Avenue, La Jolla, Calif. 92037.

Pogrebin, Letty Cottin. *Getting Yours—How to Make the System Work for the Working Woman*. New York: David McKay Company, Inc., 1975.

Ruddick, Sara, and Daniels, Pamela, eds. *Working It Out: 23 Women Writers, Artists, Scientists and Scholars Talk about Their Lives and Work*. New York: Pantheon Books, 1977.

The Spirit of Houston. First National Women's Conference Report. March 1978.

Taetzsch, Lyn, and Benson, Eileen. *Taking Charge on the Job—Techniques for Assertive Management*. Executive Enterprises Publications Co., Inc., 1978.

"*. . . To Form a More Perfect Union. . . .*" Report of the National Commission on the Observance of International Women's Year. 1976.

Trahey, Jane. *Jane Trahey on Women and Power*. New York: Rawson Associates, 1977.

Walters, Barbara. *How to Talk with Practically Anybody about Practically Anything*. New York: Dell, 1970.

Wertheimer, Barbara Mayer. *We Were There: The Story of the Working Women in America*. New York: Pantheon Books, 1977.

Window Dressing on the Set: An Update. Report of the United States Commission on Civil Rights. January 1979.

Zunin, Leonard, M.D., with Zunin, Natalie. *Contact—The First Four Minutes*. New York: Ballantine Books, 1972.

Index